Viking History and Norse Mythology

An Enthralling Journey of Exploration to Uncover the Secrets of the Vikings along with Nordic Myths, Gods, and Goddesses

© Copyright 2023 - All rights reserved.

The content contained within this book may not be reproduced, duplicated, or transmitted without direct written permission from the author or the publisher.

Under no circumstances will any blame or legal responsibility be held against the publisher, or author, for any damages, reparation, or monetary loss due to the information contained within this book, either directly or indirectly.

Legal Notice:

This book is copyright protected. It is only for personal use. You cannot amend, distribute, sell, use, quote, or paraphrase any part, or the content within this book, without the consent of the author or publisher.

Disclaimer Notice:

Please note the information contained within this document is for educational and entertainment purposes only. All effort has been executed to present accurate, up-to-date, reliable, and complete information. No warranties of any kind are declared or implied. Readers acknowledge that the author is not engaging in the rendering of legal, financial, medical, or professional advice. The content within this book has been derived from various sources. Please consult a licensed professional before attempting any techniques outlined in this book.

By reading this document, the reader agrees that under no circumstances is the author responsible for any losses, direct or indirect, that are incurred as a result of the use of the information contained within this document, including, but not limited to, errors, omissions, or inaccuracies.

Free limited time bonus

Stop for a moment. We have a free bonus set up for you. The problem is this: we forget 90% of everything that we read after 7 days. Crazy fact, right? Here's the solution: we've created a printable, 1-page pdf summary for this book that you're reading now. All you have to do to get your free pdf summary is to go to the following website:

https://livetolearn.lpages.co/enthrallinghistory/

Once you do, it will be intuitive. Enjoy, and thank you!

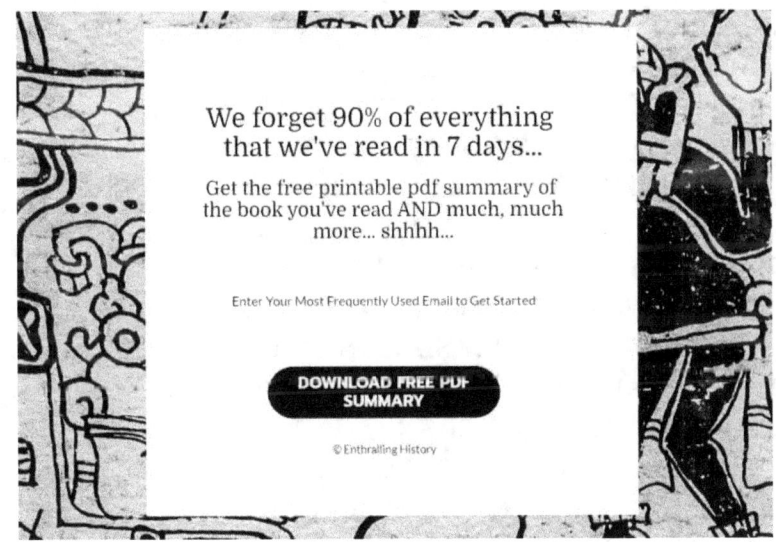

Table of Contents

PART 1: HISTORY OF THE VIKINGS 1
   INTRODUCTION 2
   SECTION ONE: THE VIKING AGE: AN OVERVIEW (793–1066 CE) 4
   CHAPTER 1: WHO WERE THE VIKINGS? 5
   CHAPTER 2: WHAT WAS THE VIKING AGE? 13
   CHAPTER 3: VIKING CONQUESTS 20
   CHAPTER 4: THE FALL OF THE VIKINGS 29
   SECTION TWO: REGULAR VIKING LIFE 37
   CHAPTER 5: SOCIETAL STRUCTURE 38
   CHAPTER 6: VILLAGE LIFE 45
   CHAPTER 7: LITERATURE AND THE RUNIC ALPHABET 53
   CHAPTER 8: ART, DESIGN, AND ARCHITECTURE 60
   SECTION THREE: WARFARE AND WEAPONRY 68
   CHAPTER 9: KEY VIKING BATTLES 69
   CHAPTER 10: ARMOR AND WEAPONS 75
   CHAPTER 11: VIKING SHIPS 82
   CHAPTER 12: MORE THAN WARRIORS - VIKING TRADERS 90
   SECTION FOUR: MYTH AND MYTHOLOGY 97
   CHAPTER 13: CUSTOMS, RITUALS, AND RELIGION 98
   CHAPTER 14: WARS OF THE GODS 106
   CHAPTER 15: THE NINE REALMS IN NORSE MYTHOLOGY 113

CHAPTER 16: SYMBOLS AND POSSESSIONS OF THE NORSE GODS AND GODDESSES 121
CONCLUSION 129
PART 2: NORSE MYTHOLOGY 130
INTRODUCTION 131
CHAPTER 1: THE BEGINNING OF THE NORSE COSMOS 134
CHAPTER 2: YGGDRASIL AND THE NINE WORLDS 140
CHAPTER 3: THE CREATION OF HUMANS AND THE WAR OF THE GODS 149
CHAPTER 4: ODIN AND THOR 157
CHAPTER 5: TÝR AND LOKI 166
CHAPTER 6: HEIMDALL AND HERMOD 174
CHAPTER 7: BALDUR AND VIDAR 181
CHAPTER 8: FREYJA AND FRIGG 186
CHAPTER 9: HEL AND SIF 194
CHAPTER 10: VALHALLA AND THE VALKYRIES 202
CHAPTER 11: THE FORTIFICATIONS OF ASGARD 211
CHAPTER 12: ODIN'S SACRIFICE AND THE MEAD OF POETRY 217
CHAPTER 13: THE BINDING OF FENRIR 224
CHAPTER 14: THOR IN THE LAND OF THE GIANTS 231
CHAPTER 15: THOR AND MJÖLNIR 241
CHAPTER 16: BALDUR'S DEATH AND LOKI'S BINDING 249
CHAPTER 17: RAGNARÖK 258
CONCLUSION 265
HERE'S ANOTHER BOOK BY ENTHRALLING HISTORY THAT YOU MIGHT LIKE 267
FREE LIMITED TIME BONUS 268
BIBLIOGRAPHY 269

Part 1: History of the Vikings

An Enthralling Overview of the Viking Age

Introduction

Vikings, warriors, Norse peoples, Scandinavians, and more are all terms used interchangeably when referring to the people who lived in present-day Scandinavia during the height of the Viking Age. Not all of those terms apply to the Vikings. Only those who participated in the raids were Vikings because they went "a viking." However, the people of Scandinavia and elsewhere were part of the collective Viking experience.

Because of the Vikings' amazing accomplishments and daring feats, they are one of the most well-known groups of people from our collective past. Their escapades are inspirational. An independent spirit gave these Scandinavian peoples the strength and vision to explore the world beyond their immediate shores.

Beyond raiding and pillaging, their sailing adventures fostered incredible craftsmen. Shipbuilding and the navigational tools they developed show their understanding of the natural world around them. Their weaponry demonstrated the same intellectual curiosity and ability to create devices that were well made and met their needs.

Vikings are often depicted as lawless savage combatants. Yes, they certainly left many quivering in their wake. But once they settled in an area they seized, the Scandinavians brought respect, leading to the beginnings of a democracy. They had laws they followed, retribution for lawbreakers, and assemblies in which villagers had input.

The Scandinavians had expectations of how each person should be treated. A strong work ethic and living an honorable life were among the virtues they extolled. No, they were not perfect, but they were also not bloodthirsty monsters.

Gods and goddesses helped guide their way. Deeply rooted belief systems gave their lives purpose, and their belief in an afterlife for honorable warriors in Valhalla guided combatants into battle. The nine realms of the Viking world framed their connections to their deities, ancestors, and origins.

Understanding people who came before us is important for us to know more about ourselves. We may not agree with all of their beliefs, but framing their principles in their time period is critical to gaining insight into other cultures.

SECTION ONE:
The Viking Age: An Overview
(793–1066 CE)

Chapter 1: Who Were the Vikings?

On June 8th, 793 CE, the first recorded attack by the Vikings on European soil occurred. The Vikings seemingly materialized out of thin air and brutally assaulted the monastery on the island of Lindisfarne, which is located off the northeast coast of England. The Viking Age and the terror that accompanied it began on that day.

Magic and sorcery did not cause the Vikings to suddenly appear on that island. Archaeologists have pieced together what they believe to be the origins of the Vikings, the culture that became infamous for their fearsome raids. However, their ancestors had thrived for thousands of years before the Viking Age.

Land formations that resulted from the Ice Age made parts of the area known today as Scandinavia habitable to early humans. This transformation occurred over twelve thousand years ago and is classified as the Stone Age. For thousands of years, sections of Scandinavia were populated by hunters and gatherers. Ancient peoples migrated from modern Europe, Syria, and Russia.

During the Bronze Age, the ancestors of the Vikings developed metalworking skills. They became adept at fashioning tools that were much stronger and accomplished more tasks. With the development of new tools, sturdier buildings were constructed. Because of this, a shift from nomadic hunters and gatherers occurred, with more people farming. Additionally, a more structured and hierarchical society began to emerge around 1700 BCE.

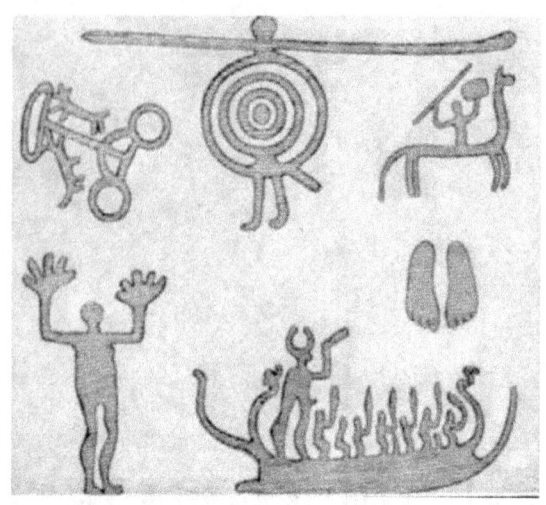

Rock carving from Sweden.
https://en.m.wikipedia.org/wiki/File:Scandinavian_Civilization_-_rock_carvings.jpg

Much of the interpretation of how the people of the Scandinavian Bronze Age lived has been provided through the analysis of petroglyphs. Petroglyphs are rock carvings. Originally, many believed the petroglyphs were etched by the ancestors of the Vikings; however, more current research shows the carvings to be from the Bronze Age. This new interpretation of the evidence suggests that cultures traded extensively with each other during the Bronze Age.

To facilitate trade and transactions, ships carried the buyers or sellers and their goods to other countries. The Norse built ships of varying sizes. From the cave drawings, it is believed that the largest ships made by Viking ancestors had the capacity for a crew of over fifty.

Due to the growing trade, other countries became acquainted with their northern neighbors. Pliny the Elder, an ancient Roman historian, is believed to have referred to the lands of Norway and Sweden as Scatinavia when he described the territories he encountered. Later, the Greek explorer Pytheas called the lands Scandiae.

The people of the lands known as Scandinavia would continue to develop their trade with other countries during the Iron Age, which occurred between 500 BCE and 800 CE. Scandinavians prospered due to increased trade with other cultures and lands during this time, including the Roman Empire. Some settlements in Scandinavia transformed into trade centers to accommodate the needs of buyers and sellers.

Iron was even stronger than the metals used by people during the Bronze Age, and the new metal transformed many ancient societies. More communities were settled during the Iron Age partly because iron tools made farming and building easier.

The application of iron went beyond its use as implements to feed, cloth, and shelter inhabitants. Iron was also utilized for weapons. With the ability to readily produce iron devices, powerful weapons were available for the multitudes. An increase in warfare was one result of the proliferation of iron-based weaponry.

Also, during the Iron Age, the demise of the Western Roman Empire occurred. In 476 CE, Rome fell. Without the strong government in Rome controlling much of Europe, regional conflicts emerged. Many smaller kingdoms arose, which all vied for power and land. Roadways between villages were no longer maintained, making traveling and trade a challenge. Seaways were no longer under the control of the Roman Empire, increasing the power of pirates and other cultures.

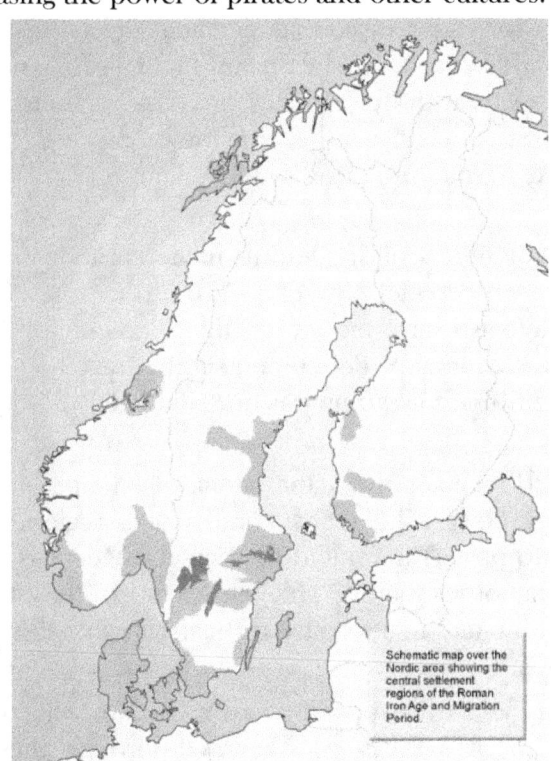

Map of Scandinavian settlements during the Migration Period.
https://commons.wikimedia.org/wiki/File:Nordic_Settlements.gif

The Migration Period helped bring about the decline and ultimate fall of the Western Roman Empire. During the years between 300 to 700 CE, thousands of tribes migrated throughout Europe. Numerous Germanic tribes, which are credited with the collapse of Rome, reshaped the political and cultural landscape of Europe. The transformation from centralized to decentralized governance caused the formation of numerous small territories or kingdoms. Continual warfare between the leaders resulted.

Scandinavia's once bountiful trade with Europe plummeted precipitously. Evidence found by archaeologists suggests that its wealth and economic prosperity declined dramatically throughout the Migration Period. Excavations of gravesites revealed many buried treasures with the dead. Hiding family valuables in this manner supports theories of political unrest, which was similar to what was occurring in Europe. It is believed that families felt they were protecting their wealth during this unsettled time.

Scandinavian society was also experiencing societal instability, with its structure being challenged. A shift from small farms and villages to a more tiered society with fewer decision-makers emerged. Influential families battled for the chance to become the ruling elite. This transitional time between the Migration Period to the Viking Age is referred to as the Vendel Period.

Information about this period and its name come from ancient burial grounds located in Vendel, Sweden. From this site and Valsgärde, Sweden, archaeologists have pieced together elements of the society that emerged from the Migration Period and set the stage for the Viking Age. Ideals valued and fostered during this time included prestige, power, and material wealth.

To gain and retain power, the rising chieftains or jarls had to consolidate their power. To retain control of a region, rulers needed strong warriors to protect them and their assets. Meetings and gatherings were held in longhouses that the chieftains built. In these great halls, the local leaders exhibited their status through lavish feasts and wearing dazzling garments.

Local farmers and tradespeople were invited to religious rituals and celebrations. The jarl's status was elevated through these displays of grandeur. Leaders also used these occurrences to demonstrate the strength of their warriors. With the continually shifting allegiances, a region and its jarl needed powerful combatants to protect their people and their lands. Chieftains continually had to prove their ability to defeat others who attacked. Any signs of weakness were detrimental to a leader's survival.

Construction of hill and ring forts for protection began during the Vendel Period. Usually circular in construction, these fortified structures stored food and animals. Villagers stayed in the forts when their homes were under attack. And this happened more and more as neighboring leaders battled each other for dominance of the region.

Military objects discovered in graves throughout the area illustrate the artistry of the people and their growing reverence for the warriors. Helmets won by warriors demonstrated the status of their military prowess. These helmets were adorned with precious gems and inscribed with scenes from myths of the Scandinavian people. Vendel Period helmets encompass the evolving beliefs and goals of the time.

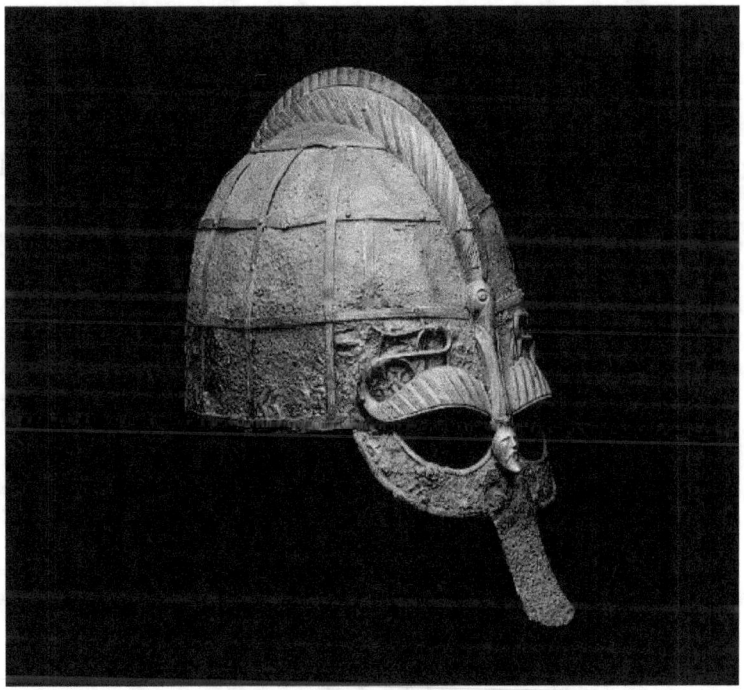

Helmet from the Vendel Period.
Ola Myrin/Statens historiska museum, CC BY 2.5 <https://creativecommons.org/licenses/by/2.5>, via Wikimedia Commons https://commons.wikimedia.org/wiki/File:Vendel_I_helmet_456059.jpg

In addition to stunning helmets, Scandinavian craftspeople were adroit at working with many metals. Artisans created works in gold, bronze, and iron, and the tradespeople were instrumental in the resurgence of trade, which had floundered since the fall of Rome. The ability to trade goods and import treasures from other lands added to the status of the jarl or chieftain. Winning victories in battles, displaying wealth, hosting lavish feasts in the longhouse, and protecting the people in his region ensured that the chieftain retained his position of power. Longevity and support of the locals were required by the jarl if he wanted to become king.

The glorification of warriors in the Scandinavian culture leading up to the Viking Age can be found in the epic poem *Beowulf*. The only known written version of the poem is from 1000 CE. Though it was one of the first pieces of Anglo-Saxon writing, the setting of the tale is the lands of Scandinavia. Historical figures, such as Danish King Hrothgar, provide researchers with an estimate of when the bards told the poem.

No evidence exists that Beowulf was an actual person. Perhaps he was a compilation of various warriors who ate, drank, and celebrated victories in the great halls of the Scandinavian kings. The traveling storytellers would have shared the incredible feats accomplished by Beowulf as they journeyed from village to village. Good fought evil in the form of Beowulf conquering monsters. He eliminated Grendel, "a creature of darkness," as well as Grendel's mother. To save others, Beowulf slayed a dragon, which ended his life.

The first page of Beowulf, dated roughly 1000.
https://commons.wikimedia.org/wiki/File:Beowulf_Cotton_MS_Vitellius_A_XV_f._132r.jpg

The looting and plundering that characterized the Viking Age were depicted in the story of *Beowulf*. Beowulf's larger-than-life exploits would transfer into tales of real-life warriors taking on the world.

At the inception of the Viking Age, the Vikings did not refer to themselves as Vikings. They were also not unified under the auspices of one king or leader. Each region was separated into different tribes or clans. People were loyal to their local chieftain or jarl. Most villagers lived and worked on their farms or as tradespeople. Karls were the free landowners of Scandinavian society who participated in Viking raids. Servants and enslaved people were referred to as thralls.

The people's lives followed the seasons and the cycle of farming. Spring was planting season, and crops were harvested in the fall. Cold and dark winters were times of sheltering in longhouses. Stories of the summer exploits of trading and pillaging were shared over winter fires. These tales perpetuated the glory of raiding and ensured the sequence would repeat itself the next summer.

The definitive origin of the term "Viking" is unknown, but many scholars feel its root is the Norse word *vík*. Other words closely related to *vík* include *víka* and *víkja*; these words are all connected to the sea. *Víkingr* was used to denote a seafaring adventurer in Old Norse. This term has been found in stories, poetry, and runestones, which were written using the runic alphabet. These inscriptions detail the exploits of people during this time. When the term *Víkingr* is carved, it indicates a seafaring warrior, not an entire group of people.

Some of those impacted by the Viking invasions began to refer to the attacking forces as Vikings. Wiccinga or Wiccingi, which is the singular and plural form of Viking in Latin, has been discovered in the writing of monks living in England during the attacks. Initially, other countries called the warriors the Danes, though not all Vikings were from Denmark. The foreigners, Northmen, Majūs for mysterious and misunderstood, heathens, and other monikers have all been replaced by the term Viking.

The majority of Scandinavians were not Vikings and never participated in any raids. Only those who partook in the pillaging adventures at sea were Vikings. Other Scandinavians traveled as merchants, trading and bartering goods from their homeland with those in other lands. The tradespeople that the Scandinavians encountered called them Northmen or Norsemen to refer to their region of origin.

Saga Oseberg, a replica of a Viking ship.
https://www.pexels.com/photo/close-up-of-the-saga-oseberg-8876097/

For almost three hundred years, the Vikings ruled the seaways. When their impressive ships approached, shouts of the "Vikings are coming!" or the "Vikings have arrived!" sent waves of fear and terror throughout the land.

The Vikings landed in more than forty countries and territories. They founded market towns to trade their goods and initiated a global trading network. Their influence on laws and instilling justice have had a lasting impact. Their shipbuilding skills and spirit of adventure led them to discover lands that were unknown to them, such as Greenland and Iceland. Scandinavian technology enabled them to reach North America before Christopher Columbus.

Numerous theories have been explored to determine the events that precipitated the Vikings to begin their raids. Overpopulation, lack of quality farmland, a desire for silver, and a sense of adventure may have all contributed to the raids. Regardless of the reasons, the Vikings had an indelible impact on communities in Europe, especially in England. After the days of surprise attacks on villages ended, Vikings effected changes throughout all levels of society.

Chapter 2: What Was the Viking Age?

The years from 793 to 1066 CE are the dates typically associated with the Viking Age. The year 793 saw the first documented Viking raid. The Vikings attacked Lindisfarne, a monastery off the coast of England.

The Vikings were notorious for their sudden and frightening attacks on towns throughout Europe. They did more than raid and pillage. Vikings also settled in villages, vastly expanded their trading routes, and explored lands previously unknown to them.

Especially at the beginning of the Viking Age, the Vikings did not sail as a cohesive group representing all of the current Scandinavian countries. Scandinavians shared a common language, ancestry, and skill in navigation and shipbuilding. The geography of their region dictated the development of their ability to build ships and traverse waterways.

People living in Sweden, Norway, and Denmark had vastly different land formations to contend with. However, the territories all had watercourses, thickly forested regions, and impenetrable mountains.

Picture of a Norwegian fjord.
https://unsplash.com/photos/W1FIkdPAB7E

Waterways included fjords, which were formed from glaciers. Fjords are incredibly deep inlets and provide narrow openings to the sea. They are bordered by steep sides of rocks that form cliffs. These challenging topographical features necessitated water travel as the most effective method of transportation.

Other topographical features of the land created a natural separation between tribes. Norsemen in Norway contended with narrow strips of farmland between the edges of fjords and mountains. Similarly, Sweden was challenged by small sections of fertile land situated between waterways and mountains. Colder temperatures added to the difficulties of farm life. Denmark had the best land for growing crops and was in a good location for contact beyond Scandinavia.

These geographical conditions developed strong regional ties in Scandinavia as the people entered the Viking Age. Some of these circumstances may have fostered the need to explore other regions. Numerous factors are believed to have led to the initial raids that are emblematic of the Viking Age. The Scandinavians' navigational and ship-making prowess contributed to the expansion of the Scandinavian world and the success of the raids.

The growing population in the years preceding the Viking Age, along with limited farmable land, may have been one of the contributing factors to the Viking raids. Young men were likely willing to sail on Viking ships with the hope of finding new lands to farm. Adding to the complexity of sufficient farmable land was the practice of primogeniture. In this system, the eldest son inherited the family's entire estate. Any other sons in the family were left landless. This may have inspired males without land to inherit to join the expeditions.

Landowners held the power in Scandinavian societies. However, for a family to differentiate itself from other landowners, it had to amass more wealth than farming alone would have provided. For those seeking the role of local chieftain or jarl, he had to seek materials obtained from other lands and countries, which would add to his status. Fine clothing, unusual treasures, lavish feasts, and an ornate longhouse advanced one's position and importance. Goods obtained from Viking raids provided a means for new landowners to secure more power.

Continual struggles for control and shifting alliances created political turmoil. Chieftains sought to add land to their regions of control. Kings pursued even more dominance and strove to consolidate multiple chieftains under their rule. Jarls who did not want to be controlled by a king relinquished their power. These jarls joined Viking treks and settled new lands in other countries. Some jarls were exiled when they lost a power struggle; others voluntarily left to begin anew.

Not only chieftains desired adventure. The Scandinavians' spirit of independence and bravery led them to be enticed by the sea. Visiting faraway lands gave those seeking escape from their structured and tiered society new ambitions. They would return to their homeland with extraordinary tales of new worlds and exotic goods, adding invaluable status to these legendary pioneers. An added benefit for the explorers was the belief in Valhalla, the Norse religion's equivalent of heaven. Dying in battle ensured the deceased would be escorted to Valhalla by Odin, the Norse god of war and the dead.

Though not clearly documented, it is thought that the initial Viking raids sailed from Norway and arrived in England and Ireland in 750. In the years that followed, ships launched from Denmark and often disembarked in southeastern England, the Netherlands, and France. Vikings who voyaged from Sweden typically sailed east toward the Baltics and Russia. It is believed that during the early years of the raids, the ships frequently followed the coastline. However, due to the talent of the Vikings, their shipbuilding expertise, and advancements in nautical technology, the open seas soon became navigable.

Exploratory raiding parties of Vikings are thought to have begun as early as 750. There is some evidence of Norse ships landing in Kent and Wessex in 753 and 788 or 789, respectively, which supports the theory of raids occurring before 793. Over the next few decades, northern England experienced bouts of looting and small-scale raids. The intensity of the raids grew, with the first documented large-scale invasion occurring in 793. For many, this date marks the official commencement of the Viking Age.

Information about the earliest raids and the attack on Lindisfarne Priory was documented in the *Anglo-Saxon Chronicle*. In approximately 890, King Alfred the Great commissioned the recording of events that had occurred in England. The *Anglo-Saxon Chronicle* recounts events beginning in 60 BCE.

The Viking Raiding Stone is known by many names, including the Lindisfarne Stone or Doomsday Stone. This gravestone is believed to depict the events that transpired on that June day in 793. The gravestone was discovered at the priory. Carvings in the stone depict a group of warriors with Viking-like weapons. The other side of the stone reveals celestial images and figures that appear to be praying. Conjectures imply that the side of the stone with warriors represents the Vikings who attacked; the other face of the grave marker depicts the monks in prayer.

Adding to the validity of details of the raid that launched the Viking Age are the writings of Alcuin of York. A well-known scholar, clergyman, and Palatine school educator at Charlemagne's court, Alcuin was contacted via letter by the bishop of Lindisfarne with details of the attack. In Alcin's reply to Bishop Higbald's correspondence, he expresses his grief and horror over the ghastly raid on the monastery.

Only Alcin's letter still exists. In it, he included details about the attack being made by pagans, which is a reference to the Vikings. He also expressed his surprise that a raid could happen at the priory due to its distance from the sea. Alcin noted that St. Cuthbert's Church, which was at Lindisfarne, was desecrated with the blood of the monks and looted of its chalices, crosses, and other goods that demonstrated devotion to God.

While the strike on the monastery shocked the monks and others, many researchers do not believe it was a random act executed by the

Vikings. The priory was founded by St. Aidan in 634 CE and was well-known within the Christian community. Visitors frequently worshiped there.

In addition to being houses of worship, Christian monasteries provided areas for learning and literature. Collections of indelible books and manuscripts, often hand-copied by monks in beautiful calligraphy and ornate decorations, were located at these holy sites. Hand-woven and embroidered fabrics, golden chalices, and gem-ladened goblets, which were all used in religious ceremonies, were housed at thriving monasteries.

As a hub of worship, Lindisfarne flourished in 793. However, the Kingdom of Northumbria, where the Holy Island of Lindisfarne was located, was undergoing turmoil in its leadership. In the fifty-eight years leading up to the attack and for almost a decade after the Vikings' arrival, ten different kings led the territory. Continual battles between rivals caused the deposition of each king.

Ominous storms started the year for the residents of Northumbria, followed by a deadly famine. Both seemed to be a foreshadowing of the catastrophic events of June 793.

Norsemen often sailed their regular trade route, which was along the coast of England. This provided the Vikings with a familiarity of the area's terrain, the ongoing upheaval in Northumbria, and experience with the sea route to and from the Holy Island. It is thought the Vikings planned their attack on the monastery because of their depth of knowledge of the situation.

Most likely, three or four ships with a total of upward of one hundred Vikings participated in the raid on Lindisfarne. Vikings sailed in longships when going on raids. In addition to speed, these ships could land on beaches, allowing the Vikings to attack more easily. Prows, the forward section of the ship's bow that was above water, were often carved to look like dragons.

On the morning of June 8th, 793 CE, the monks may have been sleeping, in the church praying, illuminating manuscripts, or tilling the fields. Suddenly, the chapel bells rang out, warning all of the inhabitants of the island. Monks looked over the walls of the monastery and heard the sounds of ships grinding against the sandy beaches. But all they could see were the ominous dragon heads glaring up at them.

Ruins at Lindisfarne.
https://pixabay.com/photos/ruins-lindisfarne-priory-lindisfarne-2021105/

But then they saw the Vikings surging from the ships. Battle cries roared from the brawny warriors as they swarmed the monastery. Monks scattered and hid but to no avail. Many religious community members were massacred during the attack. Some were taken as prisoners. Before the Vikings returned to their ships, they pillaged St. Cuthbert's Church and the priory. Ransacking and looting resulted in treasures of gold and silver religious relics. Embroidered silken vestments and embellished manuscripts were also seized by the invaders.

The unexpectedness and brutality of the raid alarmed and outraged the Christian world. The Holy Island was an especially important and symbolic location for the early Christians. St. Aidan founded the priory at Lindisfarne in 635. From there, the teachings of the church spread. St. Cuthbert was buried at this site, which added to the importance of its role in the church. Cuthbert was considered the patron saint of Northumbria and had served as the bishop of the abbey. Known for performing miracles as a healer, Cuthbert was revered by Christians. His grave was not destroyed in the raid, and his body was subsequently moved from the island.

The Holy Island also held another treasure of the early church: the Lindisfarne Gospels. Eadfrith, a bishop of the priory, spent at least five years creating this medieval manuscript. The Lindisfarne Gospels were filled with stunning illustrations and impeccable calligraphy. Thankfully, these gospels survived the 793 raid. However, its gem-studded cover did not; speculation is that the cover was stolen during the looting.

Since the Lindisfarne Monastery contained such a wealth of treasures and had such a rich history, it was able to survive and continue its mission until 875. At that time, the monks left the monastery because of the continuous threat of Viking incursions.

For this being the Vikings' first organized pillage, they were incredibly successful. Obtaining silver and gold was one of their probable motivating factors, and they surely obtained this wealth during the raid. This new wealth enabled the Vikings returning home to obtain a new status in their society. Those who participated in the raid had the resources to buy their own farmland, which improved their ranking. It also provided an incentive for others to join upcoming raids. Another aspect of participating in the raid was gaining a prestigious reputation as a Viking warrior.

Viking raids on monasteries continued for the next few summers, after which the number and intensity of the incursions grew. Places of worship were not selected because the Vikings were pagans; they tended to target remote sanctuaries. Often, the inhabitants, mainly monks and other religious people, were not armed, which made the looting and capturing of people to enslave easier to accomplish. Monasteries also contained portable treasures. Articles used as part of the liturgy and for worship were made from coveted metals.

The earliest Viking raids sailed from Norway. The early locations of the Norwegian Vikings were situated along the northeast shoreline of England. After the attack on Lindisfarne, the next year, in 794, the twin monasteries of Monkwearmouth-Jarrow were raided, resulting in destruction and looting. The following year, the Vikings pillaged and ransacked St. Columba on Iona. Vikings stole crosses, liturgical garments, chalices, candlesticks, and other portable riches from these religious establishments.

As more Scandinavian countries entered the Viking Age and joined in the pursuit of wealth and power, the attacks grew beyond monasteries. In the next century, the Vikings conquered parts of England and broadened their scope to northern Europe, Iceland, and Greenland.

Chapter 3: Viking Conquests

In the 800s, Vikings from across Scandinavia participated in raids. Norwegian Vikings tended to attack Ireland, Scotland, and northwest England. The Danes overlapped the Norwegians in England, but they also sailed to the Netherlands and France. Russia and areas to the east and south were targeted by the Swedish Vikings.

In the early 9th century, Viking raids continued. They followed a pattern similar to what had been inflicted upon Lindisfarne and other monasteries at the end of the 8th century. Throughout the 9th century, the intensity and scope of the raids increased. By the mid-9th century, the raiding Vikings began successfully invading and controlling countries. The Vikings established themselves in many countries. They built forts that were used as centers from which they organized their attacks. Also, by the middle of the 9th century, there is evidence of overwintering, which means the Vikings stayed through the winter.

Many famous and infamous leaders and warriors emerged throughout the age of Viking conquests. Viking incursions had lasting ramifications. The era's impacts spread from the shores of North America to Greenland, Paris, Istanbul (Constantinople), and Kyiv (Kiev). England, especially Northumbria, endured the most attacks.

Map of the Kingdom of Northumbria.
Hogweard, CC BY-SA 4.0 <https://creativecommons.org/licenses/by-sa/4.0>, via Wikimedia Commons; https://commons.wikimedia.org/wiki/File:Map_of_the_Kingdom_of_Northumbria_around_700_AD.svg

Ragnar Lothbrok or Lodbrok, who raided in the 9th century, was the embodiment of a Viking warrior. Fantastical stories abound detailing his larger-than-life accomplishments. Some of the claims are so extraordinary that there has been speculation about the veracity of Ragnar being one person. Perhaps some of the stories about Ragnar are about Ragnall, a composite of people, or a mythical figure. Many agree that there is sufficient evidence that supports the exploits of Ragnar since he is referenced in the *Anglo-Saxon Chronicle*.

Those living in England, Ireland, and France in the mid-9th century feared the fabled warrior. Ragnar altered the tactics of the raiders who preceded him. In addition to looting, it is believed that Ragnar was the first Viking raider who sought to control land and build settlements.

A skilled seaman, Ragnar sailed his fleet of longships on the rivers deep into current-day France. These ships were able to navigate the shallower waters. This design increased the scope of areas the Vikings could attack. They no longer needed to hover in the ocean waters close to the shore. Surprise attacks on European cities increased, many of them led by Ragnar. Fear of the Vikings spread throughout Europe, with Viking technology and shipbuilding adding to the prowess of the warriors.

Vikings first attacked the Frankish Empire in 799. The raids grew in frequency and scope in the subsequent years. After Charlemagne's death in 814, there were internal struggles for control of the vast empire. The Vikings were aware of the power void and planned their raids accordingly. The Frankish Empire suffered at least five significant raids before the siege of Paris in 845. After one of the incursions, Ragnar was granted land by the king. Over time, the king and Ragnar had a falling out, so Ragnar had his land taken away. On his way up the Seine to Paris, Ragnar and his men exacted their revenge and plundered Rouen.

After propelling his fleet of 120 ships and over 5,000 warriors on the Seine River, the siege of Paris commenced. This was Ragnar's and the Vikings' largest assault on the Frankish Empire. Aware of the assault and in an attempt to protect the Abbey of Saint-Denis, King Charles the Bald (Charles II) separated his army into two divisions, stationing them on each side of the river.

In response, Ragnar attacked and routed the army located on one side of the Seine. The Vikings paid homage to their god Odin. To send a message to the king and his remaining troops, the Vikings captured over one hundred soldiers. Then the enemy combatants were hanged and displayed on an island situated in the Seine.

Ragnar and his warriors refused to leave Paris until they received over seven thousand pounds of silver and gold from King Charles the Bald. It is believed that the payment partly reimbursed Ragnar for the land Charles had taken back from him. This is the first known payment to the Vikings to withdraw from a land that they invaded. The Vikings would receive at least twelve more such payments, which are referred to as Danegeld.

Ragnar followed the agreement and departed from Paris as soon as he was paid. However, as he and his warriors sailed back down the Seine, they looted many towns and monasteries. Ragnar's raiding adventures did not conclude with Paris. He continued pillaging areas of England and

Ireland.

The actual cause of Ragnar's death is not certain. Legends tell of the king of Northumbria throwing Ragnar into a pit of venomous snakes. Evidence does not fully substantiate the tale, nor is there proof that Ragnar's sons attacked England to avenge their father's death. However, Ragnar's legacy grew through the plundering wrecked upon England by his sons.

Inwaer or Ivar the Boneless, Halfdan, Björn Ironside, Sigurd Snake-in-the Eye, Hvitserk, and Ubba are the sons of Ragnar who led or were related to the Great Heathen Army. The legend associated with their invasion of England centers on their seeking revenge against King Ælla. Once the Viking warriors captured the king, the brothers allegedly performed a blood eagle ritual on him.

Using sharp weapons, the tormentors sliced open the back of the still-living victim, King Ælla. Then his ribs were cleaved from his spine. The captors next pulled the king's ribs through the opening to create the shape of wings. Lastly, the victim's two fully intact lungs were dragged out of his body. The lungs would have been placed on the ribs to complete the creation of an eagle. Researchers into this horrific practice believe the victim was dead by the time the lungs were removed.

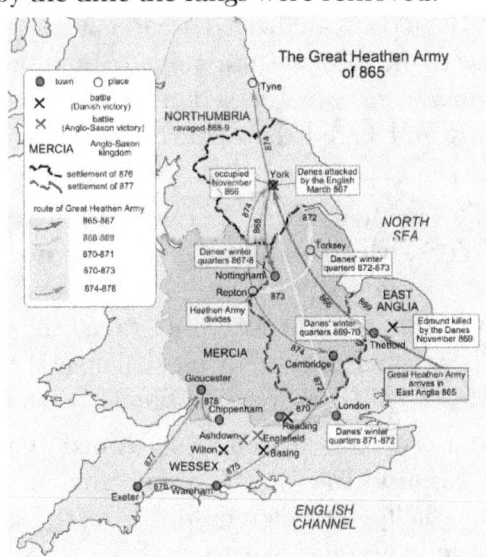

Map tracking the advances of the Great Heathen Army.
Hel-hama, CC BY-SA 3.0 <https://creativecommons.org/licenses/by-sa/3.0>, via Wikimedia Commons; https://commons.wikimedia.org/wiki/File:England_Great_Army_map.svg

Regardless of the brothers' actual motivation to invade England, the Great Heathen Army (also known as the Great Viking Army) stormed England in 865. It is not certain if all the brothers led the forces, but there is evidence to support that Ivar the Boneless and Björn Ironside were members and leaders of the formidable army.

Estimates of the army range from over one thousand fighters to thousands of Vikings from a coalition of Scandinavian forces. The army attacked England when they disembarked on the shores of East Anglia. Unlike other invasions, this force sought more than loot. The Great Heathen Army undertook the goal of conquering and controlling England.

Ivar's moniker as Ivar the Boneless is presumed to be the result of a curse. Aslaug, who was Ivar's mother and a Norse oracle, shared with Ragnar a vision she had. Before marrying Ragnar, Aslaug's prophecy told her that she and Ragnar should not consummate their marriage until after he returned from raiding. Ragnar did not listen to her forewarning. Ivar was born with what is thought to have been brittle bone disease.

However, his affliction did not soften Ivar's bloodthirsty quests as a Viking. Instead, stories were told of how Ivar Ragnarsson battled as a berserker. This subgroup of Viking warriors, berserkers, fought in a frenzied manner. Berserkers dedicated their battles to the Norse god Odin. They believed the bear's spirit joined their bodies and minds, making them invulnerable. Some berserkers wore bear skins into battle; others wore nothing and bared their skin. Their screams and intensity made berserkers beyond fearsome to their opponents.

After the Great Heathen Army's conquest of Northumbria, they gained control of York, which culminated with the devastating killing of King Ælla. But Ivar coveted all of England. On his path to control, Ivar and his men left death, destruction, and dread in their wake. The Kingdom of Mercia was their most difficult challenge. For over a year, the Vikings attacked Mercia, but they were continually beaten back.

In 869, the Vikings successfully seized the Kingdom of Mercia. Those who had fought against Ivar from inside the protective walls of Nottingham were brutally slaughtered for their resistance. Ivar's next target was King Edmund and East Anglia.

Edmund futilely led his forces against the Great Heathen Army. Some legends tell of Ivar and his invaders capturing the king. Ivar's violent killing of Edmund garnered the king the status of martyr and sainthood.

Ivar had the king tied to a tree in the village of Hoxne. Edmund was savagely beaten with clubs because he refused to recant his Christian beliefs. Then the Vikings shot Edmund until his body was filled with arrows. Finally, Ivar permitted the king to die. Once King Edmund was dead, the Vikings beheaded him. As a sign of disrespect, Ivar had his men discard Edmund's body and head into nearby thorn bushes.

The Vikings massacred other survivors and plundered homes and monasteries. Ivar controlled Britain and Ireland. Ivar continued his destructive ways until his death in 873. The leadership of the Great Heathen Army was passed to Ivar's brothers, who were also sons of Ragnar.

Image of Erik the Red.
https://commons.wikimedia.org/wiki/File:Eric_the_Red.png

Ragnar Lothbrok's family was not the only one set on exploring. Naddodd was distantly related to Erik the Red on his father's side. Naddodd sailed from Norway with the goal of settling on the Faroe Islands in the first part of the 9th century. However, he and his crew lost their way at sea and landed on the east coast of present-day Iceland. The men did not encounter any signs of human life after exploring the land and eventually returned to Norway. Naddodd shared his story, and soon others set sail to explore Iceland, although credit for discovering the land was bestowed upon Naddodd.

A few generations later, Naddodd's distant relation, Thorvald Ásvaldsson, sailed from Norway to Iceland. However, Thorvald's purpose was not to seek the Faroe Islands and sail off-course. Thorvald was banished from Norway around 960 by King Haakon the Good because of transgressions that included multiple killings. Found guilty of manslaughter, Thorvald took his family, which included his son, Erik the Red, with him to serve his sentence in Iceland.

The family lived in the wilds of western Iceland. In time, Erik Thorvaldsson (better known as Erik the Red) became infamous as a Viking with a proclivity for exploring. He was also known for having an explosive disposition like his father. With his fiery red hair and beard and a temper to match, Erik the Red was feared by many.

Erik's marriage to the well-to-do Thjodhild Jörundsdóttir enhanced his role as a leader in the community. His wife's wealth included a number of thralls or enslaved people that added to their status, which Erik received as part of the marriage. Erik's neighbor, Valthjof, lost his house in a landslide. The devastation was blamed on Erik's newly acquired thralls.

In retaliation, all of Erik's thralls were butchered by Eyiolf the Foul, a relative or friend of Valthjof. Erik took the law into his own hands, refusing to wait until the ruling council or Althing gathered. He responded by slaughtering Eyiolf the Foul and Holmgang-Hrafn, the latter of whom was involved in the murder of his thralls. Relatives of the Valthjof clan were outraged. Erik the Red and his family were expelled from the community. Like father, like son.

Erik and his family moved to the island of Oxney, which was not any more peaceful for them. Erik had possession of *setstokkrs*. These massive beams were inscribed with runic Norse pagan symbols that conveyed religious symbolism. Care of the *setstokkrs* was given to Thorgest, Erik's neighbor. However, when Erik wanted the beams returned to him, Thorgest refused. Again, instead of seeking assistance from the local council, Erik reclaimed the beams by force. In the melee, two of Thorgest's sons were killed.

The village council debated what punishment should be inflicted on Erik. For his murderous ways, Erik the Red was again banished from the community. For three years, Erik was not permitted to live in Oxney or any part of Iceland. Tired of the rules of the Viking communities in Iceland, Erik set sail.

A hundred years earlier, a Norwegian, Gunnbjörn Ulfsson, had encountered a large piece of land, a fact Erik knew. Erik sailed over nine hundred miles and is credited as the leader of the first group that settled what is today Greenland. They established their community at a fjord called Tunulliarfik. For the rest of his exile, Erik explored and mapped out Greenland. At the end of his banishment, Erik returned to Iceland, seeking to encourage others to join him in the icy tundra that he named Greenland, which he named in the hopes of attracting more settlers.

Erik the Red's children continued with their father's love of navigation and exploration. His daughter, Freydis, had a similar temperament as him. Leif Eriksson is known for being the first European to reach the shores of North America. About fifteen years before Leif sailed with a crew of about thirty-five men, North America had been sighted by Bjarni Herjólfsson when he sailed off-course.

Statue of Leif Eriksson.
Sharon Mollerus, CC BY 2.0 <https://creativecommons.org/licenses/by/2.0>, via Wikimedia Commons; https://commons.wikimedia.org/wiki/File:Leif_Erikson_Statue,_Duluth_(15290644106).jpg

Using that information, Leif's expedition landed in Newfoundland, where he established his base camp. Other excursions followed. His brother, Thorvald, and his crew lived in Vinland ("Land of Wine," with the name coming from the land's grapes) for at least two years. Thorvald was killed in a battle with the indigenous people of the area, making him the first European to die in North America. Thorstein, the third of Erik's sons, attempted to recover Thorvald's body. However, storms prevented him from doing so.

Seeking the riches the land had to offer, the last Viking male from Greenland to lead an expedition to North America was Thorfinn Karlsefni. Their settlement lasted for about three years until trading with the indigenous people was no longer peaceful.

The last voyage to Vinland was led by Freydis, Erik the Red's daughter, was the last voyage to Vinland. Legends tell of Freydis sailing in partnership with Icelandic traders and their crews. Other stories tell of her sailing with her husband and his brothers. The Vikings sought grapes from the incredible vineyards and wood from the lavish forests. Regardless of the men with whom she sailed, Freydis was much like her father. She was cold-hearted and ruthless.

Legends abound about Freydis. One is that after she gathered what she wanted from the land, she had her crew chief murder all the men they did not need to sail back with. None of her men would kill the women, so Freydis did that herself. She threatened her crew with death if they ever shared the story of what happened in Vinland. Eventually, the story was revealed. However, she was not banished, but Freydis and her family were never truly accepted after the truth came out.

The Vikings never sailed to Vinland again. It is presumed that the distance, over 2,200 miles, was too difficult to traverse. Many of the same riches that Vinland offered could be found in Norway. Greenland also lacked sufficient people to sustain villages in North America, especially due to the distance and run-ins with the indigenous people.

Chapter 4: The Fall of the Vikings

From the explosive start of the Viking Age with the ravaging of Lindisfarne Monastery in 793 until 1066 with the Battle of Stamford Bridge, the appearance of a longboat sent shockwaves through villages and towns. As with the proliferation of Viking raids, the cessation of raids happened more gradually than ending dramatically in a final battle. The people who are referred to as Vikings existed before and after 793 and 1066.

Map of Viking expansion.
https://commons.wikimedia.org/wiki/File:Viking_Expansion.svg

Most of the people who inhabited modern-day Scandinavia never sailed on a longboat or participated in raids. Thus, the end of the Viking Age did not equate to the annihilation of them as a people. However, the days of raiding, exploring, and pillaging faded away in the 11th century. Many evolving factors contributed to the demise of the Vikings as a band of warriors.

Under the leadership of Cnut the Great, also spelled Canute and Knut, the first stages of the changing landscape of the Viking raids occurred. As a young man, Cnut actively participated in Viking raids under the guidance of his father, Sweyn or Svein Forkbeard. Sweyn's style of raiding differed from the earlier raids of the 8th and early part of the 9th centuries. He was not content to just pillage monasteries; his raids had broader goals.

Sweyn's violent raids decimated much of England. Their king, Æthelred, paid Sweyn Danegeld, which was a type of extortion. Once the Vikings were paid the money, they were expected to leave. The larger forces complied, but smaller raiding parties continued to pillage the northern sections of England. In retaliation, Æthelred ordered the slaughter of all Danes in England.

A massacre on St. Brice's Day in 1002 killed Sweyn's sister. In a brutal response, Sweyn's forces invaded England the following year. Ruthless attacks were conducted by the invaders. For years, the battles raged back and forth between the English (then known as Anglo-Saxons) and Vikings. Again, King Æthelred resorted to paying Sweyn to leave England.

The raids subsided but did not conclude until 1013 when the lords and nobles of England conceded. They declared Sweyn king of England and forced Æthelred into exile. Sweyn became the first Viking king of England, adding another territory to his control (he was king of Denmark and Norway as well). This newly formed kingdom, referred to by historians as either the Anglo-Scandinavian or North Sea Empire, was short-lived, lasting for only about thirty years. Sweyn would only rule for about five weeks.

After Sweyn's death in 1014, Æthelred emerged from exile. With the support of England's nobles, Æthelred reestablished his kingdom. This forced the Viking army led by Cnut to leave English soil. However, Cnut regrouped his army and invaded England. By 1016, Cnut controlled much of England. London was ruled by Edmund, Æthelred's son. Once Edmund died in November 1016, Cnut assumed control of all of England.

Cnut gained control of Denmark in 1019, and Norway fell under his leadership in 1028. Cnut was ruthless in his quest for power and control. During the first few years of his reign, Cnut ruled through fear. However, he grew to become a great leader.

Cnut was the first king to rule all of England since the days of the Roman Empire. He successfully led his kingdoms because he blended diverse cultures and people in his courts. He recognized and rewarded those who had supported him in England, Denmark, and Norway. His unification of these lands under his rule changed the course of history for the Vikings.

Map of Cnut's realm.
Soerfm, CC BY-SA 4.0 <https://creativecommons.org/licenses/by-sa/4.0>, via Wikimedia Commons; https://commons.wikimedia.org/wiki/File:Cnut-north-sea-empire.png

It did not benefit Cnut or his kingdoms for the Vikings to loot and raid England any longer. Cnut successfully set up trade routes that benefited all in the North Sea Empire. The infrastructures in his different domains were vastly improved. The people in his kingdoms flourished. At the time of his death in 1035, England, Denmark, Norway, and parts of Sweden were stable.

Other areas in Europe also experienced different styles of leadership. This was another component that dramatically impacted the Vikings and their ability to successfully raid other countries. In part, the surge and power of the Vikings led to the restructuring of European governments.

Some leaders, such as Charlemagne, attempted to unite smaller kingdoms into larger ones under a central leadership. Charlemagne ruled over the Holy Roman Empire. However, those efforts largely collapsed after his death. The vacuum of unified leadership after the demise of the Holy Roman Empire allowed the Vikings to strike and loot lands more easily.

Gradually, Europe's system of government and its supporting military changed partly to meet the continual menace of the Viking raids. Feudalism was one of the negative factors that led to the end of the Viking Age, but this structure of ruling arose to address the rampage of the Vikings.

During the Early Middle Ages, Europe was not delineated like it is today, with defined countries or borders. Boundaries between kingdoms were often blurred. Centralized leadership, if it existed, was not able to defend or protect the entire kingdom. Without formal standing armies or militias, towns, villages, and monasteries had to find a way to defend themselves. The king's inability to effectively protect his kingdom gave rise to the hierarchical system of feudalism.

The local control of areas evolved into a system in which local lords or nobles ruled the land. On the top rung were the kings and queens. Royalty controlled all the land in the kingdom. However, the king and queen could not protect the vast lands that they ruled. In exchange for protecting the land and for loyalty, the king and queen allocated sections or units of land called a fief to a noble or lord.

The noble or lord ruled their fiefdom. In return for the land, the nobles became vassals of the king and queen, which meant they owed them their loyalty. Part of their allegiance to the crown was a pledge to protect the royal family.

Knights comprised the next tier of the system. Nobles or lords gave a section of their land to knights. Other compensation instead of land happened and could include money, housing, or equipment needed to perform their military obligations. In return, the knights were obligated to protect the nobles. The knights were trained in military operations and were called upon to fight any wars that the nobles or king and queen needed them for. Guarding the castle or providing a safe escort for the nobles and royalty also fell under the duties of the knights.

Surviving on the lowest rungs of the feudal society ladder were the peasants and serfs. Since peasants had mobility and could own land, they ranked above the serfs. Serfs were tied to the land and were comparable to thralls, although serfs had more rights. Tilling the land and providing products were the roles performed by the serfs. In exchange for their work in the fields, serfs were protected by the lord's militia.

This intricate system bonded each tier of society to each other. Dividing vast kingdoms into manageable sections that were controlled locally provided protection from the Vikings. Militias were formed and trained so they could defend their lands and people. In other areas, towns were moved away from the borders of rivers and oceans. Monasteries were relocated or built towers in which valuables could be hidden and defenses could be mounted. European towns and villages were no longer easy targets for the longships. For the Vikings, these obstacles reduced the profitability and ease of the raids.

Transformations within the Viking homelands also impacted Viking explorers and their ability to successfully continue their raiding and expansion. Similar to the rest of Europe, the boundary lines of Scandinavian countries continued to shift throughout the 11th century. During this period, Denmark, Sweden, and Norway began evolving to become separate kingdoms. As Scandinavian kings unified their lands, the culture of participating in Viking raids began to lose support.

Society at the beginning of the Viking Age was not as hierarchal as the feudal system that began to expand throughout Europe. Early raiders were often young male farmers who traveled for adventure and wealth. Upon their return, the former raiders would settle on their farms and have a family. With more centralized governments forming in the Scandinavian lands and a developing stratification of society, these young men no longer had the freedom to join the raids.

The date used by many as the fall of the Vikings was the Battle of Stamford Bridge. This battle was another contributing factor to the demise of the Vikings. After Cnut's death, his son, Harold Harefoot, became king of England. His reign was short-lived, and he died less than five years after assuming the throne. Another of Cnut's sons, Harthacnut, was named king; his tenure lasted a little over two years before his death. Before he died, Harthacnut named Edward the Confessor, son of King Æthelred, to be his successor. In 1042, Edward the Confessor became king of England.

And then things got complicated. When Edward died in 1066, he did not have a direct heir, which resulted in a dispute over who should succeed him. Three leading claimants felt they had valid rights to his throne. Promises were made to some; family connections made others viable candidates, and politics put other successors in contention. One contender was Harold Godwinson, the earl of Wessex, who was Edward's brother-in-law. William of Normandy was Edward's first cousin. And lastly, there was Edgar, the son of Edward the Exile, who was in the family bloodline but was very young.

The Battle of Hastings eventually resolved the dispute between Harold Godwinson and William of Normandy. It is uncertain if Edward the Confessor had a preference for who should succeed him. However, before that final showdown, there was a complication with another contender, Harald Hardrada, who was the king of Norway and the descendant of King Cnut. Joining and encouraging Harald Hardrada in his pursuit of England's crown was Tostig Godwinson, Harold's brother, who had been exiled by his brother and was looking to regain power. In 1066, King Harald Hardrada and Tostig led an armada of three hundred ships filled with over ten thousand warriors. On their way to battle with King Harold, the Vikings successfully fought Edwin and Morcar, the earls of Mercia and Northumbria, respectively.

Overconfident due to their recent successes, the Vikings were not fully prepared for battle. At the Battle of Stamford Bridge, both Tostig and Harald were killed. The Vikings were decimated. There were so few survivors that the Vikings needed only twenty-four of the three hundred ships they used to sail to England.

King Harold of England and his troops greatly diminished the Vikings' ability to continue inflicting their reign of terror. However, Harold's victory was fleeting in part because of the Vikings' initial successes in the Battle of Stamford Bridge.

Another leader of Viking descent also claimed that he was the legitimate king of England. William the Conqueror, who was a distant relation of Rollo, who became the first ruler of Normandy, claimed that his cousin, King Edward the Confessor, promised him the throne. William and his forces from Normandy invaded England in response to Harold not acknowledging his claims. In the Battle of Hastings, the Norman troops killed King Harold Godwinson and defeated the English troops in October 1066. William was crowned king of England on

Christmas Day, 1066.

After gaining the kingship, William faced numerous battles and challenges to his leadership before he conquered all of England. William sought complete control over England to protect his new kingdom from invasions, and he handily defeated his opponents. One of his last conquests was against King Sweyn II of Denmark.

This last Viking incursion began in 1069. English forces opposed to William requested King Sweyn's assistance. The Danish king sent his Vikings under the charge of his sons and brother, Asbjørn, to unite with Prince Edgar Ætheling, Æthelred II's great-grandson, and attack the coast of England and the town of York. They were temporarily successful in their capture of York; however, once William and his forces arrived on the scene, the rebels and Vikings were driven out. Still, the Vikings fled with the treasures they pillaged.

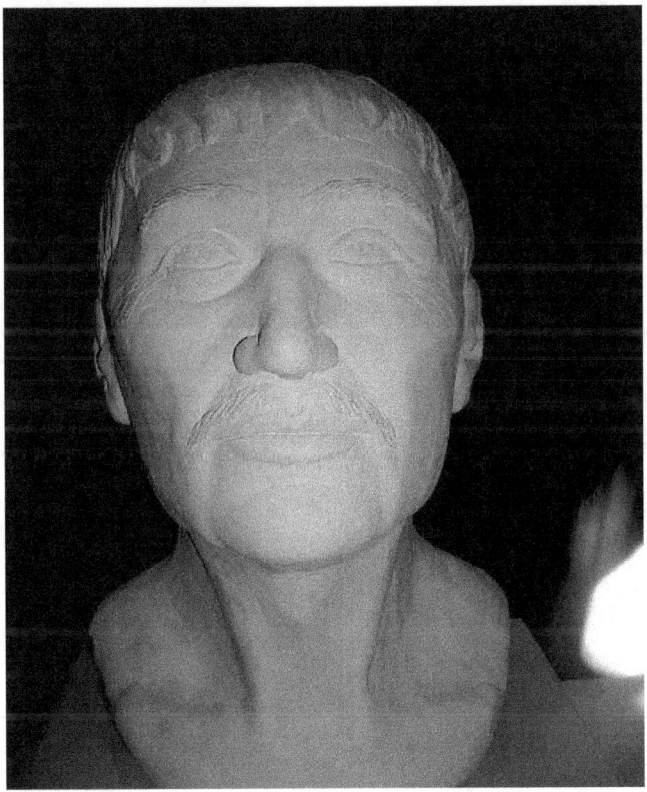

Statue of King Sweyn II.
Arne Kvitrud, CC BY-SA 4.0 <https://creativecommons.org/licenses/by-sa/4.0>, via Wikimedia Commons;https://commons.wikimedia.org/wiki/File:Svein_Estridssons_hode.JPG

In an attempt to keep the Vikings from returning, William was compelled to pay them and resorted to Danegeld. They stayed over the winter until reinforcements arrived, led by King Sweyn II. The Vikings joined forces with another rebel Anglo-Saxon leader, Hereward. Following Viking norms, they raided Peterborough Abbey. Knowing they would not defeat William, the Vikings took their treasures and set sail.

Longships would no longer suddenly appear on the shores of monasteries seeking gold and treasures as they did before. Vikings assimilated back into their homelands as farmers and craftsmen. Raids were no longer profitable due to the changing dynamics of societal structures and norms in Scandinavian and European countries.

SECTION TWO:
Regular Viking Life

Chapter 5: Societal Structure

The majority of those who lived during the Viking Age did not participate in raids. During this era, most people lived in towns and villages in Scandinavia. Warriors who did take part in pillaging returned home to their families. Their structured world has been pieced together from evidence discovered by archaeologists and other societies that wrote about the Vikings.

In many depictions of this world, there were four separate tiers. At the top of the pyramid were members of royalty, kings, and queens. This class emerged as a more powerful group as the Viking Age progressed.

Nobles and jarls formed the next class in society. Within this grouping were chieftains and military leaders who owned large estates. Jarls frequently recruited their own militia to protect their land. To foster loyalty, jarls hosted lavish feasts and festivals to honor gods and celebrate military victories and successful harvests.

The majority of the Viking era population belonged to the karls or freemen. Tradesmen, craftsmen, skilled workers, and farmers made up this group. This group, with its skilled boat builders, was essential to the success of the Viking raids. The Viking society's fourth class included slaves or thralls, who performed the most difficult work on the farms. Without thralls, farms would not have survived.

One was born into their class; however, there was some mobility to move up or down based on one's contributions or lack of to society. For example, if a jarl lost his land or wealth, he would become a karl. To protect one's status in society, many people were willing to fight to retain their class level. Violence was also inflicted on people who did not demonstrate the proper respect for someone of a higher societal level.

The structure of Viking society can be found in an ancient myth. In the poem *Rígsthula*, the Scandinavians talked about the classes. As with many stories from so long ago, there are different versions. In some depictions, Ríg and his descendants formed a four-tiered society; in other iterations, Ríg created a world with three classifications.

The god Heimdall disguised himself as Ríg and traveled to this world, which was also called Midgard or Middle Earth. During his time on Earth, Ríg stayed with three different families for three nights. While visiting, Ríg slept between each family's heads of the household. From these liaisons, a number of children were conceived. These children were the ancestors of each class of society.

Ríg in great-grandfather's cottage.

https://commons.wikimedia.org/wiki/File:Rig_in_Great-grandfather%27s_Cottage.jpg

Ríg's first stop on Middle Earth was an impoverished couple, Ái (great-grandfather) and Edda (great-grandmother). Though they were poor, the couple shared with Ríg their meager dwelling and food. Nine months after Ríg's visit, Edda gave birth to Thrall, which is believed to mean "Slave." He performed some of the more labor-intensive tasks on Ái's and Edda's land. Later on, Thrall met and had children with Thír. Thrall, Thír, and their children were all physically unkempt. They all performed tasks that required manual labor.

After Ríg's first stop on Middle Earth, he met Afi (grandfather) and Amma (grandmother). This couple lived in a modest but clean farmhouse. As with his first visit, Ríg stayed for three days and nights. Each night, he slept between Afi and Amma. Karl, which means freeman, was born to Amma nine months after Ríg stayed with the couple. Karl helped Afi and Amma on the farm. He married Snør (daughter-in-law), with whom he had children from whom farmers descended.

For his last visit, Ríg stopped at a large home that was beautifully decorated. He was invited to dine with Fadir (father) and Módir (mother). They treated Ríg to lavish feasts. Ríg slept nightly between Fadir and Módir. Nine months later, Jarl (earl) was born. Jarl learned how to communicate with runes, make and use weapons, and successfully fight in wars. Due to his prowess as a warrior, Jarl was rewarded with the ownership of eighteen farms.

Jarl married Erna, with whom he fathered several children. His youngest son, Konr (king), was the ancestor of Viking royalty. Ríg's time on Midgard provided the tiers of Viking society. He fathered three sons who each started the lineage of the class of thralls, karls, and jarls. His grandson, Konr, was the first king of the Norse lands.

Kings were not selected based on their bloodlines, nor were they a powerful force at the beginning of the Viking Age. Throughout the era of the Vikings, the countries of Denmark, Norway, and Sweden emerged as separate entities. With that evolving structure, the role of kings and queens also transitioned.

During the Viking Age, Norse royalty was expected to be brave, exhibit leadership, and be fierce warriors. Most Viking kings were selected from local chieftains. They were chosen based on their accomplishments. Wealth also contributed to their power, as chieftains were able to finance more men for their army. The ability to create and retain bonds of loyalty was important for chieftains to maintain their role and be elevated to royalty.

Allegiance to the king or chieftain was also important. Without loyalty, it was difficult for a leader to provide protection for his kingdom. The area over which a king ruled in the Viking Age does not correspond to modern-day boundaries for any of the Scandinavian countries. The domains kings ruled over were compilations of small kingdoms and various chiefdoms. His ability to stay in power necessitated frequent battles with other local leaders.

As the Viking Age and the reach of the Vikings grew, the role of royalty changed. Kings became leaders of larger and larger swathes of land and people. With a more centralized power base, they were able to conscript more men to join the military. Since there was not a bloodline lineage of royalty at the beginning of the Viking Age, they relied heavily on the support of the people they ruled. Warriors' loyalty was often based on how much the king shared feasts, weapons, and mutual alliances with them. Leaders who were not generous with their riches were susceptible to being overthrown.

Due to their wealth and power, earls or jarls became an influential class in Viking society. Many kings emerged from this group. Jarls were often landowners, successful traders, or merchants. The jarls used similar methods as the kings, rewarding those who worked their lands with celebrations centered around food and drink. Jarls also shared treasures from Viking raids to ensure the loyalty of those living in their chiefdom. These powerful men did not just spoil the villagers to show their wealth; they expected allegiance from the freemen to join them in battles or on Viking raids.

Early on in the Viking Age, there were more jarls than kings. Controlling smaller estates was more manageable than large kingdoms. Additionally, when Vikings settled the new lands they conquered, these settlements were ruled by jarls. Powerful jarls sought to find lands they could rule while on raids. Once in charge of the lands they captured, the new leaders could impose rules that were important to them.

Neither the kings nor the jarls could stay in power without the support of the karls or freemen. This third tier of Viking society fought battles with the jarls as they sought to conquer neighboring land. They followed their jarls onto ships to participate in raids and settled the lands that were captured in other countries.

Most of the members of this class were farmers. The early days of raiding were planned around the planting and harvesting seasons because of this. On these pillaging expeditions, karls were expected to provide their own weaponry. Karls needed shields, spears, and axes. Unlike jarls, the karls were not trained in combat. Jarls also entered battled better equipped. Only the wealthy warriors had spears and protective garments to wear into battle.

Replica of a Viking era farm.
Mark Voigt, CC BY 3.0 <https://creativecommons.org/licenses/by/3.0>, via Wikimedia Commons;
https://commons.wikimedia.org/wiki/File:The_Viking_Farm,_Avaldsnes_05.2010_-_panoramio_(1).jpg

Though the karls were freemen, they relied heavily on their local leaders. Either the jarls or kings provided protection for the karls. Additionally, the top two tiers of society also controlled the wealth. Shares from raids provided the karls with income, but that amount was determined by the leaders. Also, if kings or jarls needed to increase their revenue, they could control the amount of goods that merchants sold. They could also demand tribute or protection money to permit merchants and traders to enter their lands.

As freemen, karls were able to own their own land. If they could not afford to buy their land, karls could rent land from the kings or jarls. They could choose to live where they wanted. Karls could also choose whether to start their own family or business.

In return for their freedom, karls were expected to swear an oath to promise their commitment to the local jarl or king. This pledge had to be taken when a boy reached adulthood. This allegiance also meant the karls had to fight on behalf of the jarl. Anytime the jarl needed assistance on his farm for planting or harvesting, he could summon the karls to help. In return, the jarls would keep the karls safe. Karls paid taxes in silver or gave a portion of their harvest to pay for the jarls' support.

The last tier of Viking society consisted of people referred to as thralls or slaves. The basis of the word "thrall" is Old Norse from *þræll*, which refers to a person who lived in a state of servitude. It is believed that the word slave is rooted in Slavic because many Slavic people during the Middle Ages were captured and sold into slavery.

In Viking society, a person was a slave if they were born to parents who were slaves. A person could be sold into slavery as punishment for certain crimes. If a family became financially destitute, they could sell themselves to another family to be their thralls. Many people became slaves because they were captured during a battle between two jarls; the prisoners of the victorious jarl were sold as slaves. Lastly, prisoners of Viking warriors became slaves when they arrived in Scandinavia.

People in this tier of society were not able to own land and were forced to work for their owners. The success of a farm depended on the people who worked the land. Therefore, slaves were not usually mistreated in the Viking Age. Slaves were permitted to marry and have children. Most thralls were allowed to have their own possessions. Farmers sometimes let slaves work for themselves and make money. Sometimes, slaves could share the earnings from raids. Some Vikings freed slaves as a reward for their work, and other slaves were able to save enough money to buy their freedom.

Women were not identified as a separate tier in Viking society, but they did have important roles in ensuring the smooth operation of daily life. As with other cultures of the same time period, men were considered superior to women. Men were responsible for fighting in battles, joining raids and other expeditions, farming, and hunting. Women controlled the household. Though wives were not equal to their husbands, women had more freedom than their contemporaries. Norse women were permitted to own property in their own names. They could also share their husband's wealth. Though marriages were often arranged, a woman could seek a divorce.

In some households, women had thralls who helped with the daily tasks of running a home. Maintaining a house included all aspects of food preparation and serving the food. Women had to manage the inventory and preparation of food that was stored for consumption between growing seasons. Women also ensured the family had sufficient provisions for the long winter. Milking the cows and producing butter and cheese were part of their daily tasks. Women also had to spin and weave to create cloth; then, they had to shape the cloth into garments and sew clothing for everyone in the house.

When the men of the village left to go raiding, the women were in charge. Symbolically and publicly, a husband would hand his household keys to his wife before setting sail. All in the village were informed of who was responsible for the farm and house while he was away. If her husband died, she was fully in control of the farm or business.

Everyone, regardless of societal ranking, contributed to the success of the village. Even children participated and had daily chores to complete. Children did not attend school. Instead, they learned the skills they needed to survive as an adult and had their own families. Boys would spend time with their fathers learning how to farm, fight, and fish. If their father were a craftsman, the son would be taught that trade. Girls learned how to prepare and store food, make clothes, sew, spin wool, knit, and brew ale.

Chapter 6: Village Life

In areas where the Vikings settled after raids, they installed their societal foundations. Part of their world was the structure of their class system. The Vikings also had an organized village life. Framing the workings of their communities was their method of governance, which was so effective that the Scandinavians instituted their legal system in the areas they settled.

One key component of the Viking judicial system was an assembly called the Thing or Althing. Various iterations of the spelling of "Thing" can be found in different regions. All variants are from the Old Norse word þing, which refers to a governing body or assembly. Governments in parts of Scandinavia continue to be based on Things. Denmark's Folketing or People's Thing, Norway's Storting or Great Thing, and Iceland's Althing or General Thing guide each country today. Iceland's Althing was established in 930 and is the oldest national parliament still in existence.

Althing in Iceland.
https://commons.wikimedia.org/wiki/File:Law_speaker.jpg

Throughout Scandinavian lands, including Viking colonies, Things were held in each village or community. All freemen, including jarls, were expected to attend and participate in their area's Thing. If they were not able to attend, a representative was sent instead, or the freemen had to pay a fine. Women also attended their village assembly unless they were widowers. Those who worked or lived alone were not required to attend unless the agenda for the meeting included selecting a king or deciding a murderer's fate.

Assemblies were held twice a year and lasted for many days. As a communal event, Things were a much-anticipated social gathering. Craftsmen brought goods to sell. Barrels of ale and mead were made by the local brewmaster. Meetings were arranged to be near sources of water. Fields were accessible for animals to graze, and hunting and fishing supplied food for all attendees. Community members shared the latest news about their families, which often led to the arrangement of marriages. Alliances were strengthened or dissolved.

Though these assemblies had a festive air to them, their main purpose was to craft new laws and to determine the guilt or innocence of anyone accused of crimes. Anyone in the community could bring a grievance before the Thing. Local chieftains presided over these early democratic assemblies. The lawspeaker assisted him in deciding cases or situations presented to the assembly.

Though Vikings did not record their laws and write them down, they did have a set of agreed-upon rules and regulations that governed their society. A lawspeaker attended each Thing. The lawspeaker could recite all of the Viking laws from memory. He could also recall decisions made at previous meetings. Lawspeakers would provide this information to those in charge of deciding the fate of the accused. Neighbors and those attending the Thing could voice their concerns about the charges being discussed before the final decision was made. The comments by the public unofficially assisted in the decision-making process.

If the offender was found guilty, they were fined, made a partial outlaw, or completely outlawed. Partial outlaws were banished from society for no longer than three years. Anyone fully outlawed was exiled for life. In addition to having to leave their town or village, full outlaws lost all of their property, although their families were not always exiled along with them. No one was permitted to assist an outlaw. This punishment was considered a horrific feat.

The Things had no power to enforce the decisions that were made. However, each Viking was bound by a sense of duty to their community and typically did as was expected.

In addition to meting out justice, Things set tax rates for people in the community. They also made certain that each man in their jurisdictions was properly equipped with weapons to protect the villages. Things also voted for kings. Lastly, these assemblies created new laws if deemed necessary. At the conclusion of the meeting, the people's agreement was demonstrated by shaking and clanging their weapons (*vápnatak*).

Another way disputes were resolved was through a duel or *hólmganga*. Duels had extremely strict rules that were enforced and monitored by a referee. *Hólmgangas* could only be fought on a ten-foot square space of a cloak. Stepping off the cloak was viewed as a spineless act (a *nithing*). Swords and shields were the weapons of choice by duelers. The man with the most wounds at the end of the duel lost, and he had to pay the winner with silver. If one dueler died, the winner or survivor assumed control of all of his property. Most *hólmgangas* resulted in the death of one of the combatants.

Dueling was deemed illegal during the reign of King Cnut. As the role and power of the kings grew throughout the Viking Age, more legal decisions were centralized. Loyalty and honor were two important traits for Vikings. Most members of Scandinavian societies followed rules of conduct. The desire to be respected guided one's daily decisions.

Societal norms dictated the behavioral expectations of villagers during the Viking Age. This included standards of comportment for banquets and other events. Feasts were held to celebrate various occasions, such as weddings, funerals, festivals, and successful raids and harvests.

The sharing of one's bounty was important for those hosting any feast. The success of the feast due to the host's hospitality could elevate a person's status in society. Guests were seated according to their status in the town. A stranger or visitor to a feast was required to recite his family's lineage so it could be determined where they should be positioned at the table.

Seating for a feast in the king's great hall or the local farmer's table was not done by chance. Valued guests earned a seat next to or across from the host. Whether the host was the king or the head of the house, they sat in the seat of honor (*hásæti*). The lowest-ranking guest was assigned the seat farthest away from the host. Errors in seating could lead to angry exchanges if it were perceived that one was not respected by the host.

Regardless of the wealth of the person holding the feast, the celebrations were lavish affairs. Some feasts and festivals lasted for days. During that time, attendees ate and drank copious amounts of food and beverages. Mead and ale were consumed along with vegetables and meats from farms.

Farming was essential to the survival of the Vikings. Yes, farming supplied food for feasts, but successful farms and the storage of food were needed to sustain Vikings through the cold, dark winter months. Most Viking farmers were self-sufficient, meaning they raised enough livestock and grew enough crops to survive without outside help. They supplemented meat from the animals they raised with hunting and fishing.

The majority of people during the Viking Age were farmers. Everyone in the family participated in agricultural activities. Most farms had slaves who assisted with some of the more challenging daily tasks. Those who did not farm, such as blacksmiths, traded their goods and services for food.

The lack of fertile and level land made growing enough food to feed a family challenging. Long, dark, cold winters added to the complexities faced by the Scandinavians. Though the summers provided long sunny days, the summers were brief, and the growing season was short. Participating in Viking raids added income for some of the Scandinavian farmers. Others took advantage of captured land in areas with better conditions for farming and resettled in new countries.

In the early days of Viking raids, prosperous villages consisted of six to eight farms. These homesteads were separated from each other and the village center. Farms in less flourishing areas were not centered around a village; instead, they were isolated farmhouses. Often, farms had fences that identified the land boundaries of the farm. Within the fenced area was a longhouse, which was the dwelling of the family and the farm animals. Keeping the animals in the longhouse protected the valuable livestock during the frigid winters and added warmth to the family home. Food storage, the farmer's workshop, and farming utensils were also stored in the longhouse.

As farms grew, the longhouse remained the focal building of the family farm. However, other outbuildings were added over time. Workshops, stables, and barns were constructed. The longhouse transitioned to becoming the family home. Most family farms operated independently. Farmers grew their own food, made their own tools, and constructed their own buildings.

Reconstructed longhouse.
Sven Rosborn, CC BY 3.0 <https://creativecommons.org/licenses/by/3.0>, via Wikimedia Commons; https://commons.wikimedia.org/wiki/File:Viking_house_Ale_Sweden.jpg

Buildings were erected near sources of water. Structures were also located on higher ground to allow for better drainage. Situating buildings on an elevated site also provided the farmer and his family greater visibility. Not everyone who approached the farm was a welcome visitor, so the inhabitants had time to gather their weapons for protection. Signal fires were lit to warn nearby farms of dangerous situations or summon assistance. Everyone on the farm was expected to support and defend each other. Local chieftains and neighbors assisted one another.

Fields for grazing and growing crops surrounded the buildings located on the farm. The most important livestock was the cattle. Runic symbols and the word for cattle, the *Fehu* rune and *fé*, respectively, equate these animals to money and wealth. In order to plant crops, oxen were needed to plow the fields. A range of foods was produced from dairy cows, some of which could be made into foods that the Vikings stored and consumed throughout the winter. Cheese, butter, and *skyr* (a product similar to yogurt) sustained Vikings throughout the winter. Some dairy products were also used to preserve meat for winter consumption.

Another animal raised by many Viking farmers was the sheep. In addition to sheep being a food and milk source, their wool was used to create fabric and clothing. During the summer months, livestock was herded and driven to pastures located higher in the mountains. They roamed freely and fed on the fertile lands. Small stables and huts were built near the summer grazing lands.

Someone from the family farm or a farmhand stayed up in the highlands with the herds. They milked the cows and ewes. Milk was stored and transported to the main farm in skin sacks. Often, the herds from different farms mingled together. At the end of the summer season, the herds had to be separated by its farm. They were then driven back to the family farm for the winter. Usually, dairy cows were housed in a barn during the winter and fed hay. Otherwise, there was the potential for starvation if they were left outside.

Other farm animals raised on Scandinavian farms included goats, horses, pigs, chickens, and ducks. All of them required hay to sustain themselves throughout the winter. Hay was vital to Viking life. Laws were agreed upon that necessitated the growing and harvesting of enough hay to feed the animals. It was against Scandinavian law to let land on which hay was growing to decay and not be harvested before it rotted.

Replica of a Viking farm.
Mark Voigt, CC BY 3.0 <https://creativecommons.org/licenses/by/3.0>, via Wikimedia Commons; https://commons.wikimedia.org/wiki/File:The_Viking_Farm,_Avaldsnes_05.2010_-_panoramio_(1).jpg

Farmers were tasked with ensuring they had an adequate supply of hay for the winter. At the end of the harvest season, they inventoried their hay and livestock. If there was not enough hay to feed all the animals for the entire winter, the farmer slaughtered the weakest animals.

Grains were the most common crops. Barley, rye, and oats were ground into flour. Women made bread, which was preserved and stored for consumption during the winter. Grains were also used to make porridge, flatbreads, and ale. Flax was also grown on farms and used to make textiles.

Vegetables were sown in the spring and harvested in the late summer and early fall. During the harvest season, Vikings consumed freshly harvested vegetables. Some of the crops were saved for the winter; those vegetables were dried. Women and children also collected wild berries, herbs, and other plants. These greens and fruits were eaten during the summer and fall. Some were set aside and prepared for the winter via salting or drying.

The Norse people ate twice a day: the *dagmal*, or day meal, and the *nattmal*, or night meal. The food served at each meal was similar, although the time of the year greatly influenced the availability of food. Stewed vegetables, meats, and fish were the most common dishes and were served with mead or ale. Water was not often consumed because one risked illness or death due to unclean water. Food not consumed at the meal would have been stored in the coolest part of the house. The leftovers were reheated and re-served at the next family meal.

Vikings worked long, arduous hours. Therefore, they needed to eat foods high in calories and fat content so they had enough energy to complete their daily tasks. While the Vikings consumed food without the benefit of refrigeration, they were healthy. The remains of the Scandinavian people do not show they were lacking in vitamins or minerals.

Chapter 7: Literature and the Runic Alphabet

Vikings were industrious workers and made the most out of the land they farmed. During village and family feasts, Vikings entertained themselves with storytelling and sharing poetry. The long, dark winter provided time for families and villagers to perform maintenance on their homes and farms. Warriors practiced their skills for the next season of sailing and raiding.

Adults and children played a variety of games. The Scandinavians were a competitive group. *Hnefatafl*, which was similar to chess, could end up as a physical match. Many of their activities involved challenging each other in feats of cliff jumping or rock climbing. Swimming matches could lead to attempts to drown each other.

Though the Vikings enjoyed physical and aggressive activities, they also valued the skills of poetry and storytelling. These two skills framed the enjoyment of many feasts. The hosts of feasts served the best food they had. Guests were expected to wear their finest garments. Tables were set, and hand-embroidered tapestries were displayed on the walls. Even the dirt floors, which usually were strewn with trash, were covered with straw.

Meats were frequently roasted on the spit over an open fire or boiled. The people used all the parts of the animals. For instance, sausages were made from the organs and blood of animals. Women and thralls prepared fish in many ways, including pickled, smoked, and dried.

The host's daughter(s) and the family thralls served mead and ale to the guests. Many Vikings drank from horns, which could not be placed down until they were emptied. Inebriation was common during feasts and festivals. In this spirited setting, the *skáld* or poet performed stories. Sometimes, the poet would compose pieces to honor the cause for celebration.

Poets were important people in Viking society. Their ability to retell their culture's myths, heroic tales, and oral histories was valued, especially since poets emphasized the traits that were important in the warrior tradition. "Saga" is an Old Norse word for "saying." The stories shared by the poets were done in the oral tradition. Each generation passed its narratives to the next generation. Influential families from the Viking Age hired their own family *skáld*. It was the family poet's role to learn and memorize the family history to share with future generations. The reciting of the family saga was often embellished by the poet, and over time, more embellishments and accomplishments were added.

Later in the Middle Ages, these tales were collected and recorded. The main bodies of sagas were written well after the events occurred. Stories from the Viking Age are an intricate fusion of adventures and historical events that included the politics of the time. As with many tales written years later, they are a blend of fact and fiction. But with evidence from archaeological discoveries, some of the events, such as the Vikings sailing to North America, have been verified.

The *skálds* wove such incredible tales that their format influenced the development of prose in literature. Most literature committed to writing during the Middle Ages was poetry. But the Scandinavian tales were about everyday protagonists. Kings, queens, gods, and goddesses did not fill the pages of Scandinavian narratives.

The lead characters in the tales included shipbuilders, farmers, warriors, and others from everyday life. Sagas from the Norse focused on telling people's actual stories. The Norse sagas were categorized by genre, depending upon the topic of the narrative.

Stories about legendary or heroic figures are grouped as fornaldarsögur. Listeners would hear about people from the ancient past. Elements of fantasy were part of the plot line and included dragons, dangerous quests, and mythical creatures. Kings and queens were prominent in the stories known as konungasögur. In these stories, actual events framed the narrative, along with details about leaders from the time period. Another genre of sagas was family sagas or the Íslendingasögur. In these narratives, the stories and struggles of everyday people and the complexity of the human experience provided listeners with real role models.

Title page of the Prose Edda.
https://commons.wikimedia.org/wiki/File:Edda.jpg

Another grouping of stories based on the Scandinavian oral storytelling tradition is the Eddas. These collections tell of the gods and goddesses of the Viking world. There are two groups of Eddas. The *Elder Edda*, also called the *Poetic Edda*, is based on a document from the Middle Ages, the *Codex Regius*. The *Younger Edda*, which was also referred to as the *Prose Edda*, was written by Snorri Sturluson. Together, the *Poetic Edda* and the *Prose Edda* provide rich sources of Norse mythology and ancient belief systems from long ago. Materials in both Eddas were formed into manuscripts in the 13th century.

Works included in the *Poetic Edda* are tales from Norse myths. It is the most extensive written compilation of stories from the oral tradition of Scandinavian tales. Poems in the anthology tell of the Norse gods and the world's origins, as well as legends and heroes of the Viking world. Snorri Sturluson wrote the "newer" or *Younger Edda*. In this volume, Sturluson shared tales that show the beliefs and customs of the Scandinavian people. Stories of incredible warriors and their fantastic feats are available for today's readers, allowing them to access the Vikings' heroic past and other worlds.

Part of what influenced Sturluson to compose his text was the desire to preserve the poetic past of the Viking world. Poetry was used to memorialize incredible occurrences and the people involved. His textbook taught others how to continue creating skaldic poetry in the Scandinavian tradition. His work, sometimes referred to as *Snorra Edda*, provides information on myths from the Norse world, a guide to writing poetry, how the skaldic poets chose their words, and the rhythm schematics employed by the ancient poets.

The people of the Viking Age did not write manuscripts. Similar to the lawspeakers, who were responsible for memorizing laws, poets used verse as a means for ideas to be recalled and shared. This proved to be an effective method of communicating between distances and time. Poems and their messages ranged from words of praise and adulation to insults and vilification.

The words created by poets were so important that kings had their own poets as part of their entourage to memorialize their great deeds. Poets were key figures in Viking society. They held the power to preserve events and affect history. They also entertained at feasts and festivals. If a poet wrote a verse about a person, their accomplishments or misdeeds were recorded for all time. This either elevated or deflated one's status and their family's ranking in their community.

To enable poets to view events, kings created shield walls or *skjaldborgs*. Poets observed battles from a safe distance. They took notes and composed poems that retold the sequence of events and highlighted memorable deeds of warriors and leaders.

In addition to creating new verses, poets were also a source of past knowledge. Queries about past events, leaders, or families could be posed to a local poet, who was expected to be able to accurately answer any questions. Snorri Sturluson shared the details of how verses were expected to be formatted. The patterns of alliteration, rhythm, and internal rhyme served as cues for those reciting the poems. Intricacies in word choice and construction enabled the conveyors of information to recall numerous verses correctly.

Kings and leaders used poems to inspire warriors before battles. The creative fusions of words entertained people at royal and village feasts. Ordinary people were honored through artistic expression, while others were scorned for their actions by poets.

Another means of memorializing people and events was through words engraved on stone monuments. Messages written in runes were inscribed on a variety of materials for a number of distinct purposes. Unlike poems, which allowed for lengthy messages, runes were usually brief and concise. Similar to poets, a rune writer was viewed as having valuable skills that they learned and mastered.

Sixteen runes or characters comprised the basic Viking alphabet. Each letter was formed from a distinct sequence of lines. The various patterns of lines represented each of the sixteen letters. Sometimes, the runic alphabet is called Futhark, which is the first six letters (f, u, th, a, r, and k) of the full alphabet, which contains sixteen letters.

Lines were used to form letters since they could be easily chiseled into many different materials. Each glyph or symbol represented a sound. Each vertical line that was part of a letter was called a stave. Diagonal markings were called twigs. Horizontal lines were not used in the letters because they could be misconstrued as part of the woodgrain.

ᚠᚢᚦᚭᚱᚴ ᚼᚾᛁᛅᛋ ᛏᛒᛘᛚᛦ
ᚠᚢᚦᚨᚱᚴ ᚺᚾᛁᛃᛁ ᛏᛒᛗᛚᛦ
fuþąrk hnias tbmlR

Image of runes.
https://commons.wikimedia.org/wiki/File:Yngre_futharken.svg

Runic inscriptions were used to communicate many different ideas in the Viking world. Some messages simply identified the owner of an object. Merchants and traders used rune sticks to track the selling and buying of goods. The costs were recorded, and the buyer of the goods or the seller of the merchandise was identified through the use of runes. Informational messages, love notes, and complaints were shared using runes. Due to the broad usage of runes, many historians believe the Vikings were fairly literate.

In addition to runes' uses for common, everyday notes and messages, they were also a means to memorialize the dead. Sometimes, these brief yet remarkable lines are classified as another category of Viking poetry. Elite families could have memorials with runic inscriptions that detailed the accomplishments of the deceased.

Two of the most well-known runestones are located in Jelling, Denmark. The older of the two stones, dating back to the 10th century, was raised by King Gorm the Old to honor his wife, Queen Thyre. One translation of the runes celebrating Queen Thyre acknowledges her as the savior of Denmark.

Picture of the Jelling runestones.
Alicudi, CC BY-SA 3.0 <https://creativecommons.org/licenses/by-sa/3.0>, via Wikimedia Commons; https://commons.wikimedia.org/wiki/File:Runesten_i_Jelling.jpg

It is believed that while King Gorm and other leaders were participating in Viking raids, Thyre led Denmark. To fight off Saxon invasions, the queen continued building the defensive Dannevirke. The construction of this protective wall began in the 6th century. The largest sections of Dannevirke were constructed during the Viking Age.

After King Gorm and Queen Thyre died, their son, Harald Blatand (better known as Harald Bluetooth), became ruler. He had a runestone constructed to pay tribute to his parents. A tribute to King Harald is also on the stone. Harald ruled both Denmark and Norway. Harald inscribed a portrayal of Jesus on the stone to acknowledge his role in bringing Christianity to Denmark. Both Jelling stones are now UNESCO World Heritage Sites.

Part of King Harald Blatand's legacy was his ability to unite people. During his reign, King Harald united many Viking tribes. This unification framed the country of Denmark. His runic symbols are used today on all Bluetooth devices. The founders of Bluetooth chose his runic initials for their company icon.

Another impressive example of a runestone can be found in Sweden. The Rök runestone is a massive structure. It is over eight feet high and weighs over five tons. The runic etchings on the Rök runestone include 28 lines of text that incorporate 760 runes. Deciphering the runes has been a challenge since there are different styles of writing and versions of the Futhark woven through its script.

Varin, a local chieftain, erected the monument to honor his son, Vamoth. The cause of Varin's son's death remains a mystery. The stone includes Norse myths, Viking legends, and family sagas, which all overlap each other. References to historical events are included on the Rök stone. In the 6th century, the sun was obscured for years because of volcanic eruptions. It is not known if this caused Varin to believe that his son's death was inevitable or not. However, inscriptions commissioned by Varin suggest that his son was destined to die. Once Vamoth was dead, he could join the armies of the gods.

Many Vikings believed the runes were magical. The power that came with the ability to write added to the mystical aura of communicating through runes. Runes were believed to provide protection from illnesses, in battles, and against sorceresses. Many thought that the messages inscribed using the runic alphabet contained layers of meaning. Secrets and mysteries were thought to be hidden within the letters and glyphs.

Chapter 8: Art, Design, and Architecture

Viking art and design wove together utilitarian purposes and images that spoke to a deeper meaning. Similar to the use of runes, which were letters and symbols for sounds, to communicate daily ideas, design elements intertwined layers of meaning like the runes' power beyond the literal use of the Futhark. From the Old Norse word for secrets, runes imparted supernatural forces into warriors' shields, amulets, and talismans.

The runic alphabet is closely associated with the god Odin. It was believed that Odin gave this sacred communication to the world. Therefore, the staves and twig impressions were part of the message of and connection to the other world. Casting runes on sticks in a particular manner was a way to understand the world, assist with troubles, and help solve problems. Skilled readers could untangle the message and help people find the symbolic meaning sent in the rune cast.

Runes were not the only means used during the Viking Age to communicate multiple layers of meaning. Visual images intertwined the belief system of the Scandinavian peoples with their cultural icons. Symbols represented the themes and morals that were shared orally through poetry, narratives, and songs. Many Vikings believed in the impact of putting symbols on talismans and artifacts. These mementos with powerful symbols provided the holder reassurance that they could successfully face upcoming challenges.

Vikings used many powerful concrete images to represent intangible concepts. Animals, crosses, depictions of nature, and talismans of the gods frequently appeared in Viking designs. Each of these provided protection and support on one's journey in this world and the next. Evoking assistance from the mystical realm was an important part of the use of amulets.

Decorative patterns combined a mix of emblematic and pragmatic designs. Depictions included on objects and in Viking art revealed beliefs about their gods and goddesses, societal structure, and warrior culture. Viking art is typically examined as six different stylistic periods. The dates and elements of each era overlap each other. Usually, the name of each grouping of art styles is based on the location where the most famous example was found.

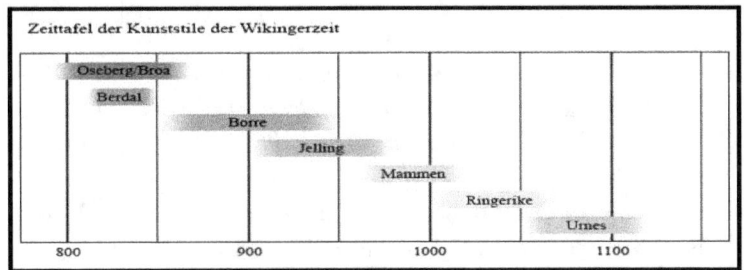

Timeline of Viking art.
Stefan Bollmann, CC BY-SA 3.0 <http://creativecommons.org/licenses/by-sa/3.0/>, via Wikimedia Commons; https://commons.wikimedia.org/wiki/File:Kunststile_der_Wikingerzeit.jpg

The first category of Viking art dates from about 750 to 850 and is referred to as Oseberg/Broa. A Viking burial ship was found at the Oseberg farm in Norway, while a twenty-two-carat gold-leaved horse bridle was discovered at Broa in Gotland, Sweden.

Animals were often depicted in the decorations throughout all six periods of Viking art. Animals etched during the Oseberg/Broa period were abstract and shown in a deconstructed manner. Animals had elongated, looping limbs, oversized protruding eyes, and undersized heads. They are known as ribbon-animals. A mixture of thick and thin lines and knots blended in with the animal shapes.

Art from the Broa area.
Elisabet Pettersson, Historiska museet/SHM, CC BY 4.0 <https://creativecommons.org/licenses/by/4.0>, via Wikimedia Commons; https://commons.wikimedia.org/wiki/File:Stora_och_Lilla_Ihre_Grave_174_Pommel_(310203).png

Variations of the animal shapes were noted in the Oseberg area. Illustrations more clearly show the animal's claws grasping one edge of the carving. Within the animal's talons were decorative designs that enhanced the motif. The details are more noticeable due to the variants in surface area.

The Borre period dated from 850 to about 950. Significant artifacts from a burial ship and cemetery were unearthed in Borre, Norway, that contained designs that frame this style of art. Gripping animals continued from the Oseberg style; however, the heads were transformed into triangular shapes.

Artifacts show an increase in geometric designs. Tighter weaves of intricate and interlaced almost-symmetrical lines showcase the animal motif. The ring-chain or ribbon weave designs were created by a continuous looping of the braids and spirals. Some of the swirls and twists are distortions of the animal's body.

Overlapping the Borre style was the Jelling style, which emerged toward the end of the 9th century and concluded before the close of the 10th century. As with the other Viking art styles, Jelling denotes where the items were found. A silver cup with elements of the Jelling style was discovered in burial grounds in Jelling, Denmark.

The characteristics of animals are more ribbon-shaped and less tightly formed than the Borre style. More fluidity was assigned to the S-shaped beasts. Varying geometric lines and images were used to denote the body parts of the animals. More similar to the Broa artifacts, the bodies and heads of the beasts were drawn showing their profile; however, the lines of the illustrations were cleaner, which made the background more prominent. The Jelling style was different from earlier periods of Viking art because of the tendrils or lappets that emanated from the neck of the beast.

Discoveries in a grave site in Mammen, Denmark, provide the naming of the next chronological style of Viking art. An ax head found in the grave is the archetypical representation of this time period, with imagery weaving together Christianity and paganism. The years 950 to 1000 overlap the reign of King Harald Bluetooth and the infusion of Christianity into the lives of the Vikings. Inscriptions on the Jelling runestone, which were commissioned by King Harald, included the Great Beast. King Harald Bluetooth's powerful accomplishments, bringing Christianity to Denmark and controlling Norway, are shown in the motif of the Great Breast.

The Great Beast is a fusion of many animals and emanates strength. It is depicted as a four-legged creature with claw-like feet. Coiled and expanding serpents are woven around the Great Beast. Designs similar to garlands and plants spiral with the snake, creating a sense of robust movement.

Depictions of the Great Beast continued into the Ringerike era, which closed out the 10th century and greeted the 11th century. Commemorative burial stones discovered in Ringerike, Norway, provide the name and style of this grouping of art. Energetic poses of forceful animals were the basis for the stylistic elements. However, Ringerike illustrations were more streamlined and less hectic than Mammen etchings.

Animals continued to be shown in their profile with more complexity than in previous etchings. Thinner whorls of plant-like tendrils coil around beasts. The movement created with the symmetrical strands or antlers emerging from an animal's head gives it a graceful flow.

The culminating period of Viking art is the Urnes style. Relief carvings found on a stave church in Urnes, Norway, exemplified this period's characteristics. This last period is also referred to as the runestone style since depictions were often found on memorial stones throughout the region.

Picture of carvings in Urnes.
Eduardo, CC BY-SA 2.0 <https://creativecommons.org/licenses/by-sa/2.0>, via Wikimedia Commons; https://commons.wikimedia.org/wiki/File:La_pared_original_de_la_Urnes_stavkyrkje_(I).jpg

Sophisticated imprints of the Great Beast were sketched during the Urnes period. Flowing asymmetrical lines formed the animals. The serpent-like creatures were thinner than previously seen and drawn in figure-eight configurations. Elongated features generate a majestic posture in the greyhound-like animal.

Throughout all the art eras of the Viking Age, craftsmen and artisans used art as a means to add decorative elements to everyday objects. The materials chosen to craft the objects were durable and readily available. A vast array of functional objects was transformed through intricate animal designs and abstract lines. Items ranging from shields, weapons, parts of ships, runestones, drinking vessels, jewelry, and more were etched with illustrations.

Relief carvings and engravings were the most common techniques employed by Viking craftsmen. Juxtaposing different materials and colors was another method to create ornate decorations. Some evidence of the use of vivid paints remains, but most of the paint has disintegrated.

In addition to using materials that were easy to find, Vikings also enjoyed working with and wearing adornments made from different metals. Men and women during the Viking Age wore jewelry constructed from gold, silver, and bronze. To obtain these precious metals, Viking merchants and warriors traded for or pillaged these resources. Jewelry was fabricated from locally sourced wood, beads, amber, and glass. Often, the same geometric and animal designs that were used to decorate useable goods were etched on jewelry.

Some jewelry was worn to indicate wealth and status. Other pieces were functional and held together clothing, such as brooches. Valuable adornments served two purposes. Decorative silver jewelry could be used as a means to purchase goods. The value of the silver's weight permitted the wearer to exchange the jewelry to buy other items.

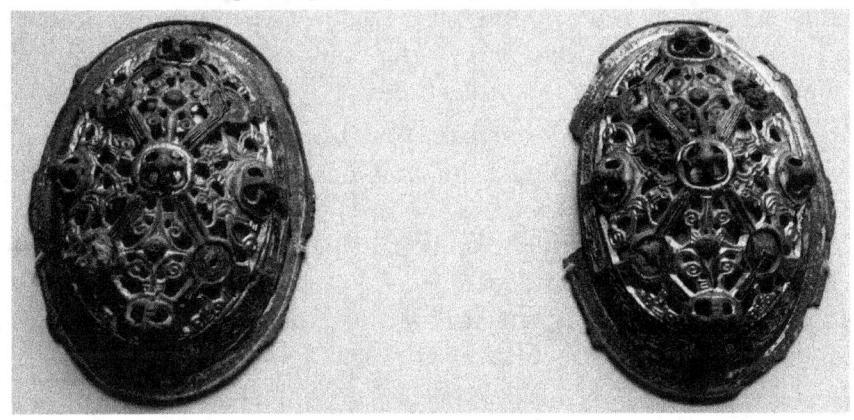

Brooches worn by women.
Johnbod, CC BY-SA 3.0 <https://creativecommons.org/licenses/by-sa/3.0>, via Wikimedia Commons; https://commons.wikimedia.org/wiki/File:Brit_Mus_17sept_015-crop.jpg

Other evidence of the Vikings combining functionality and design is in how they structured and built their villages, hamlets, and towns. One style of building that conveys Viking ingenuity and craftsmanship is the longhouse. The design of the longhouses was similar to the ships in which the Viking warriors sailed. Viking longhouses were constructed with curved walls, which made them appear like inverted ships.

On average, longhouses were between fifteen and twenty-five feet wide. However, longhouses could vary dramatically in length. Most ranged from fifty to sixty-five feet long. Longhouses constructed for the local chieftain or jarl could have extended to 250 feet. Regardless of the longhouse's size, the construction elements were consistent.

Although erected from locally available materials, most longhouses were framed with oak timbers. Areas that did not have readily accessible wood built their homes from stone or peat, creating a different style of house. Two rows of wooden posts were installed throughout the entire length of the home. These wooden timbers bore the weight of the roof.

House roofs were either wood shingles or thatched; sometimes, the roofs were made from vegetation and had moss and grass growing on them. Viking roofs were effective and kept the occupants warm and dry during the cold Scandinavian winters. A hole was shaped in some roofs over the inside fire pit to release smoke.

Walls were often constructed using a method called wooden wattle or wattle and daub. To connect the gaps between the wooden frame, thin strips of wood or sticks woven together (known as wattle) were lashed together between each post. Mud, peat, clay, or animal manure (known as daub) was added to this base layer. The daub created a tacky layer that dried and hardened to form a protective cover.

Inside the longhouse was one large open space. Roof support columns provided a means of separating the area lengthwise into threes. Packed dirt served as the floor. The ashes from the fire pit(s) in the house were added to the earthen floor. The embers helped absorb the moisture and smells. Fires were used for cooking and heating. Some longhouses had multiple fire pits, while others had one centrally located fire; it really depended upon the length of the longhouse.

Benches were embedded in the walls and stretched the length of the longhouse. These wooden benches served multiple functions. They provided extra reinforcement for the walls. The benches also supplied a place for the residents and visitors to eat, work, sit, and sleep. The space under the benches was used for storage. Often, the houses lacked the space for any other furniture. Tables used for eating were collapsible and stored in the rafters when not in use.

Since most Vikings did not have stables for their animals, they were kept at one end of the longhouse. Tools were also stored with the animals. Opposite the barn area of the longhouse was the workspace. Weaving, sewing, and other household work were performed there. Equipment needed to produce materials, such as a loom, would be located in this section of the longhouse.

Vikings often lived as multigenerational families, so dozens of people might have lived together under one roof. Almost all activities occurred within these crowded homes. The people worked, played, slept, ate, and cooked within the home, especially in the winter. During other seasons, the farm animals would graze outside. The fields would need to be tended, and the animals would need to be cared for.

The open fire was the central gathering area within the longhouse. In addition to providing warmth and a means to cook, fires provided most of the light. Candles were too expensive for most Viking families to afford. After meals, families shared stories and myths of the Viking gods and played games by the light of the fire. However, without chimneys, homes were frequently filled with smoke. The roof vent did alleviate some of the smokiness, but Viking homes were not always healthy places to live.

The longhouses of local leaders were grander than a typical family home. Lavish feasts and banquets were held in the larger and finer longhouses since they had the space and amenities to host impressive social gatherings. These longhouses were the equivalent of medieval castles.

SECTION THREE:
Warfare and Weaponry

Chapter 9: Key Viking Battles

The Vikings made their first appearances on the world stage as talented raiders and warriors with their 793 attack on Lindisfarne Monastery. Their swift and often ruthless strikes led to centuries of assaults along the European coastline, Britain, and Ireland. During these years, the Vikings gained control of the coasts and accessed inland regions, where they established settlements. Numerous clashes occurred as the Scandinavian leaders and kings battled European kings and leaders for dominance.

During the early years of the Viking Age, leaders of raids did not coordinate with others. Raids were often executed with the goal of securing payment to leave the country. However, this changed in 865. The Great Heathen Army arrived in England. Under the coordinated leadership of Ragnar Lothbrok's sons, this army sought to conquer as much of England as they could. Additionally, they sought to seize as many riches as possible from the monasteries.

Though the Kingdom of Northumbria had a larger contingent of soldiers, the battle-tested Vikings were successful. The Great Heathen Army captured the Kingdom of Northumbria and its capital, York. By forming the Kingdom of Jorvik, the Vikings created their first permanent settlement in Britain. The Vikings maintained control of Jorvik until 954. From this location, the Vikings conquered the kingdoms of East Anglia and Mercia.

Only the Kingdom of Wessex was immune to the Vikings' power, part of which was due to the Danegeld paid by King Alfred. This payment ensured the Vikings would leave the Kingdom of Wessex unscathed.

By 878, the Great Heathen Army and its leader, Guthrum, occupied the northern and eastern sections of the Anglo-Saxon world. With this control, Guthrum forced the king of the Anglo-Saxons, Alfred, into exile.

Tired of continually losing land to the Vikings, one of King Alfred's local leaders, Odda, the ealdorman (a high-ranking noble) of Devin, gathered an army to battle the Vikings. Odda led his troops in the Battle of Cynwit, named after the hill on which the battle was fought. The Viking leader in Devan, Ubba, and his warriors surrounded the West Saxon troops. The Anglo-Saxons knew they would perish in their fortress without food or water or die in battle.

The Anglo-Saxons roared out of the fortress with such savage intensity that they surprised the Vikings. Odda and his soldiers killed hundreds of Viking warriors and Ubba, their leader. The win was a moral victory for the Anglo-Saxons. However, their king was still hiding from Guthrum.

Guthrum pursued Alfred, entering the eastern and southern access points of the Kingdom of Wessex. This surprise winter attack forced Alfred and his court to escape to Athelney. While in hiding in the marshes, Alfred and his supporters built a fort. From here, Alfred recruited more troops. He had reassembled his army by the time spring arrived.

After calling a formation at Egbert's Stone, Alfred and his troops marched to Edington. This location was chosen because its boundary was the Viking stronghold of Chippenham. The Anglo-Saxons formed an effective and solid shield wall. The Vikings were hounded back into the fortress and were now the ones faced with starvation. For two weeks, Guthrum and his troops lived under siege. On the fourteenth day, the Vikings surrendered.

Under the treaty Alfred and Guthrum made (the Treaty of Wedmore), the Vikings were forced to withdraw from Wessex. Men and women from Denmark could only live in lands they already controlled in England. Alfred remained king of Kent, Wessex, and West Mercia. The Vikings continued to rule the northern and eastern regions of England, which became known as the Danelaw. People living in the areas stipulated as the Danelaw followed Viking laws and customs. The control of England was now legally divided between the Vikings and the English.

Alfred the Great fully understood the power and fury of the Viking forces. In addition to the provisions in the treaty, Alfred altered his military tactics. He shored up his defenses and began installing border fortresses. The settlement and the growth of burhs, which were fortified towns, were actively advanced. This provided another layer of protection against any future Viking attacks.

The blending of Viking and Anglo-Saxon cultures occurred as part of the Treaty of Wedmore. Another provision of the treaty was that Guthrum and his leaders converted to Christianity. Once Guthrum was baptized, he became Æthelstan. Guthrum also began minting coins following the Anglo-Saxon methods. This stimulated an increase in trade between the Danelaw areas and Anglo-Saxons.

Not all was harmonious between the two groups, especially after the death of Alfred the Great in 899, who strove to unify England. Two claimants declared their right to the throne. One was Alfred's son, Edward the Elder; the other petitioner was his nephew, Æthelwold. When Æthelwold's father and Alfred's older brother, King Æthelred I, died, it was decided that Æthelwold was too young to assume the throne. So, Alfred was declared king instead.

Now that Alfred was dead, Æthelwold wanted what he viewed as his birthright. The Battle of the Holme ensued as a fight for the throne. Æthelwold allied with the Vikings. He was accepted as a leader by the Vikings and led the assault against the Anglo-Saxons in Mercia and northern Wessex. In response, Edward attacked the Vikings in East Anglia, causing the Norsemen to flee to their own lands.

Considering the battle over, Edward withdrew. However, some of Edward's troops remained. The bloody battle continued as Æthelwold and the Viking warriors slaughtered the Anglo-Saxons. However, Æthelwold was killed in the Battle of the Holme, ending his fight for the crown.

Edward's son, Æthelstan, who became king in 924, and his brother, Edmund, led the first unified English forces in their next major battle. The brothers combined their troops from Mercia and Wessex against the invaders. Combined forces from the kingdoms of Dublin, Scotland, and Strathclyde attacked the Anglo-Saxons.

At this time, the land that is now Great Britain was configured differently. Earls of Northumberland, who were of Viking descent, ruled the northern section of today's England. Ireland was led by the Scandinavian Olaf or Anlaf Guthfrithsson, who was king of Dublin. Farther north, in today's Scotland, was the Kingdom of Alba, which was ruled by Constantine II, King of the Scots. The last part of the coalition was from Strathclyde, which was led by Owen I. Strathclyde was on the land that is part of Scotland and Wales.

Another battle between the Vikings and the Anglo-Saxons raged at the Battle of Brunanburh in 937. One of the deadliest battles ever fought on British lands, this was referred to as the Great Battle for years after it occurred. Brunanburh was a pivotal victory in the ongoing hostility between the Scandinavian forces and the Anglo-Saxons. The effects from the battle had lasting effects, some of which are still felt today.

Before the Battle of Brunanburh, Anglo-Saxon territories were ruled by many. Earls continually sought power, land, and leadership roles, resulting in a lack of unification against the invading Vikings. After this battle, the Anglo-Saxon kingdoms transitioned into becoming a unified kingdom. They began working to better secure their borders to the north and west. Eventually, the countries of Scotland, Ireland, and Wales were formed outside of England's boundaries.

While the Great Heathen Army engaged in some battles and other bands of Vikings combated the Anglo-Saxons and others, parties of Vikings continued raining and pillaging. Fear and dread gripped many vulnerable towns and villages along the coast. Many leaders believed the best response to the Viking incursions was to pay the invaders to leave. Others thought they should protect their land and people.

One such leader was the ealdorman of Essex, Byrhtnoth. In 991, as many as three thousand Vikings disembarked on Northey Island off the coast of Essex. Separated from the mainland by the Blackwater Estuary, King Olaf Tyrggvasson and his men waited for the river to recede with the tide.

Tyrggvasson and the Vikings shouted for payments of gold and silver, saying they would leave if their demands were met. Though Byrhtnoth had fewer warriors, he rejected their demands. So, the Battle of Maldon commenced.

As the tide ebbed, the Vikings began their assault. Byrhtnoth's men trapped the Vikings on a narrow strip of land, so the Vikings retreated. After being trapped back on the island, the Vikings asked to be permitted safe crossing so the battle could be fairly fought on one side of the waterway. Very nobly, Byrhtnoth acquiesced and surrendered his advantageous position.

Once the Vikings encountered Byrhtnoth's troops, ferocious fighting ensued. The battle resulted in Byrhtnoth's beheading and a convincing victory for the Vikings. After the battle, King Æthelred paid the Vikings in silver. Some researchers estimate that the Vikings left with up to five tons of silver, worth more than three million dollars today. In addition to soundly defeating Byrhtnoth's men, the Vikings' ability to extract ransom, referred to as Danegeld, made raiding an extremely profitable business.

Relentless Viking raids and demands for Danegeld proved debilitating for King Æthelred. His ability to retain his power and reign were diminishing. In response, Æthelred set up his marriage to Emma, who was of Norman and Viking descent. The king thought Emma would be able to unite the Danes and the Anglo-Saxons.

Æthelred's next political maneuver to address his waning power and belief that the Vikings were plotting his death was to order the deaths of the Scandinavian people living in England. Towns bordering Saxon and Danelaw territories were targeted. Æthelred's directive was enacted on November 13th, 1002, which was St. Brice's Day. The event is now referred to as the St. Brice's Day massacre. Though it was supposedly ordered to be a round-up of men, women, and children, archaeological evidence supports that mainly experienced Viking warriors were targeted.

The total death count is unknown; however, it has been established that the king of Denmark's sister and her husband were killed in the carnage. Sweyn Forkbeard's sister, Gunnhild, and the ealdorman of Devonshire, Pallig Tokesen, her husband, died that day.

Sweyn was known for his brutality, which included the violent toppling of his father's reign (his father was King Harald Bluetooth). For decades, Sweyn had continually raided England, creating a climate of terror. Now that King Æthelred had murdered his sister, Sweyn bombarded England with persistent attacks as retaliation. His attacks were so merciless and relentless that the people of England conceded and named Sweyn their king in 1013. King Æthelred, Emma, and their sons were forced to escape and live in exile.

Sweyn's five-week reign as the first Viking king of Anglo-Saxon lands ended with his death in February 1014. Æthelred and his family returned from exile and coerced Sweyn's son, Cnut, to leave the country.

Cnut began his quest to regain the English throne in 1015. A series of battles with Æthelred's son, Edmund Ironside, for the crown of England climaxed in the Battle of Assandun in October 1016. In the previous four encounters between Cnut and his warriors and Edmund and his troops, Edmund was the victor of three of the battles. Sherston was considered a draw.

Going into Assandun, the numbers of Cnut's forces had been greatly diminished. However, many historians believe a traitor from Edmund's ranks, Eadric Streona, influenced the results at Assandun. Cnut did not trust Eadric, and a year later, Cnut had him killed.

Edmund was not willing to concede the crown and throne but was forced to flee. One last battle stood between Cnut and the power over England. The Battle of Dane's Wood finalized the results of the two-year contest for the throne of England. Cnut soundly defeated Edmund.

In their agreement to cease fighting, King Edmund and Cnut agreed to divide England between themselves. Edmund retained control over Wessex, and Cnut gained the rest of the Anglo-Saxon lands. Also detailed in the treaty was the longevity of the deal. The pact would be enforced until one of the two men died. The surviving man would assume control over the deceased's territory.

Just a couple of months after they made peace, Edmund died. Cnut was now the leader of England. His coronation was held in December 1016. Adding to his power grab, Cnut married Edmund's mother, Emma.

Chapter 10: Armor and Weapons

Weapons were an essential tool during the Viking Age. They added to the ferociousness of the Viking warrior. When attacking villages and pillaging for silver and other valuables, Viking fighters were armed with a variety of weapons. Axes were the most common tool in their arsenal. Access to other weaponry was often dependent on one's wealth and status in society.

Not only were weapons relied upon when raiding, but all free Viking men also wore weapons. All men, other than thralls, were ready to defend their communities, families, and farms. Thralls or slaves were prohibited from carrying any type of weapon. Since most Scandinavians lived on farms during the Viking Age, women and children had knives for their work; in many gravesites of women, there were axes that had been used on the farm.

In a society that valued an honorable reputation, Scandinavian men believed it was not only their right but also their duty to carry a weapon. At night, weapons were kept by each man's bedside. If an attack occurred at night, men were able to readily defend their community.

Since axes were the most affordable, they were the most common weapon. Men from all tiers of society carried an ax for protection. Swords were the costliest weapon, so only the wealthiest men had access to them. Some Vikings also adorned themselves with helmets, spears, knives, and bows and arrows.

When local chieftains or magnates knew they were going raiding, they would conscript the men in the area. Sometimes, it was through a messenger sent by a king. As mentioned before, this king was different than today's royalty. They did not rule an entire country. These kings might have had more power, land, and money than the local earls, so he was able to form an army. All men, including thralls, were expected to respond.

Within five days of the messenger's proclamation, all men met at their leader's ship. Freemen were expected to arrive with weapons, but all were required to appear cleaned, fed, and ready for battle. The warriors used their skills and weaponry to amass treasures. After the raid, the riches were divided among the crew based on rank.

Men of all ranks carried their ax with them to the ship and into battle. Axes used in battle grew to differ from the axes used as farm implements and in shipbuilding and construction. From the commencement of the Viking Age until their power waned, axes used by the Scandinavian warriors became more advanced. An owner's wealth determined the style, size, and shape of axes.

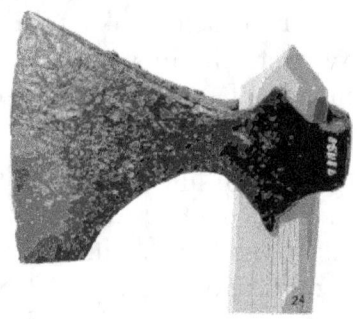

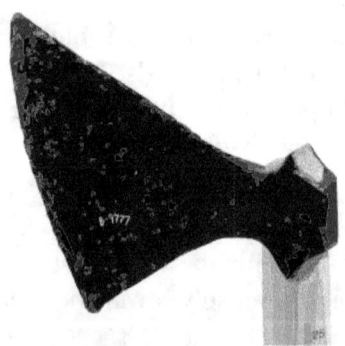

Viking axes found in Norway.
https://commons.wikimedia.org/wiki/File:Viking_axes_Norway.svg

Normally, axes were worn by Viking men on their waists. Belts were fashioned to hold the ax in place. Axes designed for battle had long handles and broader blades than their tool counterparts. Initially, battle axes had steel cutting edges that ranged from three to six inches. Eventually, warriors fought with nine to eighteen-inch sharp steel ax heads. With lightweight handles and a well-balanced wide ax head, Vikings had a deadly advantage in battle. Axes provided the warriors with a broad striking range and agile handling.

Weapons were so important to the Vikings that they often named them (just like many do with their cars or boats today). One of the most well-known battle axes belonged to King Magnus. In 1042, Magnus was named king of Denmark. Sweyn Estridsen disputed this claim. The night before the Battle of Lyrskov Heath, King Magnus believed that his father, Olaf Haraldsson, appeared to him in a dream. Using the dream as a sign, Magnus took up arms against Sweyn for control of Denmark.

Leading his warriors in battle, Magnus used Hel, the battle ax left to him by his father, Saint Olaf. Trusting that Olaf and Hel would guide his men to victory, Magnus and his troops decimated Sweyn's forces, killing over 15,000 men. Snorri Sturluson captured the victory and use of the ax in his collection of sagas about early Scandinavian kings. In *Heimskringla* (*Orb of the World*), Sturluson shared numerous stories about Olaf's reign as king, which included his mystical axe, Hel.

Another weapon commonly used by Viking warriors was the spear. Spears were a versatile weapon for the Scandinavians. Since spears were made using less iron than swords, they were more readily available for the lower classes. Spears were made in two styles. The lighter spears were thrown at enemy combatants. Heavier spears were thrust into the enemy in arm-to-arm combat.

Spears held a special significance to the Vikings. Odin, the Norse god of war and ruler of Valhalla, commenced his battles with Gungnir, his spear. In the first battle of the gods, Odin hurled Gungnir over the enemy and shouted, "Odin owns each of you." Other Viking leaders replicated this act at the start of battles. Viking warriors believed that this offered the enemy to Odin. In return, Odin would protect the Vikings and watch over them. Participating in this ritual would ensure victory with the aid of Odin and his spear.

As with spears, there were two styles of knives used by the Vikings. The most commonly found tool in the tactical belt of the warriors was a knife. Smaller versions of these knives were used as tools. Almost everyone in the Viking Age carried a knife, including thralls. Wealthier warriors used the seax, which was a larger and more deadly knife. Seaxes acted more like a machete in combat.

A picture of a seax.
British Museum, CC0, via Wikimedia Commons;
https://commons.wikimedia.org/wiki/File:British_Museum_Sittingbourne_Seax.jpg

Bows and arrows were used for hunting and combat. Bows and arrows balanced out the tools used in hand-to-hand combat. This weapon allowed Vikings to shoot at the enemy when they were farther away. From the bows and arrows recovered from the time period, it is believed the draw force of these Viking weapons reached 90 to 120 pounds of force. This force created a range of between six hundred and seven hundred feet of striking distance.

As part of the Vikings' tactics, Vikings bombarded their adversary with bows and arrows, announcing their arrival. Most Scandinavian warriors could load and reload their bows at rapid speed, shooting twelve arrows a minute. Once the Vikings disembarked from the ships, close-quarter combat began. At this stage of fighting, Vikings relied on other weapons in their arsenal.

The most highly valued weapon of the raiders was the sword. Since swords required the most iron to make of all the weapons, they were the most expensive to produce. Therefore, only the elite had access to swords, which made them a symbol of status and distinction in the Viking Age. Owning swords had such a glorious reputation that they were given as gifts or handed from one generation to the next in the same family.

After participating in a Viking raid or two, the treasures pillaged and distributed among the crew usually enabled a raider to buy a decent sword. Those of higher status were able to have their swords produced with elaborate embellishments. The creation of a sword could take up to one month. In the Icelandic saga about the people of Laxárdalr, the cost of a sword is equal to the value of sixteen dairy cows.

Swords were not carried as part of the Viking utility belt. They had special holders called scabbards. These cases were made from leather or wood. Scabbards were strapped across the warrior's right shoulder. While this made the swords readily available, they were not often used in battle. Instead, many warriors wore their swords to show their rank.

Swords smithed for the initial Viking raids bent easily in battle because they were produced from poor-quality iron. When the process of pattern welding began to be used by Viking blacksmiths, the quality of swords improved.

By using pattern welding, a more durable blade was crafted. Blacksmiths pieced together sections of iron with varying compositions. They were then coiled together and shaped under extreme heat. A talented blacksmith could distribute the iron of varying levels of carbon to generate an equilibrium of maneuverability and hardness in the metal. Then they shaped the sword from the molten mixes of iron.

An even higher quality sword appeared in the armaments of Vikings in the early 9th century. Just over 170 of these swords have been found by archaeologists. Evidence shows that the production of the Ulfberht swords ended around the year 1000.

How the steel was forged for these swords remains uncertain. There are credible theories that explain how the steel was produced. There is evidence of crucible steel, which is what the Ulfberht swords were fashioned from, being used in the area of modern-day India around 300 BCE. The steel appears again in the Viking era and then not again until the 1740s.

Scholars believe the Vikings encountered this material in their travels, either to the Frankish kingdoms nearby or from central Asia. Many researchers believe the Vikings learned the technology needed to produce this superior metal and weapon. They also gathered necessary materials on their voyages, which was why production ceased around 1000. This timing coincides with Russia interfering with the Viking trade routes.

Regardless of how the Vikings acquired this technology and necessary materials, manufacturing crucible steel was an incredible feat. Producing steel for Ulfberht swords necessitated the involvement of many blacksmiths. Master craftsmen and their apprentices worked diligently to accomplish this task, from the fabrication of the steel to the shaping of the blade to the formation of the handles to the creation of jeweled embellishments.

These swords provided the Vikings with a superior advantage in battle. Ulfberht swords were lighter than swords made from the iron used for other weapons. Warriors could effortlessly manipulate their swords in battle. Since high-carbon steel is somewhat flexible, the swords did not break or snap as readily. Crucible iron creates a strong material, so the blades of these swords retained their sharpness throughout the fight.

The iron was liquified to eliminate impurities. No evidence exists of furnaces that could reach the level of heat required for the process, so it is thought the Viking blacksmiths hammered the impurities from the iron ore. Then carbon was added to the molten iron to strengthen it. Analysis of Ulfberht swords revealed they are comprised of almost three times the carbon of other iron used during this era.

Swords made from this steel were stamped with the inscription of Ulfberht (two crosses and a T). Initially, some researchers thought this was a blacksmith's trademark. However, since the swords were crafted for over three hundred years, it is now thought the inscription was used by those who could create this steel.

The swords fashioned from crucible iron were so amazing that forgeries were made. Swords that have been discovered have the requisite two crosses and Ulfberht without the T. Warriors who had the good fortune to use these swords and others who watched with amazement at what they accomplished believed there were supernatural elements at work in the creation of the swords.

Only blacksmiths and their workers understood the craft. This added to the mysteriousness associated with the power of Ulfberht swords and metalworking in general. In the early years of the Viking Age, most blacksmiths worked with all metals. As time progressed, blacksmiths became more specialized and worked with iron and steel. Craftsmen shared their knowledge of the trade with their apprentices, who were often family members. Shrouding their skills in mystery added to the supernatural aura connected with the swords.

Villages that had their own blacksmiths were fortunate. Smiths crafted weapons for warriors and homeowners, produced items for the home, and fashioned tools for the farm. Having someone with this level of skill added to the self-sufficiency of a community. Kings and high-ranking jarls had their own blacksmiths.

Myths depict the magical ability of blacksmiths to forge tools and weapons for the gods. The naming of weapons for gods and warriors emphasized the power of these armaments. Kennings (elaborate descriptive phrases) were often created to enhance the owner's importance and the mystical ability of the sword, ax, or spear.

Sometimes, a combination of two or three words to create a phrase, such as leg-biter, foot-biter, or hole-maker, was used for swords. For those fortunate enough to have swords with a lineage, the kenning on the sword talked about the ancestral connections to the weapon. Summoning the name of Wolf's Claws while entering battle infused the warrior with the strength and cunning of a wolf.

Chapter 11: Viking Ships

The Vikings' military tactics and ability to finesse their weapons in battle made them indomitable and feared foes for hundreds of years. However, without their shipbuilding expertise, the Vikings' dominance would not have occurred. When the longship with a snakehead on its prow sailed over the horizon into the view of those on land, the people knew they should be afraid. And that's just what the Vikings wanted.

In addition to raiding, Viking ships allowed the Norse to explore and expand their territories. Vikings discovered trade routes, which enabled them to foster their settlements and establish towns for trading.

The geographical foundations of the homelands of the Scandinavians facilitated their quest for methods to traverse waterways. Rivers, fjords, lakes, straits, and the ocean surrounded and summoned the early Scandinavians. As early as 350 BCE, early canoes were carved from local trees, providing a way to navigate the lands. Between then and the dawn of the Viking Age, Scandinavian water vessels were dramatically transformed.

During the Middle Ages, there were two main methods of shipbuilding. One was the carvel. The frames of the wooden boats and ships made in this manner were constructed first. Planks were then fastened to the frames. The timber used in the assembly was cut with saws. The sawn timber was cut across the grain of the wood, which weakened the strength of the wood beams. Therefore, boats following the carvel build had a harder time sailing the currents of the water, producing a rocky and slow passage.

With their vast timber resources, the Vikings were able to build their watercraft using the clinker style. Unlike the carvel, the outside of a clinker boat was erected first. The frame of the vessel was constructed later in the shipbuilding process. Carvel boats could be built with any quality of timber, but clinker vessels required the superior timber from pine and oak trees. Both trees were readily available for Scandinavian shipbuilding. Unseasoned or green wood was used in the formation of clinker vessels since it is pliable.

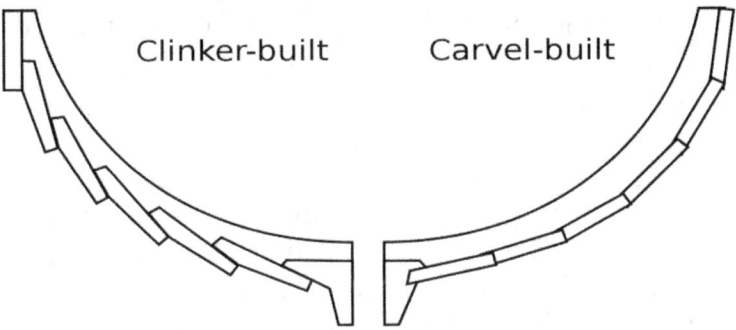

Diagram of clinker and carvel shipbuilding.
https://commons.wikimedia.org/wiki/File:Clinker-carvel.svg

Oak timbers were used for the keel, which extended the length of the ship and created the centerline. Viking shipbuilders were some of the first to frame boats with keels, which added stability to the vessel. The stern and stem were then attached to the keel. Overlying planks were attached with rivets to add durability to the hull. Animal hair and spruce roots were threaded together to tie the planks to the frame of the ship.

The additional strength from this part of the clinker method created a lighter frame. Viking ships were also more flexible, allowing them to bend and roll with the waves. Joints were filled with scrap materials and covered with tar to make them watertight. The construction of the hulls allowed the ships to sail in shallow watercourses; the heavier carvel boats were not functional for them.

Viking shipbuilders were adept at using their axes. Instead of the harshness of sawing timbers, Scandinavian craftsmen were able to create subtle incisions in the wood. By carving with the grain of the wood, Vikings created stronger, more flexible, and lighter ships. Viking warriors were able to sail in many different waterways.

Since the Vikings traveled on many different-sized waterways for a variety of purposes, many styles of boats were crafted. Most water vessels used by the Scandinavians were functional and necessary for daily chores and life. Fishing, visiting other villages, and transporting goods and people created the need for small boats for many. These sailed up and down rivers, back and forth across lakes, and short distances along the coastline.

For trading purposes, the Vikings required vessels that could withstand the power and unpredictability of the oceans. Viking trade routes were extensive. The boats that carried traders and their goods were essential to the Scandinavians' expansion of wealth and power. Longboats, which were synonymous with the Viking raiders, were not appropriate for the work of traders.

Sturdiness and reliability were the two key characteristics of merchant ships. These ships were constructed to carry cargo; therefore, they featured broader and deeper hulls for storage. Arriving at each port intact was more important than the speed of the boat. These attributes were balanced with the weight of the ships. Merchant ships sailed through different waterways, so merchant ships were often conveyed by the crew over shallow, non-passible sections of water or harbors.

To accommodate the numerous waterways that the traders navigated, they built two types of trading ships. Knarrs were designed to carry heavy cargo on long ocean voyages; some knarrs had the capacity to hold over forty tons of freight and passengers. Due to their heavy freight, these merchant ships relied on wind power and were propelled by a large mast. On days with strong winds, knarrs sailed up to seventy-mile miles. Crews averaged about thirty men, so they could maximize their weight capacity with cargo.

Model of a knarr.
Europabild,, CC BY-SA 3.0 <https://creativecommons.org/licenses/by-sa/3.0>, via Wikimedia Commons; https://commons.wikimedia.org/wiki/File:Modell_Knorr.jpg

For inland trading routes, Vikings designed the byrdings to carry lighter cargo. Scandinavian crews whose shipping lanes were more difficult to maneuver sailed in byrdings. The boats were equipped with oars and a large sail, which was similar to the knarrs. However, the crew, consisting of about fifteen men, mainly used oars to manipulate the boat. Merchandise and their merchants were transported rapidly from port to port in byrdings.

Ships designed to carry more warriors than cargo were the iconic Viking longships. Carved with elaborately designed bows, often depictions of frightening animals, longships signified that bloodshed was imminent. Dubbed dragonships by the British, the sight of one of these magnificent vessels spread terror throughout the land.

Early versions of longships were used as early as the 6th century BCE. Viking longships evolved during the Viking Age into four main classifications. However, they all followed a similar design. They were designed to navigate water ranging from rough seas to shallow estuaries. Longships could sail in rivers with water as low as three feet. This permitted the warriors to skim the surface of the water and leap out of the ship and into battle. Other vessels were outfitted with small rowboats that enabled the Vikings to get to shore without damaging the longship.

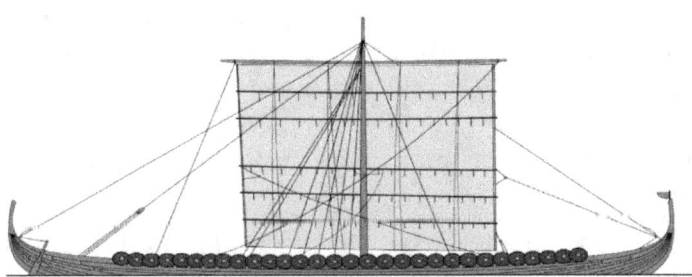

Sketch of a Viking longship.
https://commons.wikimedia.org/wiki/File:Viking_longship.png

Another characteristic of the longships that aided the Vikings in their successful raids was their ability to reverse sail without physically turning the boat around. Longships were designed to be double-ended, so they could sail forward or backward. The longships were equipped with a mast, sail, and oars, so Vikings could manually row their boats if there was no wind to propel the ship.

Piloting longships was accomplished utilizing one oar that was attached to the side of the ship. Referred to as the steerboard, the operator stood on the right stern or rear of the ship. He piloted the boat by moving the oar in the direction they sailed. Over time, the steerboard evolved into starboard or the right side of a boat.

As the scope and frequency of Viking raids grew, their longboats evolved to better meet their needs. Ships with an increased cargo capacity and the ability to carry additional crew members and sail farther distances were designed and built.

Four main classes of longships emerged from the Viking Age. The karvi class of longships was created for smaller raiding forays. Crews averaged about thirty warriors when the boats were used for battle. Due to their more diminutive size, karvi boats could not traverse as far as others on the open ocean waters. They were used in raids, but the versatile boats were often used for other domestic purposes.

The snekkja was the class of ship built and sailed most frequently. It had a crew of about forty men and was equipped with twenty pairs of oars. These ships were easier for shipbuilders to frame since they were only about sixty feet long. Though smaller than the Viking warships, snekkjas could still accommodate the rewards of a fruitful raid.

The success of the Viking raids led to the addition of new types of longships to enable the warriors to capitalize on their triumphs. The next class of Viking longship, the skeid, was bigger and more seaworthy. These intimidating vessels, which could be over one hundred feet long, were constructed to carry seventy warriors. The skeids were powered with sails and had up to thirty pairs of oars.

Viking warships, or the busse class, were the most impressive of all Viking longships. Those sailing aboard a busse ship were able to travel much farther distances across the ocean. Larger cargo areas could store supplies for long distances and the rewards garnered once the raiders landed ashore. These ships were much longer than other longships at 160 feet and could house a crew of 80 warriors. As with other longboats, the busse could be propelled by the thirty-five sets of oars or its sails.

The busse class is also referred to as the drakkar or dragonships because of the ferocious dragon or serpent head carved into the stem on the bow of the ship. The intimidating animal design was often continued to the stern of the ship with the dragon's or serpent's tail. Adding to the terrorizing visual of the ships was the addition of wings created from the sails and legs of the beast from the oars. The dragonships led the fleet and announced the arrival of the pillaging warriors.

Many Viking ships used shield lists or shield racks. These were railings on which the warriors displayed their shields. Viking shields were often decorated or painted with different patterns, scenes of Norse gods, or runic writings. The Viking ship discovered at Gokstad was found with sixty-four yellow and blue shields. The shields added to the mystique of the dragon or serpent head looming on the water. Many researchers also believe that the shields offered protection from the wind and rain. Since this added drag to the ship, other researchers surmise that the shields were not needed for weather protection since they were not hung on the wall until the ship was nearing its destination. Then the shields were mounted as protection from the enemy's arrows and spears. When the warriors disembarked, they grabbed their shields to use in battle.

Initially, powerful chieftains or jarls oversaw the raids. In the later years of the Viking Age, kings and military leaders assumed responsibility for the planning and execution of raids and retaliatory attacks against other leaders. When the Viking raids and conquests grew in complexity, they gathered a combination of all types of longships. Records indicate that the Vikings organized fleets that were comprised of hundreds of ships.

To accomplish these attacks, Viking leaders required extensive knowledge of the opposing armies. Many phases of planning were needed to gather the ships, warriors, and supplies from different villages and towns. It was an amazing strategic and logistical feat for the Vikings to accomplish.

Not only were the Vikings master shipbuilders and logisticians, but they were also highly skilled navigators. On some of their first forays, the Vikings maintained sight of the shoreline, with natural landmarks guiding their course. Their experiences were shared with other Viking navigators. It appears that as they ventured away from the coast, Vikings utilized islands as guideposts.

Their knowledge of nature aided in their ability to chart sea courses. Viking sailors used bird sounds to know when land was nearby. Floki Vilgerdarson used the assistance of ravens when he sailed from Norway in search of present-day Iceland. Vilgerdarson released three ravens. One bird flew back toward the Faroe Islands; another returned to the ship. The third raven soared off ahead of the boat; Vilgerdarson followed the raven's trajectory and sailed to Iceland.

Other elements of the natural world guided the Scandinavian sailors. The color of the water indicated changing temperatures, which provided information about their location on the water and their proximity to different types of watercourses. Directional shifts of the wind also provided seamen with information on the direction they should pilot their boats.

Looking toward the heavens and the location of the moon, sun, and stars provided a wealth of lore and data for early mariners. The least experienced navigator could use the sunrise and sunset to navigate easterly and westerly courses. With more time on the open water, a veteran seafarer could chart their course following the movement of the stars.

Tools were developed to aid the ship's navigator during the daylight hours when stars were not visible. One instrument was the bearing dial or circle. This device provided information about the latitude of the ship. An upright pin was placed in the middle of a platform with a pointer. Shadows created on the platform indicated the position of the sun.

At noon, the ship's navigator used a sun shadow board to verify their course. Sailors placed a board in a bowl of water to keep it level. A pin or gnomon indicated the location of the sun. Circles on the board noted regions to which they should sail in order to stay on course. If the shadow fell outside the circled area, the ship had sailed out of range.

To obtain navigational information on cloudy days, Scandinavian seamen employed the use of a sunstone. Calcite, also called an Icelandic spar, was held up in the light. Depending upon the color of the stone, the Vikings knew the position of the sun and their ship's location.

Sunstone.
ArniEin, CC BY-SA 3.0 <https://creativecommons.org/licenses/by-sa/3.0>, via Wikimedia Commons; https://commons.wikimedia.org/wiki/File:Silfurberg.jpg

To share the knowledge gained through experiences, the Vikings created songs, chants, and rhymes. In these mantras and tunes, directions to different locations were communicated. Routes to avoid because of navigational or other dangers could be conveyed through repetitive refrains. The Scandinavians' shipbuilding expertise, navigational knowledge and tools, and chants for easy recall aided warriors and traders.

Chapter 12: More than Warriors - Viking Traders

Vikings are well renowned for their skills as raiders. To be effective marauders, Vikings needed access to other countries to loot and seize riches and treasures, so they sailed in ships they designed and built. Their incredible ability to construct ships for different waterways and purposes made them successful traders as well. Most men during the Viking Age sailed as traders and not as part of a raiding party. What the Scandinavian people could not produce themselves, they bartered and traded with other villages and people.

Raiding ships constructed by the Vikings were known for their seaworthiness and ability to maneuver rivers and oceans. With the clinker style, Vikings widened the raiding ships to create room for cargo and built the knarr and byrding vessels for trading. Some trading ships spanned more than twenty feet in width and were seventy feet long. With the ability to transport more than sixty tons of payload, the Vikings profited handsomely from their trading routes.

The collapse of the Western Roman Empire provided the Vikings access to more trade routes. Viking trade was integral in redeveloping Europe's economy after the fall of Rome. The location of the Scandinavian lands provided the Viking traders with relatively easy access to a multitude of trade routes. To the west, the Vikings could sail the waters of the North Atlantic Ocean to Britain, Ireland, and Spain. To their east, the Scandinavians traversed the Dnieper and Volga Rivers to reach the lands of Russia, Constantinople, and much of the Middle East and Asia.

Typically, traders from today's Sweden sailed the eastern trade routes, and Danish merchants and sailors navigated the westward waterways. Whether the traders went east or west, they usually carried cargos of Scandinavian riches of fur, walrus tusks, amber, and iron. Those who sailed the western routes were also known for their raiding and pillaging. However, when the raiders encountered towns that were not suitable for raiding, those locations became part of the western trade route.

In addition to establishing trade routes and trading centers, many Scandinavians also moved their families to these locations. Up and down the coastlines, towns became settled by the Scandinavians. Dublin, Normandy, and York were just a few of the cities that the Vikings helped establish and grow.

In their new locales, transplanted Vikings recreated their workshops so they could continue to produce goods to trade. Tradesmen often created pottery, combs, leather goods, jewelry, and glass beads that had previously been made in Scandinavia. Viking armaments were also crafted in the towns where Vikings resettled. Over time, the Scandinavians and locals intermarried.

When the Vikings sailed east, they were propelled by the same motivations as their forays to the west: raiding and pillaging. However, accessing the lands via river routes limited the Vikings' ability to effectively execute their hit-and-run strikes on poorly defended coastal towns. On their river voyages, the Vikings were vulnerable to surprise attacks. These ambushes and the lack of readily accessible cities or monasteries to pillage made these expeditions costly for raiding parties. To effectively pursue their goal of gaining wealth, the Vikings needed to establish home bases from where they could operate.

As traders, the Vikings were the first to navigate the waters of the Volga and Dnieper Rivers. Profitable trading centers and routes were created along the Dnieper River to the Black Sea. Scandinavian traders sailed the Volga River to access the Caspian Sea. Similar to their western voyages, Vikings helped establish trading towns along these routes.

By the end of the height of their days of trading, the Vikings constructed a trade network that included Europe, Russia, India, the Middle East, and parts of China. Vikings had traded as far as the Baltic Sea before they expanded their reach as traders and raiders. With the development of their ships, Vikings were now able to traverse the rivers between the Black and Caspian Seas.

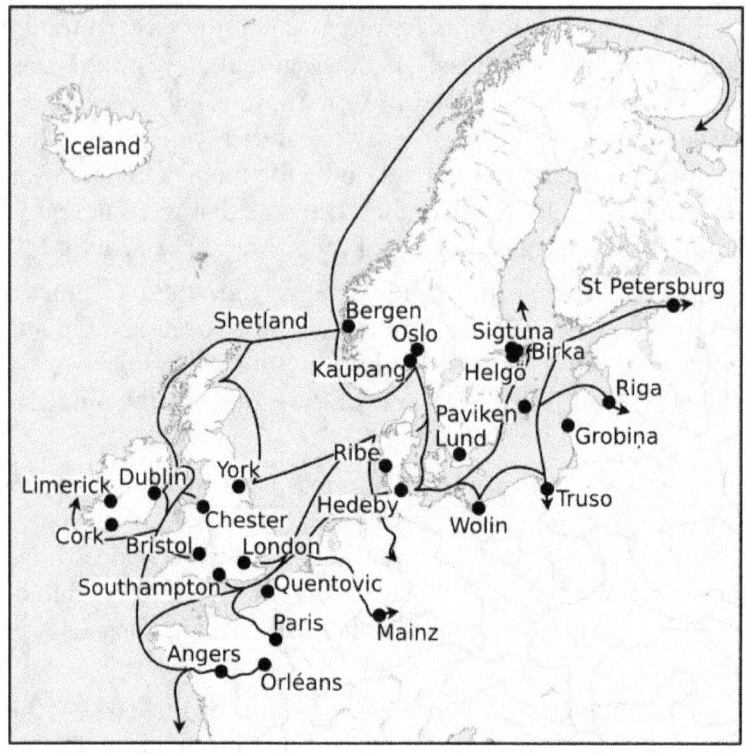

Map of Viking routes.

Brianann MacAmhlaidh, CC BY-SA 4.0 <https://creativecommons.org/licenses/by-sa/4.0>, via Wikimedia Commons; https://commons.wikimedia.org/wiki/File:Viking_Age_trade_routes_in_north-west_Europe.png

Eventually, Scandinavian traders traveled these waterways and connected to the capital of the Byzantine Empire, Constantinople, which is present-day Istanbul, Turkey. Without the interference from the Romans, the Scandinavian traders reached the Silk Road, which provided access to the Far East. Through these routes, Scandinavian traders brought back silver, silk fabrics, exotic spices, wines, and other treasures not available in Scandinavia. Viking traders created a web of trading ports that encompassed the world as they knew it.

The first Scandinavian people who established themselves along these river routes were referred to as the Rus. The Old Norse word *rópsmenn* (meaning route or rowers), which referred to how the Vikings appeared in this region, is believed to be the origin of the Rus. Another term coined by the Greeks to refer to Scandinavians was Varangians. Thought to have originated from the Norse language, Varangian has its roots in the word *vár* for "pledge." The Varangians, while associated with trade, were more often used as the noted bodyguards of the emperor of the Byzantine Empire. "Rus" is more commonly used as the nomenclature for Nordic tradesmen and merchants. However, both terms refer to Scandinavians.

The Varangian or Volga trade route established by the Norse traversed almost two thousand miles of waterways. Beginning in Sweden, the tradesmen on the route sailed over the Baltic Sea to the Gulf of Finland through different rivers and lakes to the Black Sea, ending in Constantinople. In addition to a pathway to access riches and treasures, trade along the Volga and Dnieper Rivers resulted in the growth of cities and towns.

Scandinavian traders who preferred the role of Viking warrior were able to serve as mercenaries for the Byzantine Empire. Emperor Basil II was in dire need of assistance, as he sought to fight off three challengers to his rule. So, Basil turned to the north for support. Vladimir, the ruler of Kievan Rus', which was close to Sweden, had access to Viking warriors. To support Basil II, Vladimir shared six thousand of his transplanted Vikings with the Byzantine emperor. In return, Basil promised his sister to Vladimir in marriage.

This elite fighting force repelled the advances of those seeking to overthrow Basil. Basil II established the Varangian Guard, ensuring that he had his own personal protective unit that he could trust. Basil disbanded his Greek bodyguards in favor of the Viking-based militia band. The role of the Varangian Guard varied, but they were always ready to fulfill any order from the emperor.

These men were mercilessly devoted to the emperor and accompanied Basil everywhere he or his family traveled, including church services. The mercenary force performed underhanded duties when the emperor ordered them to do so, with the guards arresting anyone disloyal to Basil. They also acted as jailers at the infamous prison of Nóumera.

Another unit of these fearsome fighters guarded the city limits. Also included in the Varangians were bands of elite Vikings. This group accompanied the emperor in battle. This unit's ability to fight successfully aided the Byzantines in numerous battles. Since only the best of the best were accepted in the Varangian Guard, it provided the exclusive group with a high status when they returned to their homelands. Being a guard proved to be an extremely lucrative job. The lure of battle and glory associated with victory made this a desirable occupation. Harald Hardrada, who became King Harald III of Norway, fought in the legendary ranks of these Viking warriors.

Scandinavians not only left their mark as warriors, but tradesmen also transformed the landscape with settlements established to foster trade. With their incredible ship-making talents, the Scandinavians were flexible about where they could dock their boats because they did not require intricate harbors. Boats could be carried overland when necessary, even if they were filled with cargo. Oars were slotted through the slots and used to lift the boats. Trade and the resulting trading centers were an outgrowth of the adventures of the Scandinavian seamen.

Many towns arose adjacent to naturally occurring harbors, which varied in size and status. The trading centers were often centrally located and began to connect the scattered farms and fishing areas. Since the goods being brought to trade were valuable, it was important for the developing areas to be protected; otherwise, traders would refuse to return to that location.

Local kings and chieftains facilitated the development of markets into towns. Taxes were levied on goods bought and sold at the market. The leaders utilized the income from taxes to pay for the costs of protecting the town. Markets grew and thrived in locations that were readily defensible and easily accessible by land and the sea. Kings and local leaders were also instrumental in obtaining land if they did not already own it.

Initially, the markets were only open for trading in warmer weather. As they grew, more people moved to the towns. Craftsmen relocated their shops to larger trading centers. Farms surrounded the marketplaces and fed the visiting traders and the people who lived in the village.

Trading centers were so profitable that it is believed that King Gudfred attacked the town of Reric in 808. Reric was located outside of his jurisdiction, but once the Danish king eliminated the competition of Reric, he helped grow Hedeby in present-day Denmark. The tradesmen who previously sold their wares in Reric were forced to relocate to land within Gudfred's domain. To make his trading center more appealing, Gudfred had the Danevirke, a Danish fortification system, rebuilt. This created a more secure boundary around Hedeby.

Another important trading town was Ribe. Located on the shores of the North Sea and the Ribe River, traders from other areas were able to access the marketplace because of Ribe's harbor. New evidence is emerging that Ribe, located in present-day Denmark, was the first Scandinavian town. Archaeologists are finding proof that Ribe was a trading center more than fifty years before the Viking warriors raided the monastery at Lindisfarne. This suggests that expeditions that originated from Scandinavian lands peacefully sailed to import and export goods with others. Ribe grew in size and importance as the Viking raids and trading increased.

The trading center of Staraya Ladoga is also believed to have been established before the attack on Lindisfarne. Situated in present-day western Russia across from Finland, Staraya Ladoga linked the Baltic and Black Seas for seafaring traders. Research indicates that Scandinavian traders first settled this market town in the 750s, again well before the first documented Viking raid in 793. Initially, Scandinavian traders arrived with their goods during the summer months. By the middle of the next century, evidence shows that craftsmen inhabited the town on a year-round basis.

As the number of Scandinavian settlements grew on the eastern trade routes, these Scandinavians became known as the Volga Vikings. Their initial forays into trade were the exchange of furs for silver and other goods from central Asia. Accounts from Arabs Abu'l ibn Khordadbeh and Ahmad ibn Fadlan describe in detail the Volga Vikings, who sailed the Volga River and traded at marketplaces along that route. Trading posts along the Volga eventually led to settlements on the Dnieper River and the Black Sea. Once traders and sailors reached the Black Sea, they gained entry to the Mediterranean Sea and a new world of riches.

Scandinavian traders sought to extend their influence beyond just the goods they sold. They established their own trading centers so they could control the goods that were traded and collect revenue. Slavic lands and areas beyond offered highly profitable items to trade, so the Norsemen began controlling the settlements that arose along their eastern trade routes. This loosely connected string of towns is often referred to as Kievan Rus'. Initial attempts by the Norse to unify the villages were met with resistance.

However, over time, the Norse gradually became the rulers of the waterways and marketplaces, including preferential trading status in Constantinople. The eastern Vikings used different tactics than their contemporaries who sailed west, but it worked out well for them since they dictated the flow of trade and items traded.

In the Vikings' conquests of market towns, raids on monasteries and unprotected villages, and after dominating in battles, the Vikings enslaved those they captured. This opened up another profitable avenue for the Scandinavian traders. The people that the Vikings seized were wanted by buyers at the markets in Constantinople and farther east. The enslaved people sold by the Vikings were from all areas of the known world.

Bartering served as the basis for many trading deals. However, as the Vikings expanded their raiding and trading routes, they had more access to coins, gold, and silver. The Scandinavians created their own dies and minted coins to use in trade. With time, the Vikings became more sophisticated as they developed a market economy. Traders often carried their own scales to ensure they received the exact amount of silver and bronze in exchange for their goods.

Coins for trading.
EttuBruta, CC BY-SA 4.0 <https://creativecommons.org/licenses/by-sa/4.0>, via Wikimedia Commons; https://commons.wikimedia.org/wiki/File:Viking_weight_combined_only_reflection.jpg

SECTION FOUR:
Myth and Mythology

Chapter 13: Customs, Rituals, and Religion

The Scandinavians who lived during the Viking Age did not leave any written texts that researchers can explore today. Much of what is known or theorized about the Scandinavians was shared by other cultures with whom they interacted. Other information was written years after the Viking Age. Many who wrote about them and their culture viewed the Vikings and their beliefs through the lens of time and other religions.

Customs, rituals, and religious practices and beliefs of the Vikings did not occur weekly at a church service. Ceremonies celebrating or commemorating life, death, or marriage were shared communally. Other beliefs differed from region to region and among people within a geographical area. Similar gods and goddesses were worshiped, but there was not a definite observance that one had to follow. Believers were free to worship deities who were relevant to their own personal life and experiences. Therefore, there were a number of ways to pay homage to one's gods and ancestors.

The local chieftain or ruler of an area often led a community's religious and ritualistic celebrations. However, they may have relied upon traveling or local seeresses. These women, also referred to as völur or *völva*, possessed mystical and magical abilities. Pre-Christian Scandinavian seeresses were proficient in their practice of magic, which was referred to as *seidr*. Seeresses would enter a trance-like state, which enabled the practitioner to enter the world of spirits. She then transported herself between this realm and the next to collect information that aided her prophecies.

Engraving of two völvas.
https://commons.wikimedia.org/wiki/File:Ed0048.jpg

The Scandinavian people believed that the seeresses could view their fate and manipulate events to influence their outcomes. With this knowledge, she could foretell their futures and work with the villagers on constructing new experiences to live within their fated world. Local leaders were assisted in ritualistic events by the seeress. Performing ceremonial rites and traditions could lead to better weather and harvests or successes in battles.

Ceremonies surrounding key life events were performed in Scandinavian communities. Births were an exciting yet dangerous event. Therefore, preparation for birth began while the mother was pregnant. Community and family members sang ritual songs that were intended to protect the mother and unborn child with their invocations to the goddesses Frigg and Freya.

After a child's birth, the baby had to be accepted into the family. First, the baby had to nurse on their mother's breast. Nine nights later, the father's ritual to acknowledge his baby was performed. The father placed the newborn on his knee, and then the infant was sprinkled with water. Lastly, the father named the child. Usually, ancestral names were selected or those of locally worshipped deities.

After these steps, the child was now a member of the family. With familial acceptance, the child had all the same rights as other clan members, such as inheritance. Children who were not accepted by their parents could be placed outside in the elements and left to die. Those born with abnormalities or to families who could not care for a baby could choose to let their baby die due to exposure. However, once an infant was accepted, the parents could not put the baby to death; if they did, they would be accused of murder.

Another significant occurrence in the Scandinavian world was marriage and its customs. Boys became men once they lived through fifteen winters; girls were of a marrying age as soon as they turned twelve. Before courting began, thought was given to whether or not the courtship would result in marriage. Otherwise, the woman's family would be humiliated if the wooing did not end with a proposal for her. If a proposal were turned down by the woman, the man's family would feel demeaned. These hurt feelings could result in violent retribution.

Once a successful courtship bloomed, the suitor and his family would go to the woman's house. A proposal for marriage would be made to the woman's caretaker; it is not known if she always had input on the decision. In essence, a contract had to be agreed upon for the marriage to proceed. As part of the betrothal, a *mundr* or bride-price was paid to the bride's family by the groom's clan. The bride's father offered a *heimangerð* or dowry, which would be brought to the wedding. The fathers of the bride and groom shook hands in front of witnesses to finalize the agreement, which included the date of the marriage ceremony.

Usually, the wedding would occur within one year from the handshake. Marriages were on Fridays (Freya's day) to ensure that the goddess of marriage bestowed her blessings of love and fertility. Frequently, the couple and their guests celebrated for three or more days with elaborate feasts at the bride's parents' house. The couples professed vows of fidelity to each other. Once witnesses saw the couple in their bed, the marriage contract was considered consummated.

At the same marriage bed, divorce proceedings could be initiated. Observers were summoned by the woman to her home. While standing next to her and her husband's bed, the wife could state her desire for a divorce. Sometimes, the marriage contract stipulated the terms of a divorce. Financial entanglements that ensued from a divorce could result in long-lasting battles between the families. However, divorces because the couple did not have children could be dissolved without complications.

Evidence from graves provides clues about ceremonies and rituals surrounding death during the Viking era. Most Scandinavian people were either cremated or buried. Very few were actually buried in Viking ships; those ceremonies were reserved for high-ranking kings, queens, or chieftains. Researchers have not discovered any evidence of ships being set ablaze and pushed out to sea. The dramatic scenes of fiery boats taking the deceased to their next life are only found in myths or the epic poem *Beowulf*.

Graves from the Viking Age that have been located show that most people were buried with goods. These artifacts varied depending upon a person's status while they were alive, but the grave goods included jewelry, weapons, and tools to assist the dead in their next life. It is believed that those who chose to be cremated were burned with their grave goods. The smoke from the burial pyre was thought to assist the deceased in their journey to the afterworld.

A Viking burial site.
Mpravink1993, CC BY-SA 4.0 <https://creativecommons.org/licenses/by-sa/4.0>, via Wikimedia Commons; https://commons.wikimedia.org/wiki/File:Lindholm_H%C3%B8je_Dec08.jpg

Framing their belief in an afterlife was the perception of one's soul. Many Vikings believed that each person's body was composed of four elements. All four parts complemented each other; none was more valuable or essential than any other part of the soul.

Physical looks were referred to as *hamr*. One's *hamr* was expected to transform throughout their life. A person's mind could influence their physical appearance or *hamr*. The belief in berserkers or warriors whose appearance became altered was due to the mind or *hugr* altering the body. Even after death, a person's *hamr* remained in this world.

Following the soul into the afterlife was the *hugr*. A person's identity or disposition was captured in one's *hugr*. A Scandinavian person's mindfulness and approach to life was part of their *hugr*. The Scandinavians believed that infants inherited their ancestor's character traits.

The *fylgja* was a person's uniqueness and individuality. The *fylgja* was depicted with a totem spirit. An animal represented a person's *fylgja*, one that was symbolic of their spirit and *hugr*. Since this part of the soul was so distinctive, it died when the person departed this world.

The fourth part of the Scandinavian soul was the *hamingja*. This aspect was inherited natural tendencies that continued from generation to generation. This quality helped shape what a person would be successful at doing and what they would be unsuccessful at or struggle to perform.

After a person died, their soul might be transported to different locations. Perhaps the most well known is Valhalla. Heroic warriors entered Odin's hall. There, the warriors prepared for the ultimate battle at Ragnarök.

Freya's domain, Fólkvangr, also housed warriors. Since Freya was able to choose those who entered, Fólkvangr, or Field of the People, was reputed to have a more notable gathering of Vikings. It is believed that warriors in this realm also spent their time readying themselves for the ultimate clash during Ragnarök.

Scandinavians who were not Vikings during their time in the living realm would have had their *hugr* transported to Helheim or Hel. The majority of the Scandinavian souls lived their eternal days in Helheim. Hel's afterworld is separated from this world with gates and a river. Therefore, after a soul enters Helheim, it cannot return. Only the goddess Hel has the power to free a person from death.

An afterworld specifically for the seafaring Norse was found in the realm of Rán. Rán was married to Aegir, the lord of the sea, and her hall in the afterlife included all of the treasures she took from sailors. She captured mariners in her nets and then drowned them, keeping their souls with her at the bottom of the sea.

Rán pulling a seafarer into her net.
https://commons.wikimedia.org/wiki/File:Ran_by_Johannes_Gehrts.jpg

It was also believed that ghosts or reanimated corpses could emanate from burial mounds. These mound dwellers could then become mystical beings. These spirits were either *haugbui* and guarded their family, or they became a *draugr* and left their graves to create problems for their living family members. Some thought *draugrs* were a result of family members not performing the funeral services correctly.

To appease the gods and goddesses, Scandinavians performed a *blót*. This ceremony was held at least four times a year. Scandinavians sought to be seen in a positive light by the gods, so, at a minimum, *blót* rituals were held seasonally. On or near the winter solstice, the spring equinox, the summer solstice, and the autumn equinox, the Scandinavians gathered for a *blót*. If a village was struggling, preparing for battle, or needing assistance, additional *blóts* were conducted.

Rituals were enacted to garner the support of the gods. Ceremonies were held on the land of the local leader or chieftain. This allowed the ruler to display his wealth and power while villagers paid homage to the gods. *Blóts* could be devoted to any or all of the gods. In addition to paying respect to deities, *blóts* could also be dedicated to ancestors or spirits that had the power to assist and guide the village.

Sacrificial feasts of horses, cattle, or pigs were prepared. Blood or *hlaut* from the slain animals was scattered on those present at the ceremony and statues of deities as a representation of life and its power. The food and drink were ceremonially blessed. Then all gathered to eat together, which symbolically included the gods, spirits, or ancestors, at the same table. Goblets of mead were drunk in remembrance of deceased ancestors.

Another connection the Scandinavians made to the gods was living a life of honor. They believed that living a virtuous life would align them with the gods. It was expected that all members of Scandinavian society would follow this code.

Virtues that guided Vikings included courage. Bravery was rewarded by the gods. Entering battles without fear was expected. Living a daily life facing and addressing hardships was a goal for all.

Secondly, everyone should always tell the truth. Lying was viewed as a cowardly action. Being truthful to others and to oneself was important. Standing up and defending one's principles was part of the code of honor. Fidelity or loyalty to one's fellow citizens, warriors, and craftsmen was the basis for all relationships in the Viking world.

Control over one's actions or discipline was another tenet of the nine Viking virtues. Being able to stay strong in challenging situations required discipline. Living within a community, which enhanced one's well-being, was another belief. Hospitality was necessary to develop and sustain relationships within one's family and between families. Treating others with respect was part of this belief partly because one never knew if a god had taken a human form and arrived in the village as a stranger.

Self-reliance was another important rule. Providing for one's family without assistance from others was considered a necessity to be a protective member of society. Everyone had to live a life that capitalized on their talents. Connected to self-reliance was industry. All tasks should be done to the best of one's ability. Laziness was viewed as shameful.

And the ninth tenet of their belief system was perseverance. When facing difficult and adverse situations, the Viking honor system called for tenacity. Through successfully confronting challenges, one's strength of character is born.

The Scandinavians who lived during the Viking Age blended their belief system with daily living. Following the code of conduct connected each person to their community and deities. Harmonizing one's individual and societal actions and inactions kept one in the good graces of the gods and their neighbors.

Chapter 14: Wars of the Gods

Scandinavians in the Viking Age believed in many godly beings. Elves, dwarves, spirits, gods, and goddesses all guided the Vikings. Supernatural creatures had humanlike qualities to them, which made these beings more relatable for the Norse (in this case, those who followed the Norse religion—those living in Sweden, Denmark, and Norway). Developing and maintaining a positive relationship with all non-mortals was important. No one wanted to endure the wrath of a mystical deity.

Gods and goddesses helped the Norse make sense of the natural world that surrounded them. A deity's actions were used to explain phenomena, such as weather events. Oceans and their tides, the flow of rivers, and how mountains rose were understood through stories of gods and goddesses. Myths made it easier to connect to the gods as though they were neighbors of the Vikings. Since the gods had their own personalities, the Norse could appreciate their own interactions with each other.

Most gods and goddesses in Norse mythology are connected to either the Æsir or Vanir tribe. Both tribes have similar gods and goddesses. Their distinction is more in their approach to life. The Æsir family was considered more physical and protective. Its members monitored and manipulated the sky. The Vanir gods were viewed as more compassionate and nature-oriented. They were caretakers of the sea and earth.

Odin was the lead god of the Æsir. This clan was structured similarly to the Viking world. Gods were assigned the task of ensuring that societal accords were followed. The Æsir were talented warriors and saw the ability to fight as an essential skill. These gods practiced and trained in the art of combat and war, which they used when they traveled the world. The Norse people called upon these gods for assistance with wars, births, marriages, deaths, and the roles of each person in society.

Gods and goddesses of the Vanir clan followed a more casual and free-spirited attitude to living. They were adept in the practice and application of sorcery and magic, so they learned spells and potions. Their ability to speak to the dead and use their mystical skills made others leery of them. They provided the Scandinavians with an understanding and appreciation of the seasons and natural occurrences. Their rules of behavior were much more open and less defined. A more laissez-faire view of the world was provided to the Norse through these deities.

The two clans of deities usually did not interact. They peacefully existed and inhabited two different realms. The gods and goddesses of the Æsir lived in Asgard; Vanaheimr was home to the Vanir. That is until Gullveig, a Vanir goddess, entered the realm of the Æsir. Some myths claim that Gullveig was actually Freya in disguise; many other stories tell of Gullveig as being a separate goddess from Freya.

Either way, the potent magic of Gullveig precipitated the first war of the gods, which was fought between the Æsir and Vanir.

Similar to earthly women who performed the magical art of *seidr*, Gullveig traveled from village to village, enchanting others with her potent witchcraft. Gullveig's spells and potions beguiled the Æsir. Initially, they welcomed Gullveig into Asgard and treated her as a special guest. However, her magic was so strong that some of the Æsir craved her spells. Beliefs of their loyalty and honor were being cast aside since they coveted her magic.

Some in Asgard recognized the alluring and dangerous reach of Gullveig. Fearful of the control she was garnering over their world, the Asgardians assembled the members of the ruling council. They unanimously agreed that Gullveig could not continue spreading her *seidr*, so the council decided to kill her.

Their first attempt to execute Gullveig was to use spears. Unbeknownst to the executioners, the talented sorceress had cast a spell on herself. She was immune to weapons penetrating her body, so she survived.

Next, the Æsir tried to burn Gullveig at the stake. The flames engulfed her, and Gullveig perished in excruciating pain. Again, her formidable talents saved her, as she arose from her cinders. Not ready to concede defeat, the Æsir tried again. Once more, Gullveig resurrected herself from her dying embers.

By this time, her fellow Vanir gods and goddesses had heard of her plight. Infuriated at the actions of the Æsir, the Vanir declared war. The war commenced with Oden throwing his spear into the troops of the Vanir. Vikings mimicked this action in their opening battle scenes. The Viking leader hurled his spear at the opposing forces and announced that Viking causalities were in honor of and sacrifice to Odin.

Intense fighting followed the opening lob. With their background and training, the Æsir were expected to be victorious. The Æsir brutally fought the Vanir. However, the Vanirs' skill in employing magical arts created an evenly contested war. The home realms of both sides suffered extensive damage. Later myths tell stories of rebuilding Asgard's fortifications. Neither side would yield.

Odin throws his spear at the Vanir host.
https://commons.wikimedia.org/wiki/File:%C3%86sir-Vanir_war_by_Fr%C3%B8lich.jpg

Realizing that no one would win, Odin signaled for a truce. Gods representing both sides met to negotiate a peace treaty. Following traditional Viking practices, the two groups agreed to swap hostages or captured gods with each other. This symbolic act was to further solidify the expectations of coexisting in peace.

In the deal, the Æsir leaders sent Hoenir and Mimir to live among the Vanir as honorary members. In exchange, Njord and his children, Freya and her twin brother Freyr, went to live in Asgard with the Æsir.

Njord, Freya, and Freyr were widely accepted among the Æsir. Freya shared her skills of *seith* or magic with her new clan. She taught others in the Æsir magic, including the power to foresee future events. The three assimilated into Asgard and became valued gods and goddesses.

In the Vanir world of Vanaheimr, the trade was not as effective. Hoenir and his counsel, Mimir, were sent to the Vanir to provide experience that the Æsir gods had. When Hoenir was invited to provide guidance, he was either silent or asked others for their input. The Vanir gods were surprised. They had been led to believe that Hoenir would be a great asset.

What the Vanir deities did not realize was that Hoenir was slow-witted. He relied completely on Mimir for guidance. To hide this from the Vanir, Mimir told Hoenir not to answer the Vanirs' questions or provide suggestions. Instead, Mimir advised Hoenir to seek the input of others. By doing this, no one would know that Mimir did all the thinking for the two of them.

After realizing that Hoenir had no thought capacity without Mimir, the Vanir became suspicious. They did not trust Mimir and knew Hoenir was not a wise leader. The Vanir believed the Æsir had cheated them in the peace treaty, so they killed Hoenir and decapitated Mimir. They sent Mimir's head to Odin.

Odin was able to revitalize Mimir's head by applying magical herbs and chanting spells. Mimir continued to advise Odin and keep him apprised of events.

The leaders of the two clans met again to avoid restarting the war. Both sides felt they had been wronged in the peace treaty. However, both the Vanir and Æsir understood that reigniting the conflict would result in more fierce fighting and damage to the kingdoms. So, they agreed to continue the truce.

This ceremonial peace was sealed with the archaic process of producing and drinking mead. All the gods were provided with berries. Each deity was expected to chew the berries they were given. Then each of them took turns spitting the mashed berries into one vessel. Magically, the mixture of the spittle from the gods transformed into Kvasir, which are fermented berries.

Kvasir was extremely intelligent and wise, and he traveled through all nine realms of the universe, sharing his knowledge. He astutely responded to all questions posed to him. Kvasir spent his life roaming the cosmos. He bestowed his insights on everyone he encountered.

Unfortunately, Kvasir was murdered by two dwarves so they could obtain his wisdom. Fjalar and Galar emptied Kvasir's body of all its blood. They then filled three separate containers with the blood. By mixing the blood with honey, Fjalar and Galar concocted a new mead: the Mead of Poetry. Anyone who drank from this special mead would be infused with some of Kvasir's wisdom and could craft poems. This was how poetry came into the world.

The peace between the Vanir and Æsir was not affected by the dwarves' actions.

Another part of the deities' agreement was to share humankind's veneration. The two clans were viewed as equal. Odin became the leader of all the gods. Vanir gods and goddesses continued to reside in Asgard, with the Vanir deities retaining their residences in Vanaheimr.

Gods were not expected to engage in combat again until Ragnarök. At the end of this last battle of the world, the world would end. Many different versions of the myth exist; however, in all iterations, humans and gods suffer dire consequences.

The bravest of the Viking warriors fought with Odin. After their deaths on the battlefield, the Valkyries selected the most talented and fiercest combatants to reside and train in Valhalla. In the spectacular hall at Valhalla, the chosen Vikings would be surrounded by glistening spears and shields made of gold. Every day, the Vikings prepared and practiced for Ragnarök. Each night, the Valkyries provided a feast for the Vikings. Then they healed all the wounds inflicted during their daily training sessions.

Signs of the approaching battle would be sent to the combatants. One indicator was three years without summer and wars in Midgard during the three winters. This would be followed by a brutally harsh winter called Fimbulvetr; snow would fall throughout the entire year. After the Great Winter, the sun would no longer shine and warm the earth. People would become desperate for food and warmth, which would lead to an abandonment of ethics and laws as humankind fought to survive.

The giants would be alerted that Ragnarök had begun when the rooster, Fjalar, crowed its warning. Another rooster would awaken the dead. Gullinkambi, Valhalla's rooster, would notify the gods. Combatants would meet in Vigrid, the realm for battles, where the battle to end all battles would begin.

The wolves, Sköll and Hati, will steal the sun and moon from the skies and ravage them. The erupting violence jolts the stars from the sky. Blackness envelops the world, and all the trees and mountains collapse when Yggdrasil, the huge tree that keeps the cosmos united, shudders.

The Wolves Pursuing Sol and Mani.
https://commons.wikimedia.org/wiki/File:The_Wolves_Pursuing_Sol_and_Mani.jpg

Loki, who had been punished for causing the death of the god Baldr, was chained to rocks on an island. The commencement of Ragnarök will loosen his binds and free him. Then he will board and captain the ship *Naglfar*, which was filled with giants. Loki will sail the ship, which is constructed from the nails of dead men, into battle. Since the earth will be flooded, Loki can navigate his ghost ship wherever he wants.

The wolf, Fenrir, will bust free from the chains that restrained him. He will rummage the earth, causing death and destruction to all in his path. Eventually, Fenrir will encounter Odin. With his valiant warriors from Valhalla at his side, Odin and Fenrir engage in a ferocious battle. However, Fenrir will be victorious. Vidar, one of Odin's sons, will seek revenge. Vidar wears a shoe sewn from all the leather scraps thrown out by shoemakers. The depth of the shoe will enable Vidar to open Fenrir's mouth. With the wolf's jaw spread wide, Vidar thrusts his sword through Fenrir's throat. This will kill the vicious wolf.

Jörmungandr, the serpent that wraps itself around Midgard, will emerge from the chaotic waters of the sea. Once in battle, Jörmungandr seeks Thor, his longtime adversary. With a mighty thrust of his hammer,

Thor massacres the massive serpent. Before Jörmungandr dies, he will douse Thor with enough venom to kill him.

Loki will die at the hands of Heimdall. The giant Surt and the god Freyr will both perish in their fight. By the end of the fighting, most of the gods will have died. Much of the world will burn, most humans will perish, and animals will die, but the monsters will depart from the world. The remains of the earth will sink into the rising sea.

Some tales say this is the end, but in most versions, the earth rises from its watery demise. The human race is repopulated by the children of Lif and Lifthrasir. The gods Vali and Vidar and the sons of Thor and Hoenir remain to guide the humans. They move to the realm of Idavoll. Balder and Hoder will be brought back from the dead to join the other gods in Idavoll.

Chapter 15: The Nine Realms in Norse Mythology

Vikings worshiped numerous gods. Polytheistic beliefs permitted and encouraged everyone from thralls to chieftains to revere different deities. The gods and goddesses had humanlike qualities that made them accessible to understand; these deities could even die. All of the gods and goddesses had their own personalities. Imperfections and flaws in their lives and decisions made them real to those who revered them.

The Norse belief system was framed around the World Tree or Yggdrasil. Emanating from Yggdrasil were the homes of all the beings that were part of the Norse world. There are different thoughts today about where each of the realms would have been in relation to the World Tree. However, the most current research agrees that the Scandinavians believed in Yggdrasil, the nine realms, and the beings who inhabited the realms.

The World Tree, Yggdrasil.
https://commons.wikimedia.org/wiki/File:The_Ash_Yggdrasil_by_Friedrich_Wilhelm_Heine.jpg

Standing at the center of the Norse universe was Yggdrasil. The massive tree was surrounded by the nine realms. These nine worlds were interconnected and held together by Yggdrasil. All the parts of Yggdrasil were significant in maintaining this cosmos. The longevity and health of the world were dependent upon the well-being of the tree.

The translation of the tree's name is Odin's horse. *Yggr* equates to the word "terrible," which is a name that was used to refer to the god Odin. *Drasil*, or "horse," is the second part of the tree's name. The tree is named for the occasion when Odin sought to understand runes. To Odin, the runes or letters represented knowledge.

Housed within the upper branches of Yggdrasil was Asgard, the realm of Odin. From his position, he could view the Norns, three women who shaped and manipulated fate. The Norns engraved runes on the trunk of Yggdrasil to control fate. Odin was jealous of their powers and sought a way to gain that knowledge for himself.

The message in the runes could only be divulged to someone who could prove themself worthy of obtaining the wisdom. So, Odin impaled himself with his spear. Odin then hung himself from a branch of Yggdrasil. For nine days and nights, one for each of the nine realms, Odin hung from the World Tree. Then, from the depths of Yggdrasil, the runes revealed their shapes and meanings to Odin. This knowledge made Odin one of the most powerful gods.

In addition to carving the runes on Yggdrasil that impacted all nine realms, the Norns were responsible for ensuring the health of the World Tree. Water from Urd's well was sprinkled on Yggdrasil's roots daily by the Norns to keep the tree healthy. Mud was gathered from the area around the well and used to repair areas of the roots that were damaged by animals and decay. Healthy roots were essential for uniting all parts of the world.

The Norns represented the past, present, and future. They were respectively named Urd, Verdandi, and Skuld. Together, the three determined the fate of one's life. One Norn spun the thread of life, the next one measured its length, and the last Norn decided when the thread should end.

The daily gatherings of the gods were held at the Well of Urd. Gods rode into the meetings on their horses, except for Thor, who arrived in his goat-driven chariot. At these daily discussions, the gods talked about justice with the Norns. The Norns captured the plans in their runic writing.

The second well feeding Yggdrasil was Mimisbrunnr, or Mimir's well, which provided insight and knowledge. Drinking this potent holy water required one to make a sacrifice to the well. Odin exchanged one of his eyes for the opportunity to drink from the well and gain wisdom. He visited the well often to confer with Mimir's head. Mimir, the god of wisdom, provided guidance to Odin during their discussions. The root from this well led to Jotunheim, which was the homeland of the frost giants.

Hvergelmir existed before time and was believed to be the original well in the Norse world. Waters from this well connected to the realm of Niflheim, where the Norse believed that the first signs of life emerged. When the World Tree lived in the great void or Ginnungagap, the icy temperature of the abyss froze the water and created Niflheim. When the realm of fire or Muspelheim arose near Niflheim, a vapor appeared. This fog was the progenitor of all beings.

The first known giant, Ymir, emerged from this mist. He produced additional giants while he slept. Icy surfaces continued to melt from the heat from which Audhumla, a cow, was uncovered. To feed herself, Audhumla licked the ice that surrounded her. The first of the Æsir clan, Buri, was discovered in the melting ice.

Buri, the progenitor of the gods, had a son named Borr. Borr married Bestla, the daughter of Bolthorn, one of the frost giants. Together, Borr and Bestla had three children. All three were part god and part giant. Their children were Odin, Vili, and Vé.

The three brothers were concerned about how rapidly Ymir could create offspring. Ymir's descendants greatly outnumbered the half-god and half-giant beings in the world. Odin and his brothers decided they needed to kill Ymir to better balance the world. The gory battle resulted in Ymir's blood drowning all but two giants: Bergelmir and his wife. They became the ancestors of all giants born after Ymir's death.

Odin and his brothers used the remains of Ymir to erect the world and the other seven realms. The flow of Ymir's blood created the waterways. His skin and muscles were transformed into soil and land. Mountains were formed from his bones. Ymir's teeth were used for rocks. Flora and fauna were shaped from his hair.

Then the brothers took Ymir's head and tossed it. From his brains came the clouds, and the sky was made from Ymir's skull. Embers of fire were snatched from Muspelheim and tossed inside his skull to serve as the stars in the sky.

Though Odin and his brothers acted quickly, Ymir's body was massive. While they worked, worms formed in Ymir's remains. The trio used the worms to form the dwarves. The brothers were concerned about the stability of what they had created, so they picked four dwarves to hold up the sky. The four dwarves were sent in four opposite directions. They were as follows: Nordi (north), Sundri (south), Austri (east), and Vestri (west).

Since their work was completed with Ymir's body, Odin and his brothers began constructing the remaining realms.

Located near Asgard is Alfheim, or the land of the elves. The Vanir god Freyr reigned over this realm. Freyr was the Norse god of the harvest, fertility, and hunting. Elves had the responsibility of assisting Freyr. They had the ability to impact the harvest. Elves could also affect fertility by impeding one's chances of pregnancy or working to assist with fertility.

The elves were incredibly beautiful creatures and illuminated their surroundings. Their presence motivated others to create artistic endeavors, including music and poetry. Alfheim was seen as a realm of brightness, harmony, and calmness.

Dancing Elves, a depiction of Alfheim.
https://commons.wikimedia.org/wiki/File:%C3%84lvalek.jpg

Also known as caretakers, the elves could be called upon for guidance, assistance, and protection. If one found themself in a crisis, these guardian angels would be there to help.

Odin created a home for himself, Asgard, and presided over it with Frigga. All the gods and goddesses of the Æsir clan live in Asgard. The realm was home to fabulous palaces and halls. Asgard was also home to Valhalla. This elegant hall with 540 doors accepted warriors who died valiantly in battle. Those selected by Odin were transported to Valhalla by the Valkyries. These beautiful female guides carried the warriors to Asgard. Warriors not chosen by Odin would go to Fólkvangr, which was located within the boundaries of Asgard. They were housed in the hall of Sessrumnir and ruled by Freya.

Valaskjalf was another hall in Asgard built for Odin. Its roof was made from pure silver. Within Valaskjalf is Hlidskjalf, Odin's throne. From this vantage point, Odin could see what was happening in the other realms.

A fiery rainbow bridge named Bifrost connected the two domains of Asgard and Midgard. Any of the gods and goddesses could move from their world to that of the humans. Asgard was a realm of law and order. Its entrance was guarded by Heimdall, who protected the world of the gods.

The realm for all the dead warriors who were not worthy of Valhalla or Fólkvangr was Hel of Helheim. Those who did not live an honorable life in Midgard were also sent here. Not to be confused with Christian hell, Hel was headed by and named for Loki's daughter, the queen of death.

Sensing that Loki's children would cause problems for the other gods and goddesses, Odin relocated them from Asgard. Odin moved each of them to areas of the world where their ability to create havoc would be minimized. Hel, which means "hidden" in Old Norse, was selected to live in Helheim. Hel's brother, the serpent Jörmungandr, was hurled into the ocean surrounding Midgard; her other bother, Fenrir the wolf, was shackled until Ragnarök.

Access to Helheim was restricted to one lengthy treacherous pathway. Traversing this desolate path included crossing a river of clashing weapons. Once one found the bridge to cross over, then, out of the ominous mist, appeared the one entranceway in the wall that enveloped the realm of Hel.

The home or realm of the giants (the Jötnar) was Jotunheim. Jotunheim is depicted as a chaotic and lawless world. It was located beyond the realm of order. Sometimes, Jotunheim is also known as Utgard; other sources portray Utgard as an area within the realm of the giants. Since Jotunheim housed the giants, the span of the land was massive, expanding from Asgard to Midgard. The River Ifing separated the orderly world of Asgard from the disorderly realm of the giants. Though Jotunheim is portrayed as a world that has a perpetual winter, the magical waterway never froze.

Since the beginning of creation, when Odin and his brothers killed Ymir, the giants sought revenge. As adversaries of the Æsir, the giants continually warred with Odin and the other gods. Frequently, the Jötnar tried invading Asgard, desiring to kill the gods who resided there. Once that task was completed, the Jötnar would kidnap the goddesses and take them back to Jotunheim to wed. Most gods and goddesses did not willingly travel to Jotunheim.

Situated between Jotunheim and Asgard was the world created for humans. Midgard, or Middle Earth, was separated from Jotunheim by Jörmungandr. The serpent was another of Loki's children that Odin could not trust; Odin cast Jörmungandr into the oceans to live until the final battle of the gods.

From Ymir's hair, Odin created flora and vegetation on Midgard. Then Odin and his two brothers, Vili and Vé, formed the first humans. The trio of brothers shaped the tree into the first humans. Ask, Midgard's first man, was shaped from an ash tree. An elm tree provided the basis for Embla, the first female. All other humans were descendants of Ask and

Embla.

The realm of fire, from which the sparks emanated to cause the creation of Ymir, is known as Muspelheim. Surtr, a fire giant, ruled this hostile world. A mortal enemy of the Æsir gods, Surtr waits for the day when he can set the other realms ablaze with his fire. At the end of the world, Surtr will play a key role in the destruction of the realms. He and his sons will set Asgard ablaze; he will also set fire to Yggdrasil, seeking to destroy all life within the World Tree.

Also part of the creation myth was the world opposite to Muspelheim. In Niflheim, or the mist world, a realm of cold, snow, and ice can be found. These two realms gave birth to Ymir from the abyss of Ginnungagap, which began all creation. A spring located in Niflheim, Hvergelmir, fed Yggdrasil and sustained all life. The dragon, Nidhogg, protected the spring of life. He acted as a sentry and kept the dead and living separate from each other.

Dwarves who arose from the bugs from Ymir's rotting corpse were provided a home in Svartalfheim. Since they emanated from insects within the giant's dead body, their world was fashioned so that the dwarves could reside in dark caves and underground. Though they were small in stature and lived in a world without much light, they produced much beauty and magic.

Dwarves were master craftsmen who were adept at a multitude of trades. They were able to make jewelry, work as blacksmiths, and shape all types of metal. The dwarves gave the gods many magical and powerful gifts. They are credited with having created Draupnir, Odin's enchanted ring, and his spear, Gungnir. For Thor, the dwarves fashioned Mjolnir, his hammer. A ship that could be folded into a pocket, *Skidbladnir*, was created for Freyr.

The last of the realms was Vanaheimr, the home of the Vanir. These tranquil gods immersed themselves in the world of untamed nature. Vanaheimr was where the Vanir continued to reside after their war with the Æsir. The Vanir were known for their ability to see into the future. They were called upon by mortals living in Midgard to assist with good harvests, as the Vanir were able to affect the sun, rain, and wind.

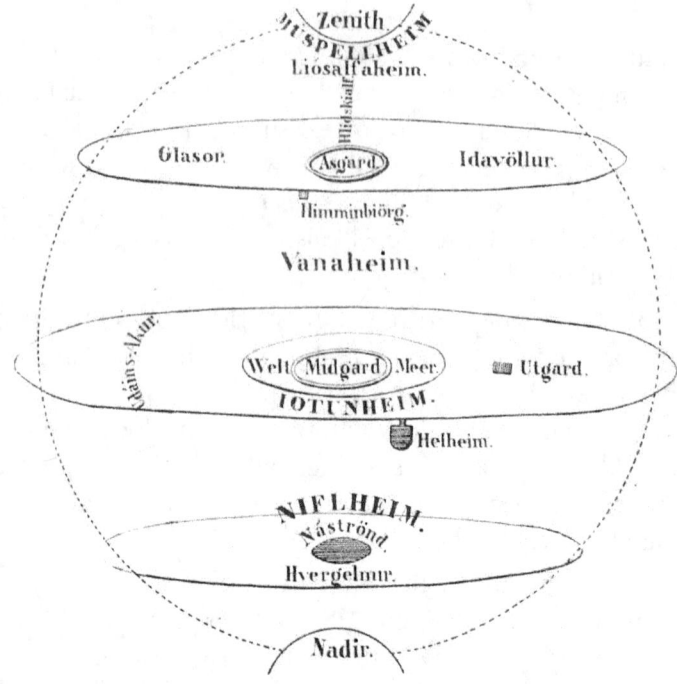

Cosmos of Norse mythology.
https://commons.wikimedia.org/wiki/File:WHEATON(1844)_The_Cosmos_in_the_Norse_mythology.jpg

The nine realms will coexist until the day of judgment when Ragnarök commences.

Chapter 16: Symbols and Possessions of the Norse Gods and Goddesses

Connecting all nine realms of the Norse world was Yggdrasil, also known as the World Tree. This one tree bound together life and death, good and evil, and heaven and earth. Therefore, Yggdrasil was one of the key symbols of the Norse people.

Vikings believed that Yggdrasil and other symbols were a way of asking the gods for assistance. Each symbol had its own meaning and purpose. Depending upon the situation in which Vikings found themselves or knew they were embarking upon, they carried their symbol for support and protection.

One symbol the Vikings warriors believed would assist them on their raiding and pillaging voyages was the *vegvisir*. The word for the symbol has roots in *vegur*, for "road" or "path," and *visir*, which means "guide." The *vegvisir* was also referred to as the Viking compass. It has a circular center from which emanates eight rune staves. Many believe these represent compass directions: four staves for the four cardinal points on the compass. The other four symbols correspond to the intercardinal directions.

Vikings began to develop navigational technology. However, for additional support during their long and dangerous voyages, the Viking compass was drawn on ships before they sailed. The *vegvisir* symbol was supposed to ensure safe passage for the ship and its passengers. Not only did the Viking compass assist ships, but it was also worn as an amulet by those who were seeking guidance in life.

Another ancient Norse symbol that provided protection for the wearer was the Helm of Awe or *Aegishjalmr*. Originating in the Old Norse language, the word *aegis* meant shield, and *hjalmr* meant helm. Similar in design to the *vegvisir*, the *Aegishjalmr* has eight tridents that radiate from a central point. The defensive posture of the spike-tipped spears gives the appearance of a shield guarding the center. Sometimes, the *Aegishjalmr* was depicted with serpents in the outer circle that would incapacitate their enemies before attacking them.

The symbol itself was thought to inflect terror in those who saw it. Vikings etched the Helm of Awe on their weapons, armor, and helmets. Some warriors drew *Aegishjalmr* on their foreheads with blood as they prepared for battle.

Scandinavian tales say that the Helmet of Awe was originally owned by Hreidmar, the giant. Hreidmar possessed much gold, which he had received from Odin. The giant had demanded the gold as payment for Odin's murder of Hreidmar's son. When Odin gave the giant the gold, he placed a curse on it. One of Hreidmar's other sons, Fafnir, killed his father for the gold. Fafnir took the gold and the helmet. With the power of the helmet, Fafnir transformed himself into a dragon so he could guard his golden treasures.

Helm of Awe.
https://commons.wikimedia.org/wiki/File:Aegishjalmr.svg

The valknut is the Slain Warrior's Knot and is often referred to as Odin's symbol. Going into battle with the power of Odin was provided to the Viking warriors by applying the valknut symbol on their bodies, wearing jewelry with it, or inscribing it on their weaponry. Valknut was a powerful symbol that offered protection in battle. If a warrior died while fighting, they were still safeguarded with the valknut symbol. Warriors believed that Odin would be there in their death to receive and greet them at the gates of Valhalla.

Since Odin was a spiritual guide, this symbol was also viewed as a passage from one realm to another or from life to death. Depicted as intertwined triangles, the valknut was also connected to the nine realms of Norse mythology. The three triangles create nine corners or nine lands on the World Tree. Each of the triangles represents different spheres in the cosmos of heaven, hell, and earth. The points of the triangles point upward to Odin's realm of Asgard.

Similar to valknut in its broad, powerful scope was Mjolnir or Thor's hammer. This hammer had the capability to kill and deliver blessings. Thor was indomitable with Mjolnir. Amulets of Mjolnir were worn by Viking warriors to summon the brawn and valor of Thor in battle. These amulets are the most often discovered artifacts at Norse excavation sites. Thor used the power of Mjolnir to safeguard the realm of Asgard from the chaos of other worlds. In his role as protector of the land of the gods, Thor and Mjolnir kept turmoil and confusion at bay with their decisive victories over the giants, trolls, and other menacing beings.

Not only did Mjolnir keep the home of the gods safe and protect warriors, but Thor's hammer was also used by the god to provide blessings. Mjolnir had the power to impede the forces of evil. With this protection from Thor, couples sanctified in marriage were given the gift of fertility. Thor's expansive reach extended to fecundity in the field, granting the people an abundant harvest.

Mjolnir was a result of the trickster god Loki's mischievousness. Always causing trouble, Loki decided to annoy Thor, so he cut Sif's hair as she slept. Sif, Thor's wife, had gorgeous golden tresses. Thor was infuriated by Loki's actions. To defend his wife, Thor threatened to kill Loki. Ever the trickster, Loki promised Thor that he would replace Sif's magnificent locks of hair with ones even more incredible. Thor accepted Loki's deal.

Loki traveled to the realm of the dwarves, Svartalfheim. The dwarves were known for their talent as craftsmen. They agreed to weave strands of gold together to replace Sif's hair. She would once again rule as the goddess of grain and fertility.

While Loki was with the dwarves, he taunted them. Loki told them that they could not make more fabulous pieces than they already had; their abilities had peaked. Accepting the challenge, the dwarves forged Mjolnir. However, Loki did not want them to win the challenge, so he shapeshifted into a fly. He buzzed around and irritated the dwarves as they worked. This caused Thor's hammer to have an unusually short handle.

Though the hammer was flawed, Thor was amazed at its abilities. Loki had fulfilled his part of the bargain and was permitted to live. To hold the handle, Thor had to wear his magical iron gloves. Mjolnir returned to Thor every time he threw it. With his hammer, Thor was almost invincible.

Picture of Thor's hammer found in Sweden.

Ola Myrin, Statens historiska museum/SHM, CC BY 4.0 <https://creativecommons.org/licenses/by/4.0>, via Wikimedia Commons; https://commons.wikimedia.org/wiki/File:Claes_Kurck_Sk%C3%A5ne_hammer_-_HST_DIG.55488_original.jpg

The prolific dwarves created other treasures for the gods while Loki was in their realm. As part of his challenge to them, the Sons of Ivaldi, who sewed Sif's golden locks, also crafted two other wonders for the gods.

One was *Skidbladnir*, and the other treasure was Gungnir.

The ship, *Skidbladnir*, had magical powers. Some tell of Loki bestowing the ship to the god Freyr; other stories say that Freyr's twin sister, the goddess Freya, was given the ship. Regardless of the owner of *Skidbladnir*, the Sons of Ivaldi, constructed a vessel that could be folded up so small that it could fit in a deity's pocket.

When the ship was unfolded, all the gods had to do was breathe on the miniature ship, and it would expand into a mighty craft. It grew so large that all the gods and goddesses who lived in Asgard could fit on it. Their weaponry, battle gear, and horses were easily stowed on board.

This ship of the Norse gods would magically transport its passengers anywhere. *Skidbladnir* could travel on land and sea in all weather conditions. Whenever its sails were hoisted, *Skidbladnir* was assured of winds that would propel it quickly and effortlessly to its destination. Once at its endpoint, the ship was refolded and inserted into a small pouch.

The dwarves also produced the lethal spear Gungnir. Gungnir was gifted to Odin by Loki after Loki returned from Svartalfheim. Similar to Thor's hammer, when Gungnir was thrown, it would return back to Odin. Also, Gungnir always reached its target and could pierce any material.

Odin used this spear to stab himself when he hung from Yggdrasil to gain knowledge of the runes. This special spear was also the one Odin flung to initiate the Æsir and Vanir war, which makes it a symbol of victory. Viking warriors replicated this action to start all their battles. They threw the first sword and invoked the power of Odin to be with them in battle and at the entrance to Valhalla.

Loki was not satisfied with the treasures he watched the dwarves create. Continuing his trickery, Loki conned two other dwarves into making him more valuables. He told Brokker and Sindri (also known as Eitri) that there was a contest in Asgard to see who was more talented: the Sons of Ivaldi or the two of them. However, these two brothers took a bit more convincing, so Loki bet his head that Brokker and Sindri were not as gifted as the Sons of Ivaldi.

Seizing the challenge, Brokker and Sindri created three masterpieces, one of which was Mjolnir. Loki transformed into a fly and pestered and distracted the brothers. However, they endured and finished all three items.

From a pigskin, Brokker and Sindri fashioned Gullinbursti, which means "golden bristles." This golden boar was quicker than all other animals except Odin's horse, Sleipnir. Not only was Gullinbursti the second-fastest of all, but it could also speed through all elements, including air and water.

Its hairs were fabricated from gold, so Gullinbursti glowed with shimmers of light in the darkness. A guiding light shined from Gullinbursti to guide Freyr in any lands shrouded in darkness. This gleaming brightness was symbolic of illuminating a pathway in battle for warriors. Many Vikings drew the image of Gullinbursti on their weaponry before battles. Boars were thought to be attendant spirits who escorted the gods to provide protection and good fortune.

Drawing of Gullinbursti and Freyr.
https://commons.wikimedia.org/wiki/File:Freyr_by_Johannes_Gehrts.jpg

Next, the brothers crafted an incredible ring called Draupnir. Every ninth night, Draupnir "dripped" eight brilliant gold rings. Every one of the newly created rings that fell from the one forged by the dwarves was the same size and amount of gold. While the latest rings could not replicate themselves, they gave their owner vast quantities of gold.

Odin, the god of abundance, now possessed a way to gain more wealth. Additional affluence equated to more power. Rings also represented a sign of fidelity, which Odin expected from others who lived in Asgard with him.

When Odin's son Baldr died as a result of Loki's actions, Odin placed Draupnir on Baldr's funeral ship. This is viewed as a sign that Odin realized that Ragnarök would soon commence. Laying the ring on the pyre was Odin's signal of the transition to the new leaders that would emerge.

Another symbol connected to Odin and Viking leaders that bridges the Norse world and the afterlife was a raven. Ravens were visual depictions of the transformation that occurred with death and appeared after battles to feast on the deceased combatants.

Other leaders in the Norse world put symbols of ravens on banners and weaponry. Ravens were perceived as shrewd birds. Their ability to observe all that was around them made them valuable to the Vikings. Kings, warriors, and sailors believed that ravens could see everything.

As Vikings traveled the world, they sailed with ravens. The ravens were caged on the ships. When Vikings needed to know if they were near land, the ravens were released from their cages. If land was nearby, the ravens flew in that direction. If there was not any land in their vicinity, the ravens flew back to the ship.

Odin's twin ravens were Huginn and Muninn. During the day, they flew to each of the realms. With their keen insight and ability to understand the human language, Huginn and Muninn reported all their findings to Odin at the end of each day. They also served as couriers, transmitting messages from other gods and goddesses, supernatural beings, dwarves, or giants to Odin.

Tapestry of Odin with Huginn and Muninn.
https://en.wikipedia.org/wiki/File:Odin_hrafnar.jpg

Huginn, which means thoughts, and Muninn, which means memory, represent Odin's desire for knowledge and learning. For the Vikings, the ravens provided a connection to their ancestors. Keeping deceased family members in one's thoughts and memory provided guidance for humans.

These symbols and more helped the Scandinavians understand their world. Creating visual representations of the gods, goddesses, and their worlds provided a sense of purpose and control. While these gods and goddesses are referred to as characters in Norse mythology, to the people of the Viking Age, these figures were real parts of their religion. Beliefs sustained the Scandinavians in battles, daily life, and death. These images supplied hope for the future and causes to celebrate happiness in life.

Conclusion

The Vikings and Scandinavians left a treasure trove for us. Though the situation in which the Scandinavians found themselves is very different from ours, there are similarities in the human experience. Each person in the Viking Age had hopes and dreams. Each person in today's world has hopes and dreams. Obstacles have hindered people of all ages. The lesson we can learn is how people persevered and adapted.

There are many myths about the Vikings that are not supported by research. One is the horned helmet. Viking warriors were much too practical to waste raw materials to add a feature that did not protect them or injure the enemy. The horned helmet is actually from a costume designer named Carl Doepler. He infused Germanic elements in his creations for Wagner's *The Ring of the Nibelung*.

The Norse gods are prominent in our days of the week. Tuesday is named for Tyr, the Norse god of war; Odin or Woden, the king of the gods, gives us Wednesday; and Thursday is for Thor, the god of the sky and thunder. We find ourselves connected to the Vikings on a daily basis. And by reading more about their exploits and myths, we can find new ways to connect with them.

Part 2: Norse Mythology

An Enthralling Overview of Norse Myths, Gods, and Goddesses

Introduction

Thor, Loki, Odin, and Asgard—these words might sound familiar, especially to those who are huge fans of comic books, superhero films, and video games. Some might know Thor, the hammer-wielding thunder god—or perhaps superhero—from the big screen. However, some might picture a golden scientific city with glimmering palaces when they think about Asgard. Some might even depict Odin as the wise, fatherly king of the Norse gods.

Hollywood has no doubt played a big role in introducing these mythical characters and places to the world; through movies, most know that Mjölnir is the name of Thor's powerful hammer and that Bifröst is the bridge that connects Middle Earth and Asgard. Through comic books, almost everyone knows that Loki is the god of mischief and that Odin is the one-eyed god. And through video games, people know that the Norse universe consists of nine different realms and that there are different races and creatures living in each one. But there is still so much more to Norse mythology than what is depicted in the media.

The *Poetic Edda* and *Prose Edda* are the two main sources of Norse mythology. Most of the sources are in the form of poetry, and they tell detailed stories of the Norse universe. *Völuspá*, the most prominent poem in the *Poetic Edda*, features a conversation between Odin and a powerful seeress about the universe—from the creation of the world up until Ragnarök, the cataclysmic destruction of the cosmos and the rebirth of a new world. Another well-known poem in the *Edda* is called *Grímnismál*. In this poem, Odin, wearing the disguise of a wandering traveler, shares a great deal of information about the world, especially the many realms in the fortified city of Asgard.

Norse mythology is also full of interesting tales and stories about the adventures of the gods and heroes. Some are entertaining, such as the story of how Thor, dressed as a bride, went on an adventure to retrieve his hammer. Certain stories have tragic endings, such as the death of the Valkyrie or Brynhild and her lover Sigurd, while there are also gruesome tales like how Loki was bound using his own son's intestines and how Týr lost his sword hand to the giant wolf, Fenrir. To put it simply, Norse mythology is both rich and peculiar but definitely well worth discovering.

While there are many legends surrounding Norse mythology, this book focuses on retelling some of the most famous tales of all time. We will start with the creation of the world and an imaginative description of all nine realms of the Norse universe before diving into the story of the first pair of humans in Midgard and the tale of how the gods waged war with each other until a truce finally reunited the two celestial tribes.

Odin, Thor, and Loki surely are not the only gods in the Norse pantheon. Freyja, Frigg, Heimdall, Týr, and Baldur are some others who each have their own unique attributes and abilities. In the second part of the book, readers will be enlightened with not only the details of each deity but also their intriguing tales and stories of their mythical adventures.

The Norse women of fate have already decided on the fates of all beings in the universe, including the mightiest of gods sitting high on their thrones—almost all of them are to meet their doom when Ragnarök approaches. The Twilight of the Gods, however, will only take place when several prophecies have been fulfilled. All of these important events that lead to the end of the world are vividly explored in the third part of the book; the binding of Odin's worst enemy, the death of Baldur, the punishment of Loki, and Fimbulwinter.

Before the existence of written manuscripts, these mythical legends, sagas, and prophecies were passed down from one generation to the next orally. So, it is safe to assume that while many tales survived to this day, many more are also gone, lost in history. Indeed, the stories that survived have been immortalized in different mediums, be it in a collection of old poems, theatrical performances, modern films, and colorful comic books. However, all of them carry different versions and depictions. We can never be sure which of these versions are the ones the Vikings passed down to their sons and daughters.

Nevertheless, this book aims to stay as close to the original as possible. Readers will be presented with not only captivating tales surrounding the Norse world but also compelling narratives about the gods and their complex profiles. Some of the lore and details you might have already known, but many others might surprise you.

Chapter 1: The Beginning of the Norse Cosmos

"Of old was the age | when Ymir lived;
　Sea nor cool waves | nor sand there were;
　Earth had not been, | nor heaven above,
　But a yawning gap, | and grass nowhere."
(*Völuspá*, Stanza 3, translated by Henry Adams Bellows)

The year is unknown. The time is not yet created. Day and night do not exist. There is no rain, no sun, not even the skies. There is nothing but a vast emptiness—a void waiting for nature to take its course. This bottomless abyss is called Ginnungagap, and this is the very beginning of the universe.

Soon, at the north and south of the yawning gap, two enormous primordial realms are formed. To the north is a land called Niflheim. This dark place is filled with nothing but extreme coldness, ice, snow, and endless mist. In the realm of Niflheim, one can also find Hvergelmir, the world's first spring and the source of all rivers and waters. This is also the spring where a vast number of serpents take refuge. These venomous serpents emit poisons in the spring, and when combined with the water, it forms eleven rivers that are known in Norse mythology as Élivágar.

These rivers flow from the land of mist into Ginnungagap. Soon, the coldness catches up with the stream and freezes the abyss. Ginnungagap is no longer a void, as frost has taken over the emptiness.

While Niflheim sits on the north of Ginnungagap, to the south is another massive realm called Muspelheim. Unlike the previous primordial land, which is even colder than the coldness itself, the realm of Muspelheim is completely the opposite. It is a land of fire, with gurgling hot lava until the air is full of soot. The land lights up with huge, red flames burning without rest.

These two elements—ice and fire—clash with each other at the center of Ginnungagap. The hot sparks and flames from the realm of Muspelheim touch the edge of the frozen void and gradually melt the ice until droplets of water and warm mists spread throughout the air.

From the melted ice, water droplets, warm mists, and venom in Ginnungagap comes the first being in the world. It is a giant named Ymir, the very first of its kind. While Ymir sleeps in the land of nothingness, the great being sweats terribly. And from the sweat under his armpits, two more giants are born: one male and one female. Ymir then moves his legs, and as they come together, he sweats again. From the sweat in between his legs, Ymir, again, spawns another giant. From this point on, more and more frost giants are born. Ginnungagap finally has inhabitants.

Just like all beings that we have come to know in our world, Ymir and the giants need food to survive. It turns out that when the elements of ice and fire met in the middle of Ginnungagap, Ymir was not the only being that resulted from the event. Auðumbla—whose name comes from the Old Norse language, meaning the "hornless cow rich in milk"—is a primeval cow that is responsible for providing nourishment to the frost giants. Ymir and the other frost jötnar or giants feed on Auðumbla's milk, which is the only way they can stay alive. Some accounts even claim that four rivers of milk came from Auðumbla's teat and that the giants drank from the river to feed themselves.

Ymir Suckling the Cow Audhumla by Nicolai Abildgaard, c. 1777.
https://commons.wikimedia.org/w/index.php?curid=639093

When Auðumbla finally gets hungry, the cow wanders around and looks for a patch of ice to lick. Since there are no grasses yet to be found in the world, Auðumbla has a particular patch of ice that she returns to every day to feed herself. On the first day, when Auðumbla first runs her tongue across the ice, a patch of hair emerges. On the second day, Auðumbla returns to feed herself. Again, when she runs her tongue on the freezing block, licking it until she is full, a head of a man appears out of the ice. Finally, on the third day, Auðumbla licks the very same ice, and a man breaks free.

This man is not just an ordinary being in the universe. This particular man who came out of the ice goes by the name Búri, and he is the first god of the Norse world. With an unknown partner, Búri soon bears a son whom he names Bor. Later on, Bor marries Bestla, a giantess and daughter of the giant named Bolthorn. From this marriage—which is considered the first marriage between a god and a giant—Bestla gave birth to three divine children. The names of these children are Odin, Vili, and Vé.

Although the population is growing—especially the giants—the land never changes. It remains empty. And so, the three brothers—Odin, Vili, and Vé—have to figure out a way to shape the world. With nothing growing on the land, the brothers have no resources to start building. And so, they come up with a vicious plan, which is to kill Ymir and use his massive remains to start building the world. While the lack of resources could be the main reason behind their plan to kill the primeval giant, some accounts also suggest that the brothers were threatened by how fast the giants could reproduce and that they believed that the giants would only lead them into chaos.

Knowing how huge Ymir is, the brothers decide to attack the giant while he is asleep. When Ymir finally rests his eyes, Odin and his brothers murder Ymir without hesitation. They stab the giant multiple times, and when he drops to the ground, his fresh wounds produce a rush of blood. Ymir's blood flows down his lifeless body so fast that it floods Ginnungagap. All of the other giants cannot escape their fate, and they all drown, except for two: Ymir's own grandson, Bergelmir, and his wife. These two giants are forced to flee by climbing on top of a lúðr, a type of chest or coffin floating on Ymir's blood.

With the brothers' plan a success and Ymir's body lying lifeless on the ground of Ginnungagap, the siblings can begin creating the world that they envision. By using Ymir's remaining blood, Odin and his brothers create the great ocean that surrounds the entire world. There was so much of Ymir's blood that the ocean was not the only result. The brothers use some of the blood to create the many lakes and pools of the land.

With Ymir's flesh, the gods then start sculpting the earth, which they filled with vast valleys and lands. By scattering the giant's bones throughout the world, the brothers create rolling hills and towering mountains. The gods make use of everything in regards to Ymir's corpse, including his broken teeth, which they use to create all the stones, rocks, and pebbles found all over the earth—from the seashores to the lakesides, riverbanks, and mountain slopes.

By using Ymir's skull, Odin and his brothers create the great sky. They lift the skull and place it over the world, creating a dome. However, the gods need to make sure the dome will hold until the end of time. And so, they begin thinking of a solution. While doing this, they see countless maggots twitching and squeezing themselves into Ymir's rotting flesh. After taking a closer look at the creatures, the gods grant them consciousness and wisdom, along with a precious gift: a deep passion and talent for crafting extraordinary things. The maggots transform into dwarves, and they live underneath Ymir's flesh, deep underground within the rocks and far below the mountains. To solve the problem regarding the mighty sky, the gods choose four dwarves and send them to four different directions, where they are tasked to hold up the sky. These dwarves are known by the names Nordri (North), Sudri (South), Austri (East), and Vestri (West).

The sky would look empty without the sparkling stars. The gods travel to the realm of Muspelheim and gather some of its shiny sparks. The sparks are then thrown into the sky, where they turn into a beautiful collection of stars. To accompany the stars in the sky, the divine brothers make use of Ymir's brain; they scatter it across the sky, and they become billowing clouds. With Ymir's hair, Odin and the brothers create the trees. Using the giant's eyebrows—or eyelashes as some sources suggest—the brothers build a great wall to protect the land from the giants. The land within this mighty wall is called Midgard, a land that human beings call home.

A pair of giants who had managed to escape the flood are banished by the gods to the mountains away from Midgard. This untamed area of dark forests and mountains is called Jötunheimr, and this is the land where the giants would rebuild their race. A descendant from Ymir who goes by the name Narfi has a beautiful daughter. Her name is Nótt, which means "night." This giantess has skin as dark as the night itself, with long hair as dark as ebony.

Said to be one of the most beautiful giantesses to ever exist, Nótt is thought to have married three times. Her first marriage is to a giant named Naglfari, and the pair bears a child named Auðr, which means wealth. Her second husband is called Annar, and she later gives birth to a daughter named Jörð, which means earth. Her third marriage is with Dellingr, whose name means dawn. Unlike her previous two husbands, Dellingr is not a giant. In fact, he is an Æsir, a god from the principal Norse pantheon. Together, the pair has a son, who they name Dagr, which means day. In contrast to his mother, Dagr has skin as bright as day, and he is as beautiful as the gods.

Of course, Odin soon learns about the birth of Dagr. And so, he takes both Nótt and her bright son and gives them each a chariot to ride across the skies until Ragnarök finally destroys the world. Nótt rides ahead of her son, and her chariot is pulled by a horse called Hrimfaxi or the "Frost Mane." Every morning, as the horse makes its way through the sky, its snaffle bit will produce foam, and this foam will drop onto the green grasses and leaves on the earth. Humans can take a glimpse of these water droplets every day before the sun rises, and they are called dew.

Behind Nótt, her son, Dagr, follows her trail in his own chariot. Dagr's chariot is pulled by another horse named Skinfaxi or the "Shining Mane." Just as its name suggests, this horse is so bright that it lights up the entire sky and the earth below.

Odin observes the sky at all times, making sure the mother and son go on their endless journey across the heavens at the same speed until the end of time. The world turns dark when Nótt passes by, and the skies brighten up when Dagr rides through on his chariot. And so, day and night are created. With Nótt and Dagr following each other in the skies, the mighty gods and humans on the earth can now tell the time.

However, Nótt and Dagr are not the only ones put under Odin's careful observation. In Midgard, a man who goes by the name of Mundilfari lives. He has a pair of children whose appearances are so fair that he names them Sol and Mani after the real sun and moon, which were created by the mighty gods. The gods, however, are enraged by

Mundilfari's boastful act. So, they take the beautiful brother and sister away from their arrogant father and give them both a task. The radiant sister, Sol, is to ride in a chariot, pulling the sun itself across the heavens. To protect the earth below from burning to ashes due to the hot sun, the gods place a legendary shield called Svalinn before the sun. While his sister controls the chariot of the sun, Mani is in charge of the chariot pulling the moon.

The Wolves Pursuing Sol and Mani *by J. C. Dollman, 1909.*
https://commons.wikimedia.org/w/index.php?curid=4722868

Of course, the siblings would love to get a rest every once in a while after their endless journey across the heavens, but they also know that they can never be able to do so—at least not until the end of times—as they are constantly being chased by two enormous wolves named Hati and Sköll. Each of these vicious wolves has but one mission: Sköll to devour the sun and Hati the moon. But they would never succeed as long as Ragnarök is just a rumor in the distance.

Chapter 2: Yggdrasil and the Nine Worlds

I remember yet | the giants of yore,
 Who gave me bread | in the days gone by;
 Nine worlds I knew, | the nine in the tree
 With mighty roots | beneath the mold.
(*Völuspá*, Stanza 2, translated by Henry Adams Bellows)

The gods, humans, dwarves, elves, animals, and the entire Norse world would cease to exist without the legendary ash tree. Yggdrasil, also known by many as the World Tree, had sprung in the middle of the Norse cosmos once the elements from Niflheim and Muspelheim met at the center of Ginnungagap. It was so tall and massive that the Old Norse poem, *Völuspá*, described it as a "friend of the clear sky." Its branches spanned across the heavens, and its gargantuan roots extended to the underworld and three sacred wells: Urðarbrunnr, Hvergelmir, and Mímisbrunnr. Yggdrasil was the tree that united all nine realms of the Norse universe. These realms are Asgard, Midgard, Vanaheim, Alfheim, Svartalfheim, Helheim, Jötunheimr, and, of course, the two primordial realms, Niflheim and Muspelheim.

Aside from uniting the nine worlds, the sacred tree itself was said to be the home to various living creatures. At the top of its highest branches was an eagle with a wide knowledge; sadly, its name has been lost in the sands of time. This eagle was unlike all the other ones we have seen flying in the skies. It was said that once it flapped its wings, a few of Yggdrasil's branches would break, and it would create a strong wind until the humans in Midgard could feel its breeze. Some accounts even claim the eagle was the one responsible for hurricanes and typhoons.

While at the top of Yggdrasil lived the mighty eagle, at the foot of the ash tree lived a serpent—or a dragon as some sources state—who spent all day gnawing at the massive roots of the World Tree. This serpent is known by the name Níðhöggr (Nidhogg)—not to be confused with Jörmungandr, the giant serpent encircling the earth—and its only aim was to topple down the ash tree and send the world back to nothingness and chaos.

The Ash Yggdrasil by Friedrich Wilhelm Heine, 1886.
https://commons.wikimedia.org/w/index.php?curid=5240798

Set to destroy Yggdrasil, Níðhöggr gained an enemy: the eagle. Every day, the serpent and the eagle would exchange insults and mockeries with each other. Since the two creatures lived far from each other—one is perched on top of the tree and the other underground, right beneath the massive root—a messenger was required. This was a task for Ratatoskr, a squirrel who would scurry up and down the tree trunk, carrying slanderous messages to provoke the eagle and Níðhöggr.

Other beings that called Yggdrasil their homes were the four stags named Dáinn, Dvalinn, Duneyrr, and Duraþrór. These stags survived by chomping at the tree's foliage and branches. Of course, with all those creatures, the World Tree suffered from several casualties, but its vitality was never depleted, thanks to the tender care of the Norns.

The Norns were female entities who controlled the fate of all beings in the world, making them even more powerful than the gods themselves. However, it is unknown how many of them there were. The Old Norse poem, *Fáfnismál*, stated that there were many of them and that they descended from the gods, elves, and possibly even the dwarves. However, in *Völuspá*, there were exactly three Norns, and they were considered mysterious yet powerful beings who descended from neither the gods nor the other beings found in the universe. The three Norns—Urðr, Verðandi, and Skuld—lived in a hall underneath Yggdrasil, next to Urðarbrunnr, also known as the Well of Fate. The Norns would draw water from the sacred well, which they mixed with clay before using it to nourish the World Tree to prevent it from rotting. When they were not drawing water from Urðarbrunnr, the Norns would leave their hall and visit newborn children to determine their fates.

Asgard

After creating the sky, the clouds, stars, the ocean surrounding Midgard, and the tall mountains, the gods needed a realm for themselves. And so, the last realm that they built was Asgard, a dwelling place for the Æsir gods and goddesses. This realm was created high up in the sky, at the top of Yggdrasil. It towered above the realm of humans. Asgard was connected to Midgard by Bifröst. To the gods, Bifröst was a bridge that they would often use to cross the two realms, while the humans saw it as a rainbow adorning the sky. No humans were able to cross the rainbow bridge since it contained a red flame that would burn any mortal should they ever attempt to set foot in the divine world.

Despite the Bifröst being one of the strongest constructions ever created by the gods and guarded by Heimdall himself, its destruction during Ragnarök had long been prophesied. There was simply no way to avoid it.

It is nearly impossible to imagine how massive the home of the gods was, but according to ancient records, there were several smaller realms in

Asgard. Each of them housed mansions and legendary halls belonging to different gods and goddesses.

At the center of Asgard was a green plain known as Iðavöllr. This was the very place where the gods would gather to discuss the world's most important issues. On this heavenly plain, one could also find the realm of Glaðsheimr. This was the realm that housed Odin's most famous golden hall, Valhalla. There was another hall for slain heroes similar to Valhalla that was called Fólkvangr. The only difference between Valhalla and Fólkvangr was that the latter was ruled by the goddess Freyja.

Near to Bifröst and home to the one and only Heimdall was another realm known as Himinbjörg, which means Heaven's Cliff. Baldur, one of Odin's sons, lived in Breiðablik (Breidablik), while in the kingdom of Þrúðheimr (Thrudheim) stood a hall of 540 rooms called Bilskírnir. This is where Thor, his wife Sif, and their many children dwelled.

Vanaheim

Translated from Old Norse, Vanaheim simply means the "Homeland of the Vanir." While the Æsir gods in Asgard were often associated with war, weapons, and justice, the Vanir gods were worshiped for something completely opposite. The Vanir were known to be powerful deities associated with nature, fertility, wisdom, and magic. It is even believed that they had the ability to predict and see the future of many beings in the universe.

However, it is unknown where Vanaheim was located in this mythic world. A majority of scholars agree that it could have possibly been situated west of Asgard. Their reasoning comes from an old poem called *Lokasenna*, where it is stated that the Vanir god Njörðr had to sail east to reach Asgard from his home. Still, other scholars believe it lay in the underworld, right underneath the roots of Yggdrasil.

There is little information that describes what Vanaheim actually looked like, but since the realm was inhabited by the Vanir themselves, we can assume that the realm was a pleasant land filled with an abundance of beautiful nature and wildlife roaming about.

Alfheim

The third realm in the Norse cosmos was Alfheim (Álfheimr), which directly translates as the "elf world." In Norse mythology, it is believed that there were two kinds of elves: the Ljósálfar ("Light Elves") and the Dökkálfar ("Dark Elves"). The Light Elves were said to be beautiful and fairer even than the bright sun itself, while the Dark Elves were, of course, the opposite. They were described to be as dark as pitch. Alfheim, however, is inhabited only by the Light Elves. This was said to be one of the three realms—with the other two being Asgard and Vanaheim—that was located on the top branches of Yggdrasil.

Even though the realm was known to be the home of the Light Elves, surprisingly, it was not at all ruled by their kind. Instead, Alfheim was ruled by the Vanir god Freyr. Whether there was a direct connection between the god and the elves remains unsure, but the old poems did explain how he gained his throne over Alfheim; the mighty gods gifted him the land when he was an infant, right after he grew his very first tooth.

However, just like Vanaheim, there is no detailed information that describes the world of Alfheim. The realm itself was only mentioned a few times in the old poems. But since it was ruled by the god of fertility and magic, many have assumed that Alfheim was a bountiful realm.

Midgard

From the empty void of Ginnungagap, the gods created a beautiful world filled with green lands, ample resources, and healthy soils for the humans to live on and make use of. Some call this realm Midgard, while others know it by the name Middle Earth. Unlike the other realms united by the World Tree, Midgard was situated neither on the branches nor the roots. Instead, it was located on its trunk. Middle Earth was connected to Asgard via Bifröst, but no human was permitted to cross the bridge. Next to the land was the dangerous realm of Jötunheimr, the world of the giants. To make sure Midgard would remain secure from unwanted attacks from the giants, the gods built a massive wall around the land. Those walls were created by using none other than Ymir's eyebrows.

However, the wall was not the only thing separating Midgard from the wildlands of Jötunheimr. A great ocean surrounded the land, and it was so vast that it was the home to the World Serpent, Jörmungandr. The serpent was said to be as massive as the earth itself; it could wrap its long, scaly body around Midgard and still bite its own tail. While Jörmungandr's ultimate nemesis was the god of thunder, Thor, every being in the universe had to be aware of its movements. Once the World Serpent let go of its tail, its entire body would drop into the great ocean, causing unrelenting floods and disasters in the world of men. Ragnarök would soon follow, and a deadly battle awaited.

Jötunheimr

When Odin and his brothers slew Ymir, his blood caused a great flood. The remaining two of his kind, Bergelmir and his wife, were forced to flee into the dark wilderness. This land was called Jötunheimr or Utgard, which means "beyond the fence." It was the only place where the jötnar were welcomed. Located adjacent to Midgard and extending to the edge of the world, Jötunheimr was separated from the fortified home of the gods by the river Ífingr, a legendary river that never froze. It had such a fast stream that it was impossible for anyone to cross it.

Some believe that Jötunheimr was a bare land filled with nothing but darkness and terrible danger, while others claim that the realm was just an untamed wilderness surrounding Midgard with towering mountains and mystic forests. However, not a single human would venture into the realm with a light heart, especially since the gods had built a strong wall surrounding Middle Earth to protect the humans from any threats lurking beyond the fence.

Other than Odin, Thor was one of the few who could easily survive in the land of the giants. During his adventures in the realm, many giants would attempt to trick the god of thunder into his own demise, but none of their plans worked. While Thor was crossing the Vimur River in Jötunheimr, he couldn't help but notice that the water level was slowly rising. In just a few seconds, both of his shoulders were already submerged underwater. Sensing something was wrong, the god looked around and saw a giantess named Gjálp standing nearby, her urine pouring continuously into the river, causing the water to rise tremendously by the second. Enraged, Thor reached for a huge rock and threw it at the giantess. His aim was precise. Gjálp immediately stopped urinating, ruining her plan to stop the god from journeying into her father's stronghold.

Thor's Journey to Geirrodsgard *by Lorenz Frølich, 1906.*
https://commons.wikimedia.org/w/index.php?curid=5163591

Svartalfheim

Svartalfheim is yet another realm that is not as well known as the others. Svartalfheim, which is sometimes referred to as Nidavellir, was the home of the dwarves. According to Snorri Sturluson, the Icelandic historian and author of the *Prose Edda*, Svartalfheim is also where the Dark Elves took refuge. However, it is not for sure whether the dwarves and the Dark Elves mentioned by Snorri are actually two different beings. Certain scholars agree that they are, indeed, the same creatures, while others believe that they are two separate races. The dwarves were short and master blacksmiths, while the Dark Elves were malevolent creatures with much darker skin compared to the Light Elves of Alfheim.

Since Svartalfheim was situated underground, the realm would be rather dark, and its atmosphere was filled with constant smoke due to the smoldering embers coming from the forges. Although the dwarves were described as strong, they were also said to be highly susceptible to the sun. Thor, who knew of this, used this weakness against a dwarf named Alviss. The wise dwarf was to marry Thor's daughter, but the god of thunder was not at all pleased by this arrangement. And so, he tricked Alviss into answering one question after another until dusk. The god asked about almost everything, from the art of crafting to cosmology and music. Not aware of the time, the dwarf left Thor's residence in the morning. Once he was exposed to the sun, he turned into stone.

Muspelheim and Niflheim

Muspelheim and Niflheim were two of the earliest realms to exist in Norse mythology. Both worlds were formed way before anything else, and they played a pivotal role in creating the universe. Muspelheim was the realm of fire, and its land was as hot as the sun itself—perhaps even hotter than that. It could easily burn any mortal who dared to set foot at its gate. Despite the extreme scorching temperatures, the flames burning all day and night, and bright red lava gurgling in the pits, Muspelheim had inhabitants. The land was ruled by Surtr, a monstrous fire giant who wielded a flaming sword called Sviga Laevi. When the time finally came, Surtr, along with his minions, were the ones destined to set the entire universe on fire.

While Muspelheim was known for the element of fire, the realm of Niflheim was where the ice came from. This primordial world had nothing growing on its dark land due to its extreme coldness and never-ending mists. Niflheim is also said to be far on the north side of the universe—do keep in mind that in the old Viking beliefs, north means down, while south means up. One of Yggdrasil's roots could still reach into the realm, uniting it along with the other eight worlds of Norse mythology.

Helheim

Helheim, also known by many as Hel, was the cold and dark realm of the dead. Believed to be located in Niflheim, it is not a surprise that the realm is described as being extremely dark with cold winds that could even make the gods uncomfortable. This land was ruled by none other than Loki's monstrous daughter, whose name is the same as the realm, Hel. It is said that under her rule, not even the gods could easily get out of the realm. There was only one way in and out: one must cross Gjöll, an ice-cold river full of sharp knives flowing through it. Then, one had to pass through a massive gate guarded by a ferocious blood-stained hound named Garmr.

However, Helheim is not at all the same as the hell we know today. This realm did not only contain those who had died without doing good deeds; it was also where those who failed to enter Valhalla continued their next stage after their life ended. Those who did not perish on a battlefield would be sent to Helheim, as did those who died of accidents, sickness, and old age. There were no tortures and torments waiting for them, as the realm was merely a place to continue life after death. But some also claim that Helheim does have a special place for the wicked ones. Those who had lived wicked lives were said to be thrown into Niflhel, the lowest level of the realm, where they would face their mistakes.

Chapter 3: The Creation of Humans and the War of the Gods

"Then from the throng | did three come forth,
   From the home of the gods, | the mighty and gracious;
   Two without fate | on the land they found,
   Ask and Embla, | empty of might."
(*Völuspá*, Stanza 17, translated by Henry Adams Bellows)

High up in Asgard, the forges never stopped burning, and the sounds of axes knocking down the trees echoed through the forests all day long. Wooden temples were built, exquisite halls were fashioned with golden thrones, and the tables were equipped with intricate plates and bowls. Every day, the gods would gather at Iðavöllr to discuss crucial matters. Afterward, they would return to their dwellings, where they enjoyed feasts and challenged each other at a game of Tafl, an ancient game of the gods resembling chess. It was the golden age, so the gods had almost nothing to worry about. Even the Norns were less busy during this period since there were not as many souls that they had to visit to determine their fate.

With the world beautifully created and no endangering threats to be seen, the gods turned their attention to Midgard. The realm had everything, but at the same time, it was empty. There were no inhabitants in Midgard to make use of everything that the gods had created. And so, Odin began to wonder. It would be such a waste to create such a wonderful world only for it to be left untouched. The All-Father then traveled to a beach accompanied by two other gods; some say he was with his two brothers, Vili and Vé, while other sources claim he was accompanied by Hœnir and Loðurr (Lodurr). While they were taking a peaceful stroll along the shore, they noticed something peculiar in front of them. It was two pieces of driftwood oddly carved in the shapes of a man and a woman. Whether it was the work of the dwarves or simply Mother Nature, no one truly knows.

Hœnir, Lóðurr and Odin Create Askr and Embla *by Lorenz Frølich, 1895.*
https://commons.wikimedia.org/w/index.php?curid=5288741

While the three gods were puzzled by the driftwood's striking resemblance to themselves, they also felt pity. Although they were shaped exactly like a man and a woman, they lacked life; after all, they were only pieces of wood. And so, the gods agreed to bring them to life and provide everything that they did not have. Odin was the first one to take a step closer to the pieces of driftwood, and he bestowed upon them the breath of life. Vili then took his turn and granted them consciousness and the ability to move. Finally, Vé gifted them with healthy complexions and their five senses. From pieces of driftwood, they turned into breathing human beings, the first pair in the world.

To protect them from the sun during the day and the cold at night, the gods gave the two humans proper clothing. The gods then sent them to Midgard, where they would spend the rest of their days. Before leaving the two, Odin and his brothers gave them names; the man was called Ask, and the woman was called Embla. The three gods asked nothing from them in return for these gifts, except for one. Within the fortified wall of Middle Earth, Ask and Embla were tasked to reproduce and populate the world. This task was, no doubt, successfully accomplished by the two, as more and more humans were born until Midgard was known as the realm of men.

The days passed, and the lives of the humans in Middle Earth evolved. From living a simple life in small settlements, tending to farms and animals, they began building ships and exploring the vast world. Kings and queens, warriors and heroes were born. They trained and waged war on battlefields, clashing swords and axes. However, the humans were not the only ones who fought among themselves. The mighty gods also threw spears at each other. This was the first war in the world, and it was one of the biggest conflicts to ever erupt between the two divine tribes: the Æsir and Vanir.

The Æsir are the principal gods of the Norse pantheon, which means these are the gods that most of us today might know, thanks to several films and video games that are inspired by the Norse world. Odin, Thor, Frigg, Heimdall, Baldur, Týr, and Loki were all Æsir. These gods lived in Asgard, and most of the time, they are associated with war, weapons, and chaos, making them the more famous pantheon, especially among warriors and heroes. Meanwhile, the Vanir were worshiped for fertility, wealth, and wisdom. Instead of dwelling within fortified walls with grand halls and banquets, the Vanir called Vanaheim, a realm believed to be rich in nature, their home. In contrast to the Æsir, the Vanir are said to be less civilized and have the ability to use magic. However, not much is known about them other than some of their well-known gods, such as Njörðr and his twin children, Freyr and Freyja.

The main reason behind this godly war is not entirely clear. There are two plausible theories. Some say that it began when the Vanir were starting to gain favor from the humans. Each day, more and more humans worshiped them and began providing sacrifices in the name of the Vanir. This, of course, caught the attention of the gods in Asgard. The Æsir grew jealous of the Vanir, even though the humans never stopped worshiping them. And so, the war began.

While the jealousy of the Æsir gods toward the Vanir could be seen as the start of the war, *Völuspá*, a poem in the *Poetic Edda*, suggests otherwise. It all began when Asgard opened its doors to a mysterious woman known by the name Heiðr. Some believe that the woman was none other than the Vanir goddess of fertility and magic herself, Freyja, who loved to travel the realm in disguise while practicing the art of seidr (seiðr) or powerful shamanic magic. One could even hire her to cast her powers and solve their troubles in return for a payment of gold.

One day, Heiðr paid a visit to the Æsir gods. In Asgard, she showcased her powerful magic until the gods themselves turned to her whenever they were drowning in problems. It turns out that the more dependent the gods were on Heiðr's powerful magical abilities, the further they strayed from their honor, loyalty, obedience, and laws. The Æsir realized this, and they put the blame on Heiðr. They claimed she was selfish and only cared about gold (Heiðr was said to have always talked about her love of gold, even from the very moment she arrived in Asgard, which irritated the Æsir greatly). Because of that, they called her Gullveig, which means "gold-greed."

The Æsir would never let Gullveig go unharmed, and they were sure that the entire universe would be better off without her. So, they captured the magic practitioner and brought her to Odin's hall. There, they set Gullveig on fire and stabbed her multiple times with spears. Right when they thought the world was rid of the greedy witch, Gullveig emerged from the burning flames, completely unharmed and without a single wound, despite the many ruthless stabs by the gods. Determined to end her life once and for all, the Æsir again threw her into the huge flame at the center of the hall and stabbed her. Just like the first time, Gullveig walked out of the flame unscathed. The same thing happened when the Æsir tried to burn and stab her to death for the third time. During all three murder attempts, Gullveig was in a magical trance, which made it impossible for her to be harmed.

A depiction of Gullveig over the fire by Lorenz Frølich, 1895.
https://commons.wikimedia.org/w/index.php?curid=4650069

To make matters worse, Gullveig was, in fact, an ally of the Vanir gods in Vanaheim. So, when the news about how the gods in Asgard treated Gullveig reached their ears, the Vanir were enraged and immediately swore that they would make them pay for the horrible act that they had committed. They began planning and preparing their vengeance, but Odin, who was sitting tall on his throne, Hliðskjálf (Hlidskjalf), could see everything and everyone in all nine realms. The All-Father knew that the Vanir would attack Asgard sooner or later, and the battle would explode to catastrophic heights. After all, the gods of the Norse world were not immortal. But thanks to Iðunn's golden apples, they would never age until the end of time.

With enough preparations, Odin and his fellow gods laid an attack on the gods of Vanaheim. The All-Father threw his spear, and it flew above the heads of the Vanir gods—an action that was later practiced by Vikings at the start of a battle. This marked the beginning of the war of the gods. Indeed, the Æsir were familiar with wars and using brute force, but the Vanir were also quite powerful. Instead of wielding heavy weapons, they used powerful magic and spells to paralyze Odin and his fellow gods. Not long after, the Vanir successfully destroyed a part of the fortified walls in Asgard. However, the war did not end there, as the Æsir managed to cause great damage and casualties to those in Vanaheim. The gods waged war with each other for as long as they could, and neither tribe was ready to back down. As the war went on, they began to realize that nothing good could come of this conflict; the entire world would be reduced to ashes before either side emerged with a victory.

Thus, the gods from both pantheons sheathed their weapons and stopped casting spells that would further destroy the world. They gathered around and chose to end the war in the most peaceful way possible. However, before they could even reach that point, the two divine tribes argued, pointing fingers at each other. After hashing out everything that may have caused the battle, the gods finally came to an agreement; they decided to coexist peacefully with one condition.

They were to choose among themselves and exchange hostages. Both pantheons had to send some of their most powerful gods or goddesses to each other's realms. To fulfill the agreement, Njord, Freyr, and Freyja moved to Asgard, while the Æsir chose Hœnir and Mimir to live in Vanaheim.

The Vanir, no doubt, had fulfilled the pact by sending three of their best gods to Asgard, but the same could not be said of the Æsir. Mimir is believed to be the wisest being to ever exist in Norse mythology. His wisdom and knowledge were as vast as the endless ocean to the point that Odin himself would turn to him for useful advice and suggestions. Hœnir, on the other hand, did not share the same attributes as the wise god Mimir. He did gain support and admiration from the rest of the Vanir, but it was his handsomeness and strength that helped him. Due to his attractive appearance, the gods of Vanaheim thought he would be a fitting leader of the realm. He proved them right by providing only the best decisions and solutions. Impressed by his skills and wisdom, the gods of Vanaheim decided to make him the chief of the realm.

Little did they know, all those decisions and solutions that came out of his mouth were not his. Despite playing a role in creating humans and sometimes described as being "the most fearful of all gods," Hœnir was actually indecisive. It was actually Mimir who had been whispering the wise words to him. The Vanir gods eventually discovered what they were up to. While Mimir was away from Hœnir, the gods would seek his advice, and due to his indecisiveness, he often replied, "Let others decide." The gods of Vanaheim felt cheated by the Æsir, and they seized Mimir and beheaded him. His body was left in the wilderness to rot, while his severed head was delivered to Odin in Asgard to express their anger.

A 19th-century depiction of Mimir's beheaded body.
https://commons.wikimedia.org/w/index.php?curid=682765

The All-Father was horrified by Mimir's brutal fate. He couldn't bear to lose someone who had possessed such tremendous knowledge. And so, Odin carried Mimir's head to safety, where he would later embalm it with several extraordinary herbs just so he could ensure the head would not decay. Then, he began chanting Seiðrhljóð (magical songs) to bring the severed head back to life. Even without his body and lungs, Mimir magically breathed again. Relieved, Odin carried the head in his hands to his hall in Asgard. Later on, Mimir would guard the legendary well of Mímisbrunnr.

This vicious incident could have restarted the war between the two pantheons. However, even the gods knew that the war would only bring chaos to the world and that neither of them would benefit. Hence, the two divine tribes peacefully agreed to stop shedding any more blood. This time around, both the Æsir and the Vanir convened and sealed another pact. The gods from both tribes performed an ancient peace ritual where they spat into a vessel. Their saliva then got mixed up, and a wise being was born. His name was Kvasir, and he was the product of the new alliance between the Æsir and the Vanir gods.

Chapter 4: Odin and Thor

Odin appearing as a wanderer by Georg von Rosen, 1886.
https://commons.wikimedia.org/w/index.php?curid=225899

It was a usual day in Midgard. Not a single threat could be seen, and the humans continued to live their lives. Nothing out of the ordinary was expected to happen until a mysterious figure arrived. From a distance, he looked just like a normal traveler who had been wandering the lands, trying to reach some destination. As he got closer, one could notice that the traveler had but one eye. His appearance was, for the most part, always the same; the traveler had a greying beard and a dark blue coat, which protected his skin from the hot sun and cold winds at night. On his head, the old traveler wore a wide-brimmed hat, and he would often walk around with a staff in his hand. People who crossed paths with the grey-bearded traveler knew him by the name Grímnir while those high up in Asgard knew him by his real name, Odin.

Odin, who is also known by many as the All-Father, was the leader of the Æsir. Snorri claimed him to be the most powerful member of the Æsir. After all, Odin was the king of Asgard, and without him, the entire universe would cease to exist. Although his appearance in Midgard did not resemble a god at all, the All-Father did this on purpose. Odin had always loved to wander the world in disguise, and he was known by many names. The third day of the week, Wednesday, is derived from one of his names; in Old English, he is known as Wōden.

As the king of Asgard, it is perhaps not surprising that Odin had several wives and mistresses. Officially, he was the husband of Frigg, the queen of Asgard and the goddess of marriage. Through Frigg, they had three children: Baldur, Hodr (Höðr), and Hermod (Hermóðr). One of the most popular partners associated with Odin was, of course, Jörd (Jörð). Unlike Frigg, who was born an Æsir, Jörd was a giantess. With her, Odin bore another child, who was the most powerful of all—Thor.

Being a warrior god, Odin is often associated with wars and death. He even owned Gungnir, a legendary spear that was said to be able to cause panic, blindness, and numbness. But those are not the only things for which he was worshiped. Odin was also the god of poetry, knowledge, and wisdom. While weapons and brute force were something with which the All-Father was very much familiar, Odin also had a vast knowledge of magic, thanks to the Vanir goddess Freyr, who came to live in Asgard after the war of the gods ended. Some sources even claim that Odin could see the future and interpret prophecies.

In Asgard, Odin dwelled in his grand hall called Valhalla, where he was accompanied by dozens of honorable warriors and kings who had fallen on the battlefield. These warriors were hand-picked by the Valkyries, and once they were sent to Odin's hall, they would spend their entire day sharpening their battle skills to prepare for the last battle, which is known as Ragnarök. Odin had other creatures by his side other than the warriors and the Valkyries. Laying by his feet were two ferocious wolves named Geri and Freki; both of their names mean the "greedy one." The All-Father took care of the wolves himself. Every day, he would feed them using his own hand. All of the food on his dining table would be fed to his wolves, leaving only the wine, as the All-Father did not need food to survive. The wine was more than enough for him.

In the hall was also a throne called Hliðskjálf (Hlidskjalf). Odin would seat himself on this throne and look over the world. The All-Father could see everything that was going on in all nine realms from Hliðskjálf. However, the throne was not the only way for the king of Asgard to receive important news and information about the universe. Odin had two crows that flew high in the skies across the realms, and he named them Huginn ("thought") and Muninn ("memory"). These two crows were his eyes—some say they were his spies—as they would return to him after scouting the world and report everything that they saw.

Whenever there was a particular event that piqued his interest, especially when it could benefit his search for knowledge, Odin would make haste and ride his loyal eight-legged steed, Sleipnir, across the sky and ocean. Odin would do anything for knowledge—even if it meant sacrificing his own eye—but it was not for the sake of his own being. When Odin met the Völva or the seeress, he was told that the gods would be killed and that the entire world he built would be destroyed when Ragnarök came. Even the All-Father would meet his fate during the Twilight of the Gods; he was to be devoured by Fenrir the wolf. Because of this prophecy, Odin pursued knowledge just so he could overcome the deadly fate looming over himself, the other gods, and the entire world.

His ability to shapeshift meant that he could travel the universe in more than one disguise. He would often interfere with various matters involving humans, especially if he saw something beneficial. However, even the All-Father was not right all the time; he would occasionally get into trouble, just like humans. One day, two boys were out in the shallows, carefully rowing their little boat to a spot where they could fish. The older boy was named Agnar, while the younger one was called Geirröth (also spelled as Geirröd). These children were the sons of a king in Midgard who went by the name of Hraudung.

While the boys were busy casting their fishing rods, the wind blew harder than usual to the point that they immediately lost control of the boat. Moments later, they drifted straight into the open sea. Terrified and with no other choice, they stayed in their boat throughout the night. When the morning finally came, they found themselves wrecked on an unfamiliar shore. In front of them stood a poor farmer. Feeling sorry for the lost boys, the farmer took them in and introduced them to his wife. Little did they know, the pair who had brought them in was, in fact, Odin and his wife, Frigg, in disguise.

Still wearing the appearance of a poor peasant, Odin took Geirröth under his wing and taught him wisdom, while Frigg took care of Agnar and raised him with compassion. When the trees began to grow new leaves, and colorful flowers started to bloom, marking the end of winter, Odin and Frigg led the boys to the very same shore that they had washed upon. After caring for them for a few months, the two gods then gifted the young boys a new boat and asked them to return to their father's land. However, before sending them off, Odin pulled Geirröth to the side and started whispering into his ear; he persuaded the boy to push his brother back to the sea and return to his home alone.

And so, the brothers began their journey home, and this time around, the wind was different—it was as calm as the ocean itself. When they were nearing the shore, Geirröth, who sat at the front of the boat, leaped up on land and pushed the boat away, causing Agnar to drift out into the open sea again. However, upon returning home, Geirröth soon found out that his father, King Hraudung, had died. Since he was the king's only heir to return home, Geirröth was welcomed with open arms and crowned as the new king. While Geirröth wore a crown on his head and owned all the riches in his land, Agnar dwelt in a cave with a giantess, with whom he had children.

Odin saw the entire event while he was sitting on his high seat in Asgard. Proud of his champion, Odin began to taunt his wife. "Would you look at your ward," the All-Father presumably said to Frigg. "What has become of Agnar? He dwells in a cave with a giantess, while my champion, Geirröth, is a respected king who rules his own land."

Frigg was, of course, irritated and not at all impressed by Geirröth's success. "Open your eyes," Frigg said. "I hear Geirröth has become nothing but the worst of his kind. Your champion knows nothing of hospitality. He would torture his guests if too many of them stood before him." Odin dismissed his wife's words and claimed them to be nothing but lies.

To prove that Geirröth was not at all what Frigg claimed him to be, Odin set out to Midgard in his most famous disguise. He wore a dark blue cloak along with a wide-brimmed hat or, as some accounts suggest, a hood. Frigg, who knew of her husband's plan to visit Geirröth's hall, ordered her most loyal servant, Fulla, to travel to Midgard and speak to the king. Fulla managed to reach Geirröth before the All-Father, and she warned the king about a dangerous sorcerer who was on the way to his land.

"And how would I recognize this sorcerer?" Geirröth asked, taking the bait.

"Once he sets foot in your hall, not even the fiercest hounds would dare to bark at him," Fulla said.

And so, the king waited for the sorcerer to arrive while keeping his eyes on his guard dogs. Moments later, an old man with a grey beard appeared in his hall. Noticing his presence, the dogs immediately took a step back and cowered in the corner. Seeing how his hounds were afraid of the old man, Geirröth heeded the false warning given by Fulla and ordered his men to seize the sorcerer. With his hands tied, Odin was questioned. Geirröth interrogated him, but the only answer he gained from the old sorcerer was his name: Grímnir. Infuriated that he refused to say anything more than his name, Geirröth ordered the sorcerer to be set in between two huge flames for eight nights without rest.

On the eighth night of this torture, a young boy approached the disguised god. The ten-year-old boy was the son of the king himself. He was named Agnar after his father's brother. Unlike Geirröth, Agnar was not at all cruel. The boy went to Grímnir and brought him a horn filled with water. Not only did he offer the old man water to ease his pain, but he also apologized for his father's ill actions. Grímnir accepted the kind offer and drank from the horn. He then began to describe in full detail the universe to the people surrounding him: how it was shaped and the names of the nine realms, along with its inhabitants. Grímnir even revealed his real name and told them of his many disguises before shifting his focus back to Agnar. He promised the boy a reward for his kindness and a terrible misfortune upon Geirröth.

The king finally realized that the person he tortured was the All-Father himself. The panicked king immediately rose from his throne, hoping he could fix his fate by pulling the god away from the burning flames. But he had already signed his death warrant. The moment he stood up, Geirröth slipped and fell on his own shiny sword. With the king impaled and dead on the floor, Odin vanished into thin air. Geirröth's son, Agnar, was hailed as the new king.

Frigg, who witnessed the entire incident—presumably from Hliðskjálf—was more than satisfied, knowing that her husband was completely wrong about his champion. Some said that upon seeing what happened to Odin in Geirröth's hall, the goddess laughed so loudly that it echoed throughout the heavens. However, on the bright side, the dead king was replaced by a better ruler. Agnar's reign was much more prosperous compared to his father's.

However, Odin was not the only godly figure to venture out of the comfort of Asgard. The same could be said about Thor, the red-bearded god of thunder. He was the son of Odin and his giant mistress, Jörd. Just like any other member of the Æsir tribe, Thor dwelled within the fortified walls of Asgard. His realm was called Þrúðvangr (Thrudvangar), and he had his very own hall named Bilskírnir. Thor was married to Sif, the goddess of fertility, and with her, they had a son named Modi and a daughter they called Thrud. Another one of his well-known sons was Magni, whose mother remains unknown—some believe that Magni was born from a giantess named Járnsaxa.

Being one of the strongest gods in Norse mythology, Thor is said to be the protector of both Asgard and Midgard. Of course, as the mighty defender of two important realms in the universe, Thor gained numerous enemies whose sole wish was to eliminate him once and for all. This included most of the giants in Jötunheimr, as well as Jörmungandr, the World Serpent, who would soon be able to kill him during Ragnarök. It is believed that although Thor successfully ended the serpent's life by hitting him in the skull one last time, Jörmungandr managed to spit his deadly poison on the mighty god, causing him to drop dead on the ground just a few moments after the serpent's death.

Thor by Johannes Gehrts, 1910.
https://commons.wikimedia.org/w/index.php?curid=4624484

Thor did not only hold the title of defender of the world, but he was also known as the god of thunder, lightning, and storms. Oftentimes, the red-bearded god would venture all over the realms wielding a powerful hammer that is popularly known as Mjölnir. This was the weapon that he used to crush the skulls of the many giants who stood in his way. But Mjölnir was not the only legendary item in his possession. Thor also wore Megingjörð ("power belt") around his waist. This belt was said to have the ability to double his godly strength. To wield his hammer, the god of thunder had a pair of iron gloves named Járngreipr. To travel from one realm to another, Thor rode in his chariot, which was pulled by two magical goats named Tanngrisnir (Snarl Tooth) and Tanngnjóstr (Tooth Gnasher). Some even believed that once the mighty Thor burst out of his hall riding this very chariot, thunder could be heard across the heavens. When the wheels of the chariot moved, lighting sparks would be produced.

However, pulling the chariot was not the goats' only task, as they also kept the thunder god nourished. Whenever there was nothing to eat during his travels, Thor would slaughter the goats and roast them over a fire before devouring them. Given that their bones were still intact, the goats would come back to life the very next day completely unharmed—except for that one time. There was a day when Thor and Loki were on their way to the land of the giants. The two gods decided to rest from their journey and made a stop at a farm located in the realm of humankind, Midgard. They were quickly greeted and invited to stay the night by a poor peasant and his family. However, the poor farmer informed the gods that lodgings were the only thing he could offer. Due to his family's poor condition, the peasant was unable to provide food on the table for his guests. Feeling sorry for the family and as a token of gratitude for letting him and Loki stay the night, Thor decided to cook his two magical goats. He then offered the meal to the family, but he sternly warned them not to break a single bone of the goats.

The dinner went pretty well, and the family was more than delighted that the mighty Thor himself had offered them dinner. However, Loki had a little something on his mind; he successfully persuaded Thjalfi, the son of the farmer, to break one of the bones, claiming that the best part of the goat was its sweet bone marrow. Curious about its taste, Thjalfi did what Loki had advised him to do. The next morning, Thor woke up to see his two goats resurrected, but something odd caught his attention; one of them was limping. Enraged, Thor turned to the poor peasant and his family and demanded answers about what had happened to his trusted goats. Loki sealed his lips, but Thjalfi admitted that he was the one who had snapped the goat's bone. As punishment, Thor took both Thjalfi and his sister, Röskva, with him. They became his most loyal servants, and they would often accompany him on his journeys to the dangerous land of the giants.

Even though Thor was the son of the All-Father himself, he did not really share his wisdom and diplomatic ways of solving a problem. The lightning god preferred action rather than hours of talks and discussions, which explains why he is often described as short-tempered. Odin, for one, was well aware of his son's short fuse, and he once took an opportunity to play a prank on the mighty god.

Hárbarðsljóð, a poem in the *Poetic Edda*, tells a story about Thor's encounter with a grey-bearded man, who historians and scholars believe to be Odin in disguise. After an adventure in Jötunheimr, Thor was on his way back to Asgard when he crossed paths with an old ferryman named Hárbarð (Harbard), who was standing by his boat across the fjord.

"Ferry me across, and I shall feed you from the basket on my back," said Thor, who was planning to cross the fjord. The ferryman, however, responded rudely and started to throw insults at the god's face. Before Thor could even express his anger, Hárbarð insulted his clothing, saying that he was nothing but a vagrant who dressed almost like a beggar without breeches.

When asked about the owner of the boat, the grey-bearded man claimed that it belonged to someone named Hildolf the Wise and that he had specifically commanded him not to ferry vagabonds and thieves. Thor, full of pride, told the old ferryman that he was neither a criminal nor a poor peasant but instead was the son of Odin and the father of Magni. Irritated that Hárbarð still refused to bring his boat over, Thor threatened him, saying that his stubbornness would only bring him misfortune, to which the grey-bearded man paid no mind.

The banter between the two continued. Hárbarð claimed that Thor's mother was long dead, which was followed up with a series of boasts about his magical abilities and sexual prowess. The old ferryman then asked about Thor's achievements, and Thor told him the stories about his battles with the giants. The mocking, however, did not stop there, as Hárbarð continued to accuse the god's wife, Sif, of adultery.

"Your mockery will bring you nowhere!" Thor exclaimed. "No wolf would howl more hideously than you if I could strike you with my mighty hammer." The god knew that there was nothing else he could do to make the old ferryman grant him passage across the fjord. And so, he asked him for another way around the water.

"It is a long way," replied Hárbarð before he explained the routes to go around the fjord.

Thor had no other choice but to take the long way home since Hárbarð refused to ferry him across the water. The god then made his way around but not before he threatened the grey-bearded man once more. "If we ever cross paths again, you will pay for your stubbornness."

Although the mighty Thor would prefer to strike first rather than stop and think of a more peaceful strategy, sometimes that was what the gods and the humans in Midgard needed in order to remain protected from the threats posed by the giants. Without Thor's brute force and powerful strength, the realms might have been crushed sooner than what was prophesied by the Völva.

Chapter 5: Týr and Loki

Some believed that Týr was the mightiest of the Æsir pantheon and that his strength was on par with the god of thunder himself. However, there is little information about this one-armed god since most of his stories have been lost to time. Týr is only mentioned several times in the old poems that have survived to this day. His name is featured in *Gylfaginning*, *Hymiskviða*, and briefly in *Lokasenna*.

Since he was a part of the Æsir tribe, Týr was associated with war and bloodshed. To some, he was also known to be the bringer of justice and order. Since the t-rune is named after Týr, heroes and warriors would carve said rune on the hilt of their swords. By doing this, they believed that their chance of achieving victory was higher than their opponents. Like Odin, Týr could also decide the outcome of any battle in the world. The second day of the week, Tuesday, also originated from his name, which means "Týr's day."

His bravery and courage on the battlefield, however, were not the only attributes he possessed, as Týr was also said to be one of the wisest gods to ever exist in the Norse world. As one of the oldest gods in Norse mythology, some even claimed that Týr was actually the initial ruler of the Æsir until Odin stepped in and gradually became worshiped by many.

However, due to the lack of detailed information about the god, no one is entirely certain of this claim. Even his bloodline has been disputed by many. Based on Snorri's writings in *Skáldskaparmál*, some scholars agree that Týr was, in fact, another son of Odin, while there are others who believe otherwise. The poem *Hymiskviða* tells another version of

Týr's family. The story began when the gods of Asgard were busy feasting in their halls all day and night. They had unlimited sources of food, but eventually, they ran out of ale to wash their food down.

And so, the gods, including Týr and Thor, traveled from the fortified city of Asgard to meet Ægir, the giant sea god who dwelled in his golden hall underneath the rolling waves. Upon their arrival, Thor burst into Ægir's hall, and while looking the sea god directly in the eyes, he immediately commanded him to brew ale for the Æsir. "I need plenty of ale for the gods, and you must prepare it at once!" Thor exclaimed.

Ægir was, of course, irritated by the god's abrupt command, and Thor's tone made it even worse. He delayed his response and began thinking of a way to outwit the gods. "I own no such cauldron that could hold enough ale for all the gods," Ægir replied. "Bring me one, Thor, and I shall brew plenty of ale fit for all the gods."

The gods, however, were puzzled as none of them owned a cauldron large enough, and they had no idea where to find one right there and then until Týr stepped in and informed Thor that he knew exactly where to get one. "My father, Hymir the Giant, owned a cauldron that is five miles deep," he claimed.

Without wasting more time, the two gods, Týr and Thor, set out for another journey to Hymir's hall, which was perched on top of a mountain across the Élivágar. Knowing how dangerous his father could be, Týr advised Thor to hide his real identity and introduce himself as Veur. When they arrived, the two godly figures first came across Týr's grandmother. Little is known about her except that she was a hideous monster with nine hundred heads and that Týr was not at all fond of her. The next being that they crossed paths with was a rather beautiful woman—presumably a giantess—with pale white skin and a golden necklace adorning her neck. This was Týr's mother, and she welcomed the two gods with open arms.

While handing the gods two goblets of ale, she warned them to be cautious of Hymir, her husband and Týr's savage father. "After all, giant blood runs in our veins," she said. Týr's mother also suggested that both her son and Thor hide in one of the cauldrons since she claimed that her husband had an unpleasant way of welcoming his guests. The short-tempered Thor, of course, was not a fan of this suggestion, but Týr persuaded him to give in and avoid unwanted conflicts.

Moments later, Hymir finally returned to his hall, tired from hunting. His wife quickly greeted him, saying that their son was finally home after all those long years of journeys and adventures. Hymir, as expected, turned to look at the cauldrons in the hall and began smashing them with his bare hands. Most of the cauldrons cracked and fell off the shelf onto the floor, except for the one in which Týr and Thor were hiding. The two gods then crawled out of the cauldron, their stares meeting the savage giant. When Hymir saw his son standing beside a mighty companion, he reluctantly welcomed them since he knew starting a fight would only lead to disaster. And so, the giant ordered his servant to cook three oxen for his guests to feast on. Thor easily devoured two of them, which astonished Hymir.

"If this is how you feast, we'll have to go hunting for more food," the giant said.

"Let's take the boat then and see what we can find," Thor responded.

From this point on, the poem no longer mentions Týr—whether it was intentional or if some part of the stanza is missing remains unsure. Nevertheless, the story continues with Thor going out fishing with Týr's father. During their fishing trip, Thor accidentally fished out the World Serpent and his fated enemy, Jörmungandr. The red-bearded god refused to loosen his grip, but in the end, Jörmungandr managed to free itself from the fishing barb and return back to its shelter deep down beneath the dark sea.

The god and the giant then returned to the shore with two whales that they had successfully fished out of the water. Thor dragged the massive boat, along with the two whales, to the land with only his bare hands until he saw Týr and his mother waiting for their return. Even after looking at the strength that the thunder god possessed, Hymir refused to admit that he was second best. And so, he challenged Thor to a test of might. The god had to break a glass goblet that was said to be extremely sturdy and strong—the goblet was even thrown into a stone pillar, but not a crack could be seen. The same could not be said of the stone pillar, as it broke into hundreds of smaller pieces.

"Throw it to his head," Týr's mother whispered to Thor. "Nothing is harder than his head." Listening to her, Thor immediately threw the glass goblet straight at the giant's head. It broke into pieces, but Hymir's skull was unscathed. Hymir finally came to terms that Thor was indeed stronger than him, and he offered the two gods his five-mile-deep cauldron. Týr rose and tried to lift the cauldron but to no avail. The second time he tried, the cauldron only moved an inch. Thor then stepped in, and he managed to hoist the cauldron on his shoulder. It was so big that its handle touched his ankle when he walked.

With the cauldron in their possession and their mission accomplished, Týr and Thor set out on a journey back to Asgard. Right before they left, Thor noticed that Hymir and several dozens of multiple-headed giants were positioned to ambush them. The two gods had no other choice but to stand their ground. Thor smashed his hammer, and when the battle cooled down, not one giant could be seen breathing, including Hymir.

Upon returning to Asgard, the other gods gathered at the Well of Urd (Urðr). Each one of the gods was amazed by the size of the cauldron, and they thanked both Týr and Thor. With the massive cauldron, Ægir's plan to outwit the gods failed.

Like many other members of the Æsir, Týr was considered a warrior god. Despite losing his right hand to the wolf Fenrir, the god was still able to emerge victorious in many wars and battles—except when Ragnarök came. During the Twilight of the Gods, the one-armed god met his deadly fate when he faced Garmr, the blood-stained hound of Helheim who bit his other hand until he bled to death. Garmr, however, also succumbed to its wounds that had been inflicted by Týr right before he perished.

While Týr was associated with justice, law, and honor, the same could not be said about Loki. Like the All-Father himself, Loki was a shapeshifter. He could turn into any sort of being, be it a giant, giantess, human, dwarf, mare, fish, or even a flea. However, he was not only known for his shapeshifting ability, as the god is more famously known for his cunning tricks and wit.

Loki was the god of mischief, tricks, and chaos, which explains why he was never worshiped by the Vikings back in those days. Some people likely regarded him as an evil entity whose ultimate goal was to bring down the gods and the entire world, while other sources suggest that Loki was neither good nor evil. The god simply loved to pull pranks on his fellow gods, although some of them did go too far and caused great havoc. But his antics were not all trouble since some of them saved the gods from bigger issues. Without his cunning tricks, the walls of Asgard would have remained in ashes after the war of the gods, and without his wit, it would have been harder for Thor to retrieve his hammer back from the giants. It was also because of his pranks that the gods ended up with various priceless treasures forged by the dwarves.

When it came to lineage, it was not at all unusual for a god to be born from a giantess—even Thor's mother, Jörd, was a giantess, as was Bestla, the mother of Odin. However, in Loki's case, it was the opposite. The trickster was born from Laufey, possibly a goddess from Asgard, while his father was a jötunn named Fárbauti. Because of this, the gods would sometimes refer to the trickster as Laufeyson, which simply means "son of Laufey."

Like the other Æsir, Loki also had a wife. He was married to the goddess Sigyn, who was loyal to him until the end. Together, they bore two sons named Narfi—sometimes also known as Nari—and Váli. Not much was mentioned about his family except that the god of chaos also had another relationship with a giantess. She was known by the name Angrboda (Angrboða), which translates as "the one who brings grief." With the giantess, Loki fathered three other children, but they were not godly like Narfi and Váli. These monstrous offspring are the Midgard serpent named Jörmungandr, Fenrir the wolf, and Hel, the ruler of Helheim. These three children of chaos were Odin's worst fears, as they were the ones prophesied to play vital roles in killing the gods when Ragnarök arrived.

Although Loki's relation with the Æsir before the events of Ragnarök was rather ambiguous—he neither sided with nor against them—the trickster was said to have a close relationship with the All-Father. In *Lokasenna*, an old poem in the *Poetic Edda*, Loki claimed that Odin was his blood-brother, which the latter never denied. This, however, was not at all surprising given that they had been through various adventures together, one that even led to the kidnapping of a goddess.

It is said that it all began when Loki, Odin, and Hœnir were traveling to the realm of humankind, Midgard. The three gods arrived at a certain region of Middle Earth where food sources were scarce. The trio finally grew hungry after their long journey, and they started wandering around the empty land, searching and keeping an eye out for any animals that they could hunt. Not long after that, they encountered a herd of oxen grazing at the grasses growing in the valley. Without wasting any more time, the gods split their tasks. Loki was to hunt and slaughter one of the oxen, while Odin and Hœnir would prepare the campsite and start a fire.

It did not take too long for the trickster to return with the slaughtered ox, and they began roasting its meat over the fire. As much as the hungry gods were delighted knowing that their dinner was being prepared, their expressions soon changed when they noticed the extremely long time for the meat to be cooked. Another hour came and went, but blood was still dripping from the meat. The ox was still as raw as when they first placed it over the fire. Puzzled, the trio turned to look around in case there was anyone nearby playing tricks on them—and they were absolutely right.

"It is I," said an unfamiliar voice. "It is my magic that is keeping your catch from cooking." The voice came from a giant eagle perched on top of a tree. "Allow me to get my share of the meat, and only then will I disperse my magic."

Seeing that there was no other way, the gods agreed. The mysterious eagle flapped his massive wings and flew down to the campsite before devouring a huge portion of the raw ox. The three gods watched as the eagle gobbled up their catch, and Loki grew angry since the enormous being had eaten way more than what they had agreed to. And so, the god of mischief began to act rashly; he quickly grabbed his staff—or a piece of a sturdy branch—and plunged it into the enormous eagle's flesh.

The staff, however, got stuck in the eagle's talon, and when he flew away, so did Loki, who was still clinging onto the other end of his staff. The god of mischief was terrified when the eagle flew higher and higher into the air. He begged for the enormous being to show mercy and let him down safely. The eagle, who was then revealed to be a jötunn named Thjazi, knew that this was an opportunity for him to strike a deal with the god. He agreed to bring Loki to safety on one condition; the giant asked for Idun (Iðunn), the Æsir goddess of youth and rejuvenation. Loki could not think of a trick to overthrow the giant, especially when he was hanging high up in the skies, so he gave his word.

After a while, the three gods returned to Asgard. Loki had no intention of breaking his deal with the jötunn. And so, instead of informing the Æsir about the incident, Loki went to see the goddess of youth with a plan forming in his mind.

Idun, who is only mentioned a few times in the old poems, was one of the most important deities in Norse mythology. Not only was she a goddess of youth, but she was also the guardian of the sacred apples. Since the gods were not immortal, they had to consume Idun's magical apples from time to time just so they could stay young until the end of time.

Loki was well aware that Thjazi not only wanted the goddess to himself but that he also wanted the goddess's magical apple. So, upon meeting Idun, the trickster lured the goddess out of the safe walls of Asgard, where the giant, in the form of an eagle, would be ready to take her.

"I might have found some fruits that you might be interested in," the trickster told her. "It's growing right outside of Asgard. Take the apples with you so you can compare them, and come with me." Idun suspected nothing, so she followed him right into a trap.

Thjazi, in disguise as an eagle, was circling the sky when he finally spotted the two gods outside of the fortified walls of Asgard. Without hesitation, he flew down and snatched the goddess from the ground. Idun was then brought to Thrymheim, Thjazi's dwelling in Jötunheimr.

However, it did not take all that long before the Æsir noticed Idun's absence since, without her magical apples, the gods began to age, and their strength deteriorated. All of the Æsir, including the fairest and strongest, began to grow grey hairs on their heads and beards, and wrinkles started to show on their divine faces. They looked everywhere for the goddess of youth, but they failed to find any trace of her.

So, one day, the gods gathered around to discuss the goddess's disappearance. One of them recalled that Idun was last seen in the company of Loki. Realizing that the trickster might have been behind the kidnapping, they summoned him to the hall. As soon as the god of mischief arrived, the other gods began threatening him with all sorts of punishments—including death—should he fail to return the goddess and her apples to Asgard. Again, scared for his life, Loki convinced the gods that he would do everything he could to fix his own wrongdoings.

When the gods let him go, the trickster barged into Freyja's hall and asked to borrow her magical coat of feathers. With the coat, Loki was able to transform into a falcon, and he flew straight to the land of the giants. Upon arriving in Thrymheim, Thjazi's dark and cold dwelling on top of a snowy mountain, Loki discovered that the giant had left his home. It was said that he had gone out to the sea to fish, leaving Idun alone and unguarded in his hall. Without delaying a single second, Loki transformed the goddess into a nut, and he carried her in his talons as he flew in the direction of Asgard as fast as he could.

Not long after the two gods had made their escape, Thjazi returned to his hall. Furious that his prize was no longer in his possession, he turned into a massive eagle and chased after the trickster. The gods in Asgard could see Loki nearing their walls with Thjazi closing in behind him. Quickly, they built a huge fire around the walls. When Thjazi passed by, his feathers burned, causing him to fall to his death. With the giant dead and the goddess of youth returned, Loki was spared.

However, this tale does not end here, as Thjazi's daughter, Skadi, stormed into Asgard with weapons in her hands, ready to avenge her father's death. The Æsir did not wish to spill more blood on that day, especially since they were celebrating Idun's return in their hall. And so, they bargained with the giantess, saying that they were willing to compensate for Thjazi's unfortunate death.

There were three compensations offered to the angry giantess. The first one was a ceremony in which Odin took Thjazi's eyes and cast them into the skies, where they later became two shiny stars. Skadi then demanded the gods make her laugh, to which the gods turned to Loki after most of their tricks had failed. The trickster then came up with an idea where he played tug of war with a goat. Instead of using his own pair of hands to pull the rope, he tied it around his testicles. When the goat pulled the rope too hard, Loki screeched and fell into Skadi's lap, and the giantess let out a laugh. The third compensation was someone's hand in marriage; Skadi was to choose one of the gods, but she would choose one just by looking at their legs. The giantess pointed to the fairest pair of legs that caught her attention, thinking that it belonged to Baldur. However, it was actually Njord, the Æsir god of the sea. Their marriage sadly did not last long, but peace between the giantess and the Æsir was, indeed, established, and not a single drop of blood was spilled.

Although Loki was the one who caused the kidnapping, he came through in the end. The trickster returned the goddess back to her hall, and in return, his life was spared. However, the same could not be said when he took his prank a little too far and caused the death of the most beloved god in Asgard, Baldur. He was punished greatly, but during Ragnarök, the god of chaos would break free from his bonds and engage in a deadly battle with Heimdall.

Chapter 6: Heimdall and Hermod

The All-Father was not the only one who had traveled across the realms in search of knowledge and gifts. Heimdall, for one, was also said to set foot at Mimir's well of knowledge and perform a sacrifice. While Odin sacrificed his eye in exchange for ultimate wisdom, Heimdall threw one of his ears into the well just so he could be blessed with exceptional hearing abilities.

Ever since the sacrifice, the god could hear everything surrounding him—no matter how low or loud the sound was. It was even believed that Heimdall could hear the grasses growing out of the earth and the wool of a sheep growing on its body. But that was not all of his powerful abilities, as the god also had keen eyesight. Heimdall could see objects from a hundred miles away, be it during the day or at night. He also required little to no sleep and could stay alert at all times with ease.

These are some of the things that made the gods of Asgard agree to appoint him as their city watchman. With his remarkable eyesight and exceptional hearing, Heimdall was given a hall in Himinbjörg, a realm right under the skies and on the very top of the rainbow bridge, Bifröst. Every day, Heimdall would mount his only horse, Gulltoppr, and ride from his hall to Bifröst, where he would stand guard without rest. In his hand was Gjallarhorn, the horn that he would sound to mark the start of Ragnarök. When the Twilight of the Gods finally happened, Heimdall was prophesied to battle Loki, where they would successfully slay each other.

There are few writings left that describe Heimdall's bloodline, but Snorri claimed that his father was none other than Odin. Heimdall also had nine mothers, which could symbolize the nine realms. Although the names of his mothers were all mentioned in the *Poetic Edda*, some scholars have also linked them to the Nine Daughters of Ægir, especially since it was said he was born at the edge of the world. This claim, however, has been disputed by many since their names do not match Ægir's daughters.

Even though Odin, Hœnir, and Lodurr (Loðurr) were the ones who created the first two humans in the world, it was Heimdall who was responsible for the social classes in Midgard. In the Norse world, the social classes were divided into four: the slaves, karls, jarls, and royals. The lowest class, the slaves, was born when Heimdall traveled to Midgard under the name Rig. After a long journey, Rig came across a dilapidated hut belonging to an old couple named Ái ("great-grandfather") and Edda ("great-grandmother"). The two humans were poor; they could only afford to wear rugged clothes and live in a small cottage. But upon seeing Rig, the two welcomed him with open arms and invited the traveler to stay the night. "We have only a little, but we can offer you a bowl of soup and some bread," said the poor couple.

Rig did not mind at all, and he was more than happy with their hospitality. In fact, he enjoyed their company so much that he stayed at their place for three days. Every night, the traveler would sleep in between the two humans on their bed. When the three days were up, Rig left the couple, and they resumed their lives. Nine months after the traveler had left, Edda gave birth to a son. His name was Thrall, which simply means "slave." The boy had a crooked back, and when he grew up, he ended up doing labor that typically belonged to a slave. Soon, Thrall married Thír, a scruffy woman with a hooked nose, several scars on her skin, and sunburned arms. Together, they bore many children, and they all grew up to be slaves. Hence, the first and lowest social class of the Norse world was born.

"Rig in Great-grandfather's Cottage" by W. G. Collingwood, 1908
https://commons.wikimedia.org/w/index.php?curid=4736123

Next, Rig (Heimdall) traveled the world again, and he stopped by another house. This house belonged to another couple, and they went by the names of Afi ("grandfather") and Amma ("grandmother"). Unlike the previous house that he had visited, Afi and Amma's house was slightly better and bigger. The couple was also dressed in proper sets of clothes. Just as before, Rig was offered food, only with better quality than the last, as well as lodgings for three nights. When his time was up, the traveler again bade farewell and left the couple. Nine months later, Amma gave birth to Karl, a red-headed boy with better features than Thrall. Instead of doing typical slave jobs when he grew up, Karl used his skills to plant wheat on the fertilized land and raise farm animals.

Soon, Karl met the love of his life. Her name was Snør, and together, they bore many children who all grew up to become peasants and farmers like their parents. And so, the second social class was created.

Continuing his journey across the land, Rig came across yet another house. This time around, the difference was obvious since the house was much bigger and comfier than the two previous ones combined. Inside, Rig was welcomed warmly by another couple named Modir ("mother"), a fair-skinned woman who wore a pretty long dress with a couple of shiny pieces of jewelry, and Fadir ("father"), a man with a neat appearance. At their dining table, Rig was served a bountiful dinner. There was perfectly sliced white bread, a plate full of cooked meats and poultry, and a generous amount of wine.

Just as before, Rig stayed with the couple for three consecutive days, sleeping with them in their bed. Nine months later, another child was born from Modir, and his name was Jarl. The boy had a beautiful pair of eyes and blonde hair. As he began to grow, his father showed him how to ride horses. He taught him all the right ways to hunt and the best ways to wield a sword, hurl a spear, and shoot arrows. When Jarl reached a certain age, Rig returned to his big house, where he taught him how to read runes and encouraged him to conquer lands. Jarl was also given Rig's name and made his heir.

With this useful knowledge taught by his own father and Rig, Jarl set out on his own journey on which he would meet Erna. After marrying her, they bore many children together. With Jarl and his children, the third social class was created.

"The Crow warns Konr" by W. G. Collingwood, 1908.
https://commons.wikimedia.org/w/index.php?curid=4736159

Following his father's footsteps, Jarl taught his many sons everything he knew, from riding horses to hunting, wielding weapons, and reading runes. However, his youngest son, Konr, proved to be more special than the others since he possessed the ability to cast spells from the runes and could understand the speech of birds. With practice, he mastered the art of runes and became even better than Rig himself. And so, the long line of heroes, kings, and queens in Midgard began with Konr.

With all four social classes created, Heimdall earned another name for himself; he was known by many as the father of mankind.

Other than Heimdall, another god of Asgard whose name is only mentioned a few times in the old poems is Hermod (Hermóðr). While the "Watchman of the Gods" was fated to die during the Twilight of the Gods, Hermod was believed to survive at the end of the deadly event. Along with a few other gods and goddesses, he would help build a new world.

As a member of the Æsir, Hermod was considered a warrior god; even his name roughly translates as the "Spirit of War" or the "Fury of War." Although there are several sources that describe Hermod as a human hero rather than a god, the more famous claim was that he was, indeed, the son of Odin and his wife Frigg, which made Baldur and Hodr his brothers. Since Hermod was raised as a warrior god, it is thought that Hermod was a brave god who loved a good fight. He could often be seen wearing a helmet and his treasured coat of mail, which had been gifted to him by his father. In his hands, the god carried a wand or a staff named Gambantein. When he was not out fighting, the god was believed to be in Valhalla, welcoming the einherjar, the fallen warriors chosen by the All-Father.

Although Hermod was considered a minor god in Norse mythology, he did play an important role after the death of his brother Baldur. Almost like Hermes from Greek mythology, Hermod was also known as the "Messenger of the Gods." The Æsir, especially the All-Father, would give him errands that required him to travel across the realms. The god was described to be the swiftest god in the pantheon and the only one allowed to mount Odin's loyal steed, Sleipnir.

His agility was attested in full detail in Snorri's *Prose Edda*. After the death of the shining god Baldur, Asgard and the entire universe were clouded with ultimate despair and sorrow. The gods and goddesses were not able to rest, not only because they had lost their beloved god but also because his death meant that Ragnarök would soon approach. After Baldur's funeral, the queen of the gods, Frigg, bent her will to bring her son back to life. She was almost certain that someone could persuade Hel, the ruler of the land of the dead, to release her son since his death had caused such great devastation and sadness. And so, Frigg asked the gods and goddesses that had gathered before her, "Which one of you is brave enough to journey to the dark land of the dead and speak to its ruler? Be my messenger, convince Hel to release my son from her grasp, and I shall forever be in your debt."

While most of the gods remained quiet to Frigg's desperate request, Hermod stepped forward. "I shall ride to Hel and release my brother from the dark realm," the swift god said in determination. Without hesitation, Hermod prepared himself for the challenging journey. Riding on Odin's greatest horse, Sleipnir, the god galloped through the skies and out of the fortified city of Asgard. For nine nights, Hermod rode across the realms and through deep valleys and passageways. It was said that his journey was so dark that he could barely see anything. The god only pulled the reins and came to a halt when he heard the loud sounds of Gjöll, the river that separated the land of the living and the dead.

To reach Helheim, Hermod had to cross Gjallarbrú, a bridge glittering in gold that spanned across the river. However, it was not an easy journey since it was guarded by Hel's trusted maiden named Móðguðr (Modgud). The giant maiden had but one task: she was to ask those who sought passage across the bridge their names and business. Once the information was given to her, Móðguðr would grant them access on one small condition—they must be dead.

"Why would someone with warm flesh and soul wish to cross this bridge? The only place that lies north of here is Helheim," the maiden said.

"I must cross and travel to the realm, for I carry an urgent message that must be delivered to your mistress," Hermod responded sternly.

Upon crossing the bridge, Hermod arrived in front of a massive iron gate that guarded the realm of the dead. It was locked, and the only way for the god to get through was to jump over. Fortunately, he was riding the greatest horse in the universe. Holding the reins tight in his hands, he spurred Sleipnir toward the towering gate. The eight-legged horse then leaped high over the gate and landed safely on the grounds of Helheim. In the realm, Hermod made his way straight to Hel's vast hall, where he finally saw Baldur and his wife sitting at a table, enjoying their feast.

"Why have you come to this land of bleak nothingness, my dear brother?" Baldur asked the swift god.

"I've come to bargain with the mistress of the dead so that I can bring you back to the land of the living."

Baldur gave him a warm smile and responded, "Return to your home, brother, as your request is, indeed, impossible. It is not yet my time to return."

Of course, the swift god refused to return to Asgard empty-handed. "Forgive me, brother, but I must succeed." And so, he stayed in the hall with his brother for three days before finally meeting Hel.

During Hermod's audience with Hel, the giantess that ruled the dead, he convinced her that Baldur's death brought nothing but heavy grief to so many beings in the world. He pleaded with the giantess to release

Baldur and his wife from the cold realm, to which she agreed if the livings could fulfill her one condition.

"If what you say is true, then show me. I want to see all things in the universe mourn and weep for the shining god's death. Only then will I release them back to the land of the living," Hel responded to the god's request. "Now, return to where you came from, as you don't belong in my realm, and deliver this message to the gods."

With that, Hermod mounted Sleipnir and rushed back to Asgard. He carried Hel's words and delivered them to the Æsir. Frigg, knowing that there was a chance for her son to be resurrected, quickly sent emissaries across the world to ensure everyone from each corner of the universe wept for her son. However, Hermod's journey to the underworld to secure his brother was not a successful one. In the end, Baldur was forced to remain in Helheim since not everyone mourned his death.

Chapter 7: Baldur and Vidar

It was almost impossible to hate the god named Baldur, which is sometimes spelled as Baldr or Balder. One could spend an eternity searching for his flaws, but it was never guaranteed that they would find one unless they believed that being too kind and forgiving were flaws. Baldur was greatly loved by many, be it those sitting high on their thrones in Asgard or those working on their farms in Midgard. Some even claimed that even the giants found it hard to despise him—all except for Thökk, the giantess, presumably Loki in disguise, who refused to weep for his death. Despite not dying honorably in battle, Baldur still received special treatment after his death. The only downside to that was that the god was stuck in Helheim instead of Valhalla.

Baldur by Johannes Gehrts, 1901.
https://commons.wikimedia.org/w/index.php?curid=4643348

The radiant god was the son of the All-Father and his wife, Frigg. He had a brother named Hodr, but this brother was far from perfect. Baldur's brother was blind, and he would later fall victim to one of Loki's treacherous pranks. Baldur was married to Nanna, another goddess of Asgard that we know only little about—some claimed she was the goddess of joy, which perfectly matched her husband's attributes. Together, they bore a son named Forseti, who was said to be the god of justice and reconciliation. While their son resided in Glitnir, a hall with a silver roof and golden pillars, Baldur and his wife dwelled in Breidablik (Breiðablik). His realm was, in fact, the fairest and most pristine among the gods.

The god's most famous attribute was his absolute fairness. Although most gods and goddesses in Asgard were said to have their own divine looks, Baldur's appearance topped all of them. He was described as the most good-looking god in the pantheon. There was not a day when he was not cheerful to the point that he had light shining out of him—because of that, he was known as the shining god. However, his fairness was not only shown in his appearance but also in his behavior and judgment. Baldur was extremely gracious and so well-spoken that he could easily resolve any kind of dispute. Even the most temperamental god, Thor, could calm down if Baldur were to speak to him. His judgment was always clear and fair that none of the Æsir would question him twice. Baldur was, indeed, respected by all.

Although Baldur was rarely depicted as a warrior god who went on long adventures across the realms like Odin and Thor—especially in the *Prose Edda*, where he was often described as more of a passive and innocent god—some claim that he was actually an exceptional fighter. The god even had his own ship called *Hringhorni* that could sail across the ocean faster than the wind itself. The Danish historian Saxo Grammaticus, for one, depicted Baldur as a strong warrior who was skillful in handling weapons. However, the most prominent tale that featured the god was, of course, the one about his death. While the tale is indeed moving, his death also set the course for Ragnarök to begin.

The Norns had spun their threads, and Baldur must die, no matter what his protective parents might do. When the god started to be plagued by an ominous nightmare, he knew terror awaited him. Odin immediately rode to the underworld to seek help from a dead seeress, but not even the All-Father could alter his beloved son's fate. Frigg, although knowing all about the prophecy, would do anything just so she could delay her son's death. But the goddess, too, would fail since Loki had already planned his schemes. It was already decided by the women of fate that Baldur would die at the hands of his innocent blind brother and that not a single force could bring him back to life—at least not until the events of Ragnarök had passed.

Vidar on horseback by Lorenz Frølich, 1895.
https://commons.wikimedia.org/w/index.php?curid=4668350

Unlike Baldur, who was favored by the gods for his cheerful attributes and fair judgments, his half-brother, Vidar, was associated with something darker. Vidar was the god of vengeance. But just like many other gods and goddesses in Asgard, not much information about him has survived the years, except that he was the product of the relationship between Odin and a giantess named Grid (Gríðr). Vidar dwelled within the fortified city of the gods, but there was no mention of the name of his own specific realm like the other members of the Æsir. The only thing we know is that his land was once filled with tall grasses and trees.

Similar to how Odin treasured his spear and Thor with his hammer, Vidar also had his own prized possession. The god had a sturdy yet magical shoe that was specially crafted for the last battle. Every day, Vidar would collect leather scraps that were left by shoemakers and attach them to his shoe. Eventually, his shoe became so thick and sturdy that it was impossible for even the sharpest blade to cut through. This was the very same shoe that he would wear to avenge his father.

Vidar was also known as the silent god. The reason behind this, however, remains unknown. Some suggest that it was because the god never bragged about his victory over Fenrir, while others claim that it was because Vidar was only featured in one tale. It is safe to say that we know nothing about his personality other than his powerful strength; Vidar was believed to be one of the strongest gods in Asgard, second only to Thor. Even though the god was only mentioned a few times in the old poems—his name was briefly featured in three poems of the *Poetic Edda* and two poems of the *Prose Edda*—Vidar undoubtedly played a huge role during the Twilight of the Gods.

Vidar stabbing Fenrir by W. G. Collingwood, 1908.
https://commons.wikimedia.org/w/index.php?curid=4657687

Ever since the beginning of time, it was prophesied that almost all of the gods would perish due to the forces of chaos, including the All-Father himself. While Thor managed to slay Jörmungandr before he died, Heimdall successfully killed Loki before he succumbed to his own wounds, and Týr and Garmr slew each other. Odin was not able to eliminate his fated foe of Fenrir. The one-eyed god was swallowed whole by the giant wolf, but his death was immediately avenged by his own son, Vidar.

The brave god, wearing his leather shoe, leaped onto Fenrir's lower jaw and held the monstrous creature's mouth open with his bare hands. According to the poem *Gylfaginning*, Vidar was said to kill the wolf by ripping his jaw apart, although there are other sources that claim he slew

Fenrir by stabbing the wolf in his beating heart.

Nevertheless, the silent god successfully put an end to the monstrous creature's life and avenged his father's death, just as the seeress had foreseen. When new land emerged from the water after the horrendous events of Ragnarök, Vidar, along with a few other surviving gods, would rebuild the world.

Chapter 8: Freyja and Frigg

The goddess Freyja was favored not only by the Æsir but also by the giants from the untamed lands of Jötunheimr. She was said to be the fairest and most beautiful goddess in Asgard, which explains why several giants tried every trick up their sleeves to get their hands on her. Once, a giant in disguise as a master builder offered to help the gods build the walls surrounding Asgard. In return, he asked for the goddess. Another giant, who went by the name Thrym, once stole Thor's mighty hammer. When the gods demanded he return the weapon back to its owner, the boastful giant asked for Freyja's hand in marriage.

However, her wondrous beauty was not the only attribute she possessed. Freyja was, in fact, associated with fertility, love, sexuality, and magic. The goddess was also considered one of the most important deities among the Æsir; thanks to her, the Æsir gained the powerful art of seidr, shamanic magic that could be used to foresee and shape the future. Freyja was initially a part of the Vanir tribe, and it was only after the war of the gods ended that she became an honorable member of the Æsir. The goddess was the only daughter of Njord, the Vanir god of the sea and an unknown mother. Freyja also had a twin brother named Freyr.

She was said to be married to an obscure figure named Odr (Óðr)—some claim that this was, in fact, Odin—and together, they had two beautiful daughters named Hnoss and Gersemi. Not much is known about her husband and two children, except that Odr once set out on a journey, leaving Freyja behind for a long time. The goddess soon grew worried about her husband, and she went to search for him but to no avail. Knowing that she could no longer see her beloved husband, the goddess wept, and as her tears fell to the ground, they turned into gold.

While her twin brother ruled and dwelled in the realm of Alfheim, Freyja lived in Asgard. She had her own intricate hall called Sessrúmnir, which stood in the middle of Fólkvangr, the same field where her handpicked fallen warriors resided. Since her status in Asgard was almost on par with the All-Father, the goddess was given the honor to choose which of the bravest warriors would enter her hall first. Once she had chosen her portion of warriors and heroes, only then would Odin take the other half to his hall, Valhalla.

An illustration of Freyja riding her boar by Lorenz Frølich, 1895.
https://commons.wikimedia.org/w/index.php?curid=5404472

Just like the other gods in Asgard, Freyja had her own ways of traveling across the realms. She would either ride her chariot, which was pulled by two black cats, or use her magical coat of feathers and turn into a falcon, which allowed her to easily fly between realms. At times, the goddess could also be seen riding a boar named Hildisvíni—the very same boar that Loki once accused of being her human lover, Óttar, in disguise.

But that was not the only accusation Loki made against Freyja. The trickster once claimed the goddess to be an immoral woman for sleeping with more than a dozen other men, be it a god, human, elf, or dwarf, even though she was, in fact, the goddess of lust and sexuality. However, although Loki did have a sharp tongue, he was not one to accuse the gods and goddesses without reason. The accusation began in the story of how Freyja gained her treasured necklace, Brísingamen.

On one fine morning, the goddess left her hall and was seen by none other than the god of mischief himself. Loki followed her as she suspiciously walked across Bifröst, through Midgard, and into the dark realm of Svartalfheim. Finally, she stopped at an unfamiliar cavern. Carefully, the goddess entered the dark cave and made her way through the narrow passage, with Loki still following quietly behind her. As they reached the end of the cavern, the temperature of the air began to change; it was slightly hotter than usual. Here, Freyja came across a forge belonging to four dwarves named Dvalinn, Alfrik, Berling, and Grer. As much as they were enthralled by the beautiful goddess, the dwarves did not stop working—they continued hammering and tempering a particular treasure.

Freyja in the Dwarf's Cave *by Louis Huard, 1891.*
https://commons.wikimedia.org/w/index.php?curid=4596949

The goddess was said to have a great love for gold, so all it took was a single glance at the shiny necklace for her to fall in love. Completely hypnotized by its sparkle and intricate patterns and twists, Freyja immediately made an offer to the master smiths. "I shall provide you with heaps of gold and silver in exchange for that fine necklace."

The dwarves, however, rejected the offer, as they claimed to already possess so much silver and gold that they had no need for more. "If so, then name your price, and I shall see to it," the goddess said again, refusing to leave the cavern without the intricate necklace.

"Spend a night with each of us, and the necklace is yours to take," one of the dwarves demanded.

Although disgusted by their wicked looks, the goddess agreed and spent a night with each of them. By the end of the fourth night, one of the dwarves approached her with the glimmering necklace and fastened it around her neck. With her heart content, the goddess bid them farewell and quickly returned to her dwelling within the fortified city of the gods. But Loki, who had witnessed the entire event, had gone back to Asgard long before her. After arriving in the city, the trickster headed straight to the hall of Odin, where he requested an immediate audience with the All-Father.

"What seems to be the problem that you must see me in such a haste?" the one-eyed god asked while sitting in his high seat, accompanied by his wolves lying by his feet.

Without hesitation, the trickster told the god of Freyja's newly treasured necklace and to what lengths she went to get it. The All-Father sprang to his feet in anger and hit the floor below him with his spear, Gungnir. "That is outrageous!" Odin roared.

Loki, on the other hand, cracked a sinister smile, but it immediately faded upon hearing the All-Father's command. "Steal it from her, Loki. That punishment alone would make her suffer."

The god of mischief grimaced. "I believe that it would be impossible to sneak inside her hall against her wishes."

Again, Odin hit the floor with his spear. "Get me that necklace, Loki, or never show your face again!"

That night, Loki sneaked into Freyja's hall and quietly made his way to her main chamber. The door, however, was locked tight, and the trickster was unable to pick it. So, the sly god did what he had to do; he transformed into a fly and scouted the area. Just as he expected, Freyja's hall was built so well to the point that there was not even a tiny hole that the shapeshifter could squeeze through. He couldn't enter the keyhole or the gap between the floor and the bolted door. Loki then flew to the roof, which was when he finally saw an opening. The crack was so small that the sly god could barely wriggle himself in.

But when he finally got into the chamber, another problem arose, as Freyja was sleeping on her back with the necklace clasped around her neck. The trickster was not able to remove the shiny necklace without waking the goddess. So, again, he transformed into a fly and stung her cheek. Freyja let out a small groan, but then she rolled to her side. With the clasp exposed, Loki successfully stole Brísingamen. Holding the necklace tightly in his hand, the god unlocked the door and slowly walked out of the hall.

The following morning, Freyja woke up to her neck feeling slightly more exposed than usual. Upon noticing that her door was ajar, she quickly touched her neck to feel the necklace. When she realized that it was gone, the goddess immediately rose to her feet and burst out of the hall. She knew that it was Loki who had stolen her treasured necklace since there was no other thief as nimble as him. She also knew he would not have done it if it was not under the order of the All-Father.

"You did this!" She stormed into Odin's hall. "Return my necklace if you wish to maintain the peace in Asgard!"

The All-Father, who was sitting on his throne with his two crows perched on his shoulders, turned to look at the goddess, his one eye filled with fire. "You, Freyja, have brought shame on yourself and the other gods! You gladly sold your body to the filthy dwarves just so you could satisfy your greed."

The goddess stomped closer to the All-Father. "You're one to talk about shame, Odin. Now, tell me, where is my necklace?"

The two gods could spend all day and night at each other's throats, but Odin came up with a plan. "You can get your prized necklace back under one condition." Freyja, still enraged, listened to the one-eyed god's words. "I want you to cause a catastrophe between two kings in Midgard. Let them battle each other for eternity. Do that, and the necklace is yours again." Freyja gave the chief of the gods a stern look before finally agreeing to his condition.

And so, the Vanir goddess stirred up hatred between the two kings of Midgard, Heidin and Hogni. The two then met in the middle of the battlefield and clanged their swords against each other until both fell, laying in a pool of their blood. However, with Freyja's powerful spell cast on them, the two kings would be resurrected the next day.

While the kings picked up their swords every morning and continued with their never-ending battle, Freyja regained her prized necklace.

Since Freyja was thought to stand almost on the same level as Odin, some sources suggest that the goddess was, in fact, the same person as the All-Father's wife, Frigg. It was said that the goddesses were initially a single entity until, at some point, they evolved into two separate beings. Frigg was widely known among the Germanic people, so it could be plausible that the Norse reimagined her as Freyja before they also adopted Frigg, which explains why Freyja was featured more in the old poems than Frigg.

The claim was also made due to the several similarities between the two goddesses. Like Freyja, Frigg was also a Völva, and she had the ability to perform seidr and foresee the future. The two goddesses also owned a coat of feathers, which could turn them into falcons. They were even associated with the same thing, fertility, although Frigg's association with fertility was more toward the earth, crops, marriage, and family, while Freyja leaned more toward sexuality, lust, and love. There are even theories of their husbands being the same person. Freyja was married to Odr, while Frigg was married to Odin, both of whom were known to embark on long journeys across the realms while leaving their wives behind.

However, this matter remains debated among scholars and historians since there are various sources that suggest Freyja and Frigg are two separate deities. In *Lokasenna*, for instance, Loki was warned by Freyja right after the trickster had slandered Frigg for her infidelity. "Beware of your own tongue, Loki! Frigg knows the fates of all beings," the Vanir goddess said. This showed that they were, indeed, two separate beings since they both were present at the feast.

Frigg was also believed to be the daughter of Fjörgynn, another obscure deity of the past, instead of Njord, the father of Freyja. The queen of Asgard even had her own realm. She called the marshland, Fensalir, her home, and there, Frigg was accompanied by four other goddesses and servants: Lofn, the goddess of forbidden love; Hlin, the goddess of protection; Fulla, her handmaiden who was also the goddess of secrets; and Gná, her messenger.

Being the queen of the Ásynjur, or the goddesses of Asgard, and the only one allowed to sit on Hliðskjálf, it was not unusual for her to outsmart everyone, even the All-Father himself. There was a time when the two decided to engage in a wager. As Odin was overseeing the realm of humankind from his high seat, he came across an upcoming battle between two Germanic tribes called the Vandals and Winnilers. Turning to his wife, Odin declared that he favored the Vandals more and would like to grant them victory in the war, while Frigg thought otherwise.

An illustration of Frigg and Odin sitting on their throne by Lorenz Frølich, 1895.
https://commons.wikimedia.org/w/index.php?curid=5734101

The goddess gave her reasoning to her husband, but the discussion quickly turned into a heated argument. Tired of the argument, Odin came up with a solution. "Let us put the argument to rest and sleep. The very first tribe that appears in my sight tomorrow morning will be the winner of the war," the All-Father said, knowing that only the Vandals would be visible from his side of the window by their bed.

Of course, Frigg knew of her husband's dirty trick, and she was not about to let him win the wager so easily. And so, as Odin was sleeping, she instructed the women of the Winnilers to arrange their long hair across their faces so that they looked like beards. The goddess then carefully turned their bed to the other side so that her husband would first spot the Winnilers through his window.

When Odin woke the next morning, he was confused to see an army of long-bearded men through the window instead of the Vandals. Thus, he was left with no choice but to honor his oath to his wife. The All-Father granted victory to the Winnilers just as Frigg had suggested.

Although Frigg always had her ways to turn the tide in her favor, she would fail to do so when it came to her son, Baldur. The goddess was well aware of the prophecy, and she knew that none could escape their fates—Baldur's death must happen. But as a mother, she went to extreme lengths just so she could at least protect her son a little longer. Even after the shining god's death, she never stopped trying to bring him back to the land of the living, which eventually failed, thanks to one of Loki's schemes.

Chapter 9: Hel and Sif

The realm of the dead was as bleak as a plain of nothingness. Indeed, some said that Helheim was not a place of torment, but it sure was not a palace with golden halls, chambers, and feasts either. However, just like the other realms of the Norse world, Helheim had its own ruler, and she was known by the name Hel.

Hel by Johannes Gehrts, 1889.
https://commons.wikimedia.org/w/index.php?curid=4624357

Hel was the daughter of Loki, the god of chaos, tricks, and mischief, and his giant mistress, Angrboda. Although her father was a god who once lived within the fortified walls of Asgard, Hel was not considered a goddess. Instead, she was identified as a jötunn. But she did not resemble her mother since she was born with half of her body blue and decomposing, almost like a corpse.

Like her two other monstrous siblings, Jörmungandr and Fenrir, with whom she might not have had a close relationship, Hel was abducted from her home in Jötunheimr by the Æsir. While Jörmungandr was thrown into the sea and Fenrir was taken to Asgard—and soon bound when he grew too big—Hel had a slightly better fate. She was cast to the deep depths of Helheim by the All-Father, where she was given full authority to rule over the dead.

In her realm, Hel was said to own a vast number of mansions, which were all surrounded by towering walls and massive gates so that none of the living beings could gain entry. Every time a newcomer arrived at the dark realm—be it the dead or a god—they would be greeted by Hel's ferocious pet named Garmr—the very same hellhound that would face Týr during the Twilight of the Gods.

Even though her realm was described to be another location where one would reside after their death, that does not mean those guilty of crimes would roam freely without paying for their mistakes. The queen of Helheim would cast these people into another hall deep down below called Nastrond, which simply means "Corpse Shore." In this unpleasant hall, those guilty of murder, adultery, and oath-breaking must wade through a stream of poisonous venom and face the dragon-like creature named Níðhöggr (Nidhogg) who would suck every drop of their blood while a wolf tore their body apart.

But not all of the halls found in Helheim were filled with long streams of venom and slithering serpents. Eljudnir, for instance, was a great hall where the queen resided. Within her dwelling was all sorts of furniture that could be found in a normal household, except that they had names and all of them symbolized misfortunes. Hel's dining table was called "Hunger," while her knives were named "Starvation." Her bed was called "Sick Bed," and there was also a long curtain named "Misfortune."

Being the ruler of the dead and a friend to no one, Hel was believed to be harsh, ruthless, and fierce. However, she never portrayed any of these traits when she heard the news of Baldur's death. Instead, the giantess prepared a lush hall for the bright god and his wife, Nanna. She welcomed them into her realm as guests of honor and served them a bountiful feast of fresh warm food. The same could be said when Hermod desperately paid her a visit.

Hermod before Hela by John Charles Dollman, 1909.
https://commons.wikimedia.org/w/index.php?curid=4780795

Hermod, who had been riding his father's mount, Sleipnir, was stopped by one of Hel's many servants, Modgud, at the end of the bridge upon discovering that he was a living being. After being granted passage, Hermod had to jump over the towering walls, where he later ended up in Hel's great hall. Upon meeting the living god, Hel listened to his request; he had asked the queen to release his brother, Baldur, back to the land of the living. The queen could have denied the request right away, but perhaps sympathy did exist in her cold heart since she agreed to do so with one condition. Hel would only let the son of Odin go if every creature across all nine realms wept for his death, a condition that was not fulfilled, thanks to Loki's trick.

With Baldur trapped in the realm of the dead, Ragnarök was set in motion. Although Hel was not present on the battlefield fighting against the Æsir, she did prepare an army out of the dishonorable dead to fight alongside her father, Loki. This undead army would soon board the *Naglfar*, a ship built entirely out of the dead people's fingernails. Steered and led by the vengeful god of mischief, the ship surged through the waves of the flood caused by Jörmungandr until they finally landed on Vígríðr (Vigrid), the battlefield of the last war. This is where Loki's army clashed swords with the einherjar, Odin's brave heroes from Valhalla, and Freyja's chosen warriors from Fólkvangr.

In contrast to Hel was the goddess Sif. Unlike her depiction in films in which Sif is portrayed as a fierce warrior goddess who would march into battles wearing armor and carrying a sword in her hand, the goddess was not known for her strength and brute attributes. Based on the old poems, Sif was associated with the earth, agriculture, and beauty.

The goddess was married to none other than the god of thunder himself, and she was said to have two children. With Thor, she gave birth to a daughter named Thrud; with another unidentified figure, she bore a son named Ullr, who was the god of archery. Along with Thor, Sif and her children dwelled in Bilskírnir, a massive hall in Thrudheim (Þrúðheimr), one of the many realms of Asgard.

Although married to the strongest and most prominent Æsir, few writings describe her in full detail, leading scholars and historians to come up with different theories of her life. Some claim that Sif was, in fact, a prominent goddess back in the days and that the Norse people would often associate her with the earth and fertility, especially since her husband symbolized the sky and rain, two things that promote fertility and agriculture. However, in time, she was overshadowed by Freyja and Frigg, the more well-known fertility deities. But there are those who disagree with the claim, especially the religious studies scholar Rudolf Simek since, according to him, there are no exact stories or tales that clearly depict Sif as the goddess of fertility and the earth.

Nevertheless, what we can be sure about was that Sif was, indeed, considered the most beautiful deity in Asgard. Even the giant Hrungnir acknowledged her beauty when he drunkenly threatened the Æsir. "I'll kill every one of you except Freyja and Sif, the fairest among all," the intoxicated giant said after he lost a horse race against Odin. "The two goddesses I'll take with me to my dwelling in Jötunheimr." The proud and boasting giant, however, did not get to realize his wish as Thor arrived just in time. Hrungnir then challenged Thor to a duel. The giant ended up dead, with his skull smashed into a million pieces.

While Sif was only mentioned once in that tale, another story that features the beautiful deity more prominently is the one from the old writings of Snorri called *Skáldskaparmál*.

Described by Snorri as the "loveliest of all women," Sif was, indeed, loved by the god of thunder. The goddess's best-known feature was her thick, golden hair—some say that this wondrous golden hair of hers symbolizes a rich field of wheat or golden corn. As tough and ferocious as the god of thunder could be, Sif was said to be his soft spot. The mighty god would even boast about his wife's beautiful hair whenever he was out drinking ale with his fellow gods. But little did he know that his wife was about to be the next victim of the trickster Loki.

Sif by John Charles Dollman, 1909.
https://commons.wikimedia.org/w/index.php?curid=4782702

Sif would spend hours caring for her hair, especially since she knew her husband loved her locks. In the morning, the goddess would rise and brush her hair with a jeweled comb, and in the afternoon, she would walk to the glimmering streams near her hall and wash her prized hair. She would spend hours caressing her hair by the river, and later on, she would lay her thick, long hair across a rock and wait for the scorching sun to dry it. This was Sif's daily routine, but it was about to change when Loki suddenly came up with yet another one of his pranks.

One lovely afternoon, Sif was out and about, sitting on the softest moss by the riverbanks while drying her hair under the sun. Nothing unusual was happening except that the goddess felt extremely sleepy. This was, in fact, the work of Loki, who had quietly followed her to the river and cast a magical spell on her. The trickster waited behind the bushes until Sif finally gave in and fell asleep against a rock. With the goddess now sound asleep, he approached her with a pair of clean, shiny sheers in his hand.

Loki knew Sif's golden hair was her prized possession and how much Thor adored it. With a sly grin carved on his face, the trickster grabbed a handful of Sif's silky smooth golden hair, and with his shiny sheers, he cut it off. The goddess, who was under a powerful spell, did not even move a muscle and was still sound asleep as Loki continued to cut her hair strand by strand until none was left. By the end of this shameful prank, Sif was left by the river with her head cropped and bare.

During this unfortunate incident, Thor was not in Asgard; the god of thunder was out on his regular journey across the realms. But when he returned that day, he was puzzled when Sif did not welcome him at the door as usual. He called out to her many times, but only his voice filled the hall. Not even the softest voice of his golden-haired wife could be heard in response to his callings. And so, Thor went and knocked on every door in Asgard, asking the other gods and goddesses where his wife could have gone. None of them had any answers, which left the thunder god disappointed and worried.

Upon arriving at his home again, Thor heard a faint voice calling him from afar. He immediately recognized the voice, so he slowly approached the dark corner. There stood Sif, who was wearing a full veil to cover her bare head. "Look away, Thor!" she sobbed the moment her husband got closer to where she was. "I do not wish for you to see me this way. I am ashamed, so I shall leave our hall and live among the dwarves in Svartalfheim."

"My dear Sif," Thor responded. "What has happened to you that makes you think you do not belong in Asgard?" The goddess revealed to the thunder god that she had lost her golden hair, which Thor had loved so very much. Sif was convinced that with her hair gone, Thor's affection toward her would also go away. Once again, she told her husband that she would leave Asgard in haste and never come back.

When Thor saw his wife ashamed and sorrowful with her hair gone, he flew into a rage. "I am the strongest among all who live in Asgard, and with all my strength, I will hunt down whoever did this to you and return your fairness back!" the mighty god exclaimed before taking his wife by her hand. Together, they headed to the Council House, where some of the gods and goddesses were sitting on their thrones, laughing and drinking mead.

As soon as Thor barged in, with Sif by his side, the laughter was replaced with complete silence. The anger flashing in the thunder god's eyes and Sif appearing with a veil covering her head was already to tell the gods that something terrible had happened. When Thor mentioned what had happened to his wife, the gods gasped, but one of them insisted that it was a prank by Loki. "No one else in Asgard would dare to perform a shameful act like this except the son of Laufey."

Thor, completely fueled by his anger, yelled that he would find Loki and hunt him down even if he ran away and hid in the cold depths of Helheim. "I shall kill him with my bare hands for what he did!" the thunder god shouted. But he was stopped by the All-Father. Odin had forbidden any of the Æsir to slay each other in Asgard; rather, he wished to summon Loki into the hall where he would make him redeem himself for his shameful prank.

When Loki arrived, he quickly noticed the fiery rage in Thor's eyes and the stern look of his blood-brother, Odin. He knew right there and then that he had to figure something out fast if he wished to live another day.

"You must return Sif's fairness, Loki," the All-Father said. "No matter what it takes."

With haste, the trickster left Asgard and made his way through dark passages underneath the earth until he finally reached the realm of the dwarves, Svartalfheim. Here, Loki was surrounded by the noisy sounds of hammers hitting anvils, hissing sounds of hot metal dropped into cold water, and the forges pumping out thick, dark soot. The trickster walked around and was astonished by some of the items being forged; one was a well-balanced spear named Gungnir, which was later gifted to Odin, and another one was *Skidbladnir*, a magical boat that could sail on any type of ocean and fold up like a piece of cloth until it could fit in one's pocket. This ship was later gifted to Freyr, the god of peace.

Of course, the trickster had his ways when it came to persuading others to fulfill his needs. So, he talked his way around the dwarves, complimenting their expertise and admiring their work. The dwarves were delighted by his presence; for once, they were not insulted and threatened. Knowing that he had gotten on their good side, Loki asked the master smiths, the sons of Ivaldi, if they were skillful enough to turn a bar of gold into fine threads. "If you could forge them into threads even finer than that of Sif's hair, the gods would be mighty jealous of you."

Ready to take up the challenge, the dwarves immediately took a bar of gold and dropped it into the fire. When it was hot enough, they grabbed it with a pair of iron tongs and banged it on the anvil with their hammers until golden threads started to take shape. The master smiths were, indeed, flattered by Loki's continuous compliments, and when the god suggested that they could ask for anything from those in Asgard, they worked on the golden threads for days, putting great effort and skill into their work.

A couple of days passed by, and the bar of gold had completely turned into a headpiece with threads as fine as Sif's golden hair. Each strand was shiny and even smoother than silk. Loki took the golden threads and put them in the palm of his hand; they were long and flowed to the ground in such soft movements. Although the headpiece was made out of a bar of gold, none could feel its weight—a bird's feather was heavier than the threads.

With his plan a success, Loki thanked the dwarves for their hard work, and he did not leave before giving them false promises. The god of mischief then made his way back to the city of the gods and headed straight into the Council House, where the Æsir were waiting for his return.

The looks on both Thor's and Odin's faces were the same as when Loki had first left, but he was no longer scared. He smiled and held the golden threads in front of him. "You can take off the veil now, Sif, as I am here to redeem my mistake," he proudly said. Once the sorrowful goddess took her veil off, the trickster carefully laid the golden headpiece on her head. The golden strands fell beautifully over her shoulders and flowed gently behind her back. With powerful magic infused in them, the golden threads would grow longer from time to time as if they were real hair growing from Sif's head. All of the gods present were amazed by how wondrous the golden threads were, and Sif was overjoyed. Sorrow no longer haunted her expression, and her cheeks flushed in redness as she held her new hair. The goddess was, indeed, the fairest of them all.

Chapter 10: Valhalla and the Valkyries

"The fifth is Gladsheimr, | and gold-bright there
 Stands Valhall stretching wide
 And there does Othin | each day choose
 The men who have fallen in fight."
(*Grímnismál*, Stanza 8, translated by Henry Adams Bellows)

It was said that once the three women of fate known as the Norns had spun the threads and weaved the tapestry of fate, not one soul could ever escape from their destiny—not even the giants from the cold, misty mountains of Jötunheimr or the mightiest of gods in Asgard. So, when Odin discovered that Ragnarök would soon fall upon them, the All-Father knew he had to prepare for the battle.

The gods alone were not enough to fend off the thousands of giants marching toward their realm, so Odin had to raise his own army out of the brave mortals who had fallen on the battlefield. These loyal warriors of Odin were called einherjar, and they were the ones who would fight alongside the warrior gods against the forces of chaos led by Loki.

To house the slain warriors, Odin built a grand hall. This hall was known in the Old Norse language as Valhǫll, but most of us know it as Valhalla, which is also translated as the "Hall of the Slain." In *Grímnismál*, Odin, in his disguise as Grímnir, described Valhalla in full detail. The ornate hall was said to stand in the realm of Glaðsheimr, right in the middle of the eternal plain known as Iðavöllr. One could easily spot this vast hall since it was one of the grandest in the realm, with its rafters made entirely out of shiny spears and its roof fully fortified with polished shields. Over the magnificent hall itself, an eagle could be seen hovering; some sources claim that eagles were a symbol of battle and that when one started hovering, it was a clear sign that a battle was nearing. In this case, the battle was Ragnarök.

Valhalla by Emil Doepler, 1905.
https://commons.wikimedia.org/w/index.php?curid=5417783

Inside the hall of Valhalla were 540 different doors. Every day, eight hundred einherjar would come out of each one, after which they would engage in long, grueling hours of training. These elite warriors would battle each other, equipping themselves with coats of mail, swords, and spears. Blood spilled, and their vitality waned in the span of their training, but when evening came, all of their wounds would heal, and their health would be restored. This also marked the time when the warriors must put down their weapons and reward themselves with a bountiful feast.

All of the warriors were served with endless supplies of meat, which came from a boar named Sæhrímnir. Almost like Thor's magical goats, this particular boar would come back to life whenever it was slaughtered. To wash down the food, the warriors would drink full horns of mead that was produced by Heidrun the goat. This mythical goat stood on top of Valhalla, consuming the red-gold leaves of the tree called Læraðr. But Heidrun was not the only animal that dwelled on top of the vast hall, as a great stag named Eikþyrnir also stood on its roof. While the creature ate the foliage of Læraðr, its antlers would drip water into the world below, producing rivers and streams.

To the Vikings, gaining entry into Valhalla was their ultimate goal. However, not all warriors who died on the battlefield were guaranteed to enter Odin's magnificent hall, as half of them would be sent to Fólkvangr, another great hall for fallen Vikings. This hall was led by the goddess Freyja. It was believed that Freyja herself would choose those she seemed worthy for her hall, while Odin put his trust in the Valkyries or the "Chooser of the Slain."

Some believed that the Valkyries were demons of death who would roam around the bloody battlefield and feast on the bodies of the fallen heroes before carrying their souls to the underworld. Some even claimed that the Valkyries were wicked creatures since they would use malicious spells and magic to kill off the warriors that they did not favor. Just like the Norns, the Valkyries were believed to have the ability to decide the fates of the warriors.

While some thought the Valkyries to be menacing death demons, some sources also suggest that they were powerful and honorable female warriors who served Odin. Their origins, however, remain uncertain to this day; certain scholars believe that they were supernatural warrior maidens whose lineage is unknown. Others claim that the Valkyries were once humans and daughters to kings, queens, and legendary warriors.

Walkyrien by Emil Doepler, c. 1905.
https://commons.wikimedia.org/w/index.php?curid=5441746

These warrior maidens were often depicted as beautiful women with golden or black hair. Whenever they were not in the skies looming above a battlefield, the Valkyries would remain in the hall of Valhalla wearing elegant dresses. But most of the time, these female warriors were pictured riding strong horses—although some said they also rode wolves and boars—wearing helmets and mail coats with a shield in one of their hands and a spear in the other.

Aside from pouring mead to the einherjar and sometimes assisting the human beings in Midgard, the Valkyries were tied to an important role, which was to choose and lead those worthiest among the slain heroes to Odin's ornate hall. The All-Father, who oversaw every single battle on Midgard from his high seat, would determine which side of the war he favored. And so, on Odin's order, the Valkyries mounted their steeds and journeyed to the land of the humans.

Once they reached the battlefield, the Valkyries were tasked with making decisions on which side of the war would emerge victorious. Some said that the Valkyries would remain in the clouds above an active battlefield with their eyes wide open. Once they sensed that their favored warriors were nearing death, the warrior maidens would swoop down and protect them from their fate. When the battle ended, the bodies of the handpicked warriors who perished on the battlefield would be carried by the Valkyries and sent to Valhalla, where they became einherjar.

Although the Valkyries were given full power to determine the outcome of the battles in Midgard, they must do so according to Odin's preference. Since they were described to be loyal to the All-Father, none of them dared to disobey his order, except for Brynhild (or Brunhilde), one of the most powerful Valkyries. She was punished to live the life of a mortal. Not only was she condemned to marriage, but her love story was also one of the most tragic ones in Norse mythology.

Brynhild was said to be the daughter of a legendary Norse king named Bulthi. Even before she was chosen by the All-Father to take on the duties of a Valkyrie, Brynhild was described as a wondrous woman who knew no fear.

One day, Odin saw a battle going on in Midgard. The war was between two powerful kings named Hjalmgunnar and Agnar. While sitting on his high seat, the All-Father declared that he favored Hjalmgunnar, the older king, rather than the young Agnar. And so, he ordered Brynhild to travel down to the battlefield and decide the outcome of the raging war.

Without delay, the wise Valkyrie mounted her steed and headed toward the land of humankind, where she remained in the skies and watched the mortals clashing swords and throwing spears. Although she was well aware that the All-Father had preferred the older king to win the victory, Brynhild thought the opposite. The bold Valkyrie decided to side with Agnar and made him victorious.

Upon returning to Asgard, the Valkyrie was faced by Odin, who was enraged by her decision. "You are a Valkyrie no more, and I shall cast you to the world of the human beings where you will continue to live as a mortal and be condemned to enter a marriage," the All-Father fiercely said since he could not accept Brynhild's disobedience. However, he did not only wish to throw her out of Asgard and cast her to Midgard, but he also wanted to imprison her within a remote keep on top of Mount Hindarsfjall. Instead of being locked behind bars, Odin planned to put her in an enchanted sleep where she would only wake to a person who wished to marry her. The bold Valkyrie then responded that she would never submit herself and marry a fearful man. "Very well," said the All-Father before he put Brynhild to a deep sleep using Svefnthorn or the "sleep thorn."

Just as Odin had threatened, Brynhild was brought to an isolated keep on top of a mountain. Since the Valkyrie refused to marry just anyone, the All-Father built a ring of fire surrounding the place where the Valkyrie was sleeping so that only the bravest among heroes could wake her.

Many years had passed since Brynhild was first put to sleep when suddenly a man approached the keep on his horse. Some knew the man only by his name, Sigurd, while some knew him as the legendary dragon slayer who descended from Odin himself. And when the legendary hero stumbled upon the keep and the blazing circle of fire, he shook the reins of his horse and made it inside, completely unharmed.

Inside the keep, Sigurd immediately saw Brynhild, who was still imprisoned in her deep sleep. He first removed the sleeping Valkyrie's helmet and was quickly enchanted by her wondrous beauty. He then noticed how tight her chainmail corset was; it looked like it almost pierced through her flesh. Gently, Sigurd loosened the laces, which allowed Brynhild to finally draw a deep breath and awake from her years of sleep.

Although she had been asleep for years, there was no need for Sigurd to introduce himself since the Valkyrie already knew who he was; she was said to have the knowledge of events that were yet to happen. Sigurd, on the other hand, did not know who he was talking to, so he asked for the Valkyrie's name and what had caused her to be imprisoned within such an isolated keep.

Upon learning that the woman he had awoken was once Odin's warrior maiden, Sigurd began asking Brynhild for her words of wisdom and useful knowledge. The Valkyrie was more than delighted to fulfill the brave hero's wish, so she taught him almost everything she knew. First, Brynhild taught him the knowledge of runes, such as their origin and what they were used for. Then, she showed him how to heal various wounds and sicknesses, as well as the ways to calm the rolling waves. Brynhild even gave him wise words for his journeys that could save him some trouble. "Do not sleep by the open road, for there are many evil spirits that dwell in the wild," said the Valkyrie. "Never trust the offspring of those you have slain," she continued, "for even the smallest of a wolf cub can bite."

Completely enthralled by the Valkyrie and her vast knowledge, the legendary hero soon fell in love with Brynhild. Before he left the keep, Sigurd proposed to her and promised that he would soon return to marry her. Brynhild, who had finally found a man who feared nothing, accepted his proposal, and together, they swore an oath that nothing would ever come between them. Many tried to warn the legendary hero that Brynhild was not interested in marriage. "After all, she was once a warrior maiden. It is impossible for her to put her helmet down and choose the game of love." They would say this to the hero, but Sigurd was so headstrong that he would never marry anyone other than Brynhild. And so, the next time Sigurd returned to the Valkyrie, he gave her a ring, one that had been worn by Odin himself. This ring was called Andvaranaut, and unbeknownst to the two lovers, it was cursed.

When Sigurd pledged to the Valkyrie by giving her a ring, which was also his most treasured possession, Brynhild wished to protect the pledge. And so, she surrounded herself with another circle of fire, and this time around, only Sigurd was allowed to pass unscathed.

Sigurd's next journey brought him to a kingdom ruled by King Gjúki of the Gjúkung clan. Upon entering his hall, the legendary hero was welcomed warmly by the royal family, especially Grimhild, Gjúki's wife, who wished to take Sigurd into the family, along with his hoards of treasure. Although Sigurd mentioned that he had already sworn an oath to marry a Valkyrie, Grimhild thought that it would be better for him to marry Gudrun, her only daughter. And so, the queen began to plot her wicked plan, which was to infuse the hero's mead with a potion that would make him forget all about his love for the Valkyrie.

All it took was a sip of his mead, and Sigurd no longer remembered his promise to Brynhild. Even the thought of their daughter, Aslaug, had escaped his mind. With her plan a success, the queen then persuaded her husband to offer the hero their daughter's hand in marriage. Sigurd was, of course, honored by the offer and immediately accepted it. Soon, he married Gudrun, and together they bore a child named Sigmund.

With her only daughter married to a legendary hero, Grimhild began plotting another one of her schemes. This time around, she was arranging a wedding for one of her three sons, Gunnar. The queen persuaded her son to marry Brynhild. "Go now and seek her hand in marriage," said Grimhild. "There's not a person in the world who could appear as beautiful as Brynhild."

Gunnar was indeed interested, but one thing bothered him. "And what if she deems me unworthy of her? After all, she was a Valkyrie," the son of Gjúki asked.

"No one would refuse such a hero as you!" Sigurd, who was still under Grimhild's spell, encouraged him.

Together, Gunnar and Sigurd traveled on horseback through the woods and up to Mount Hindarsfjall until they could see Brynhild's keep surrounded by a ring of blazing fire. Since the Valkyrie only allowed Sigurd to pass through the flames, Gunnar had a hard time trying to reach even the gates of the keep. Upon nearing the flames, his horse reared and refused to go any farther. Gunnar then attempted to ride on Sigurd's horse, Grani, but it would not move without its master in the saddle.

"Let us exchange looks," Gunnar said. "We can swap our clothes and appearances. You can ride your horse through the flames and seek the Valkyrie's hand in marriage on my behalf." After assuming Gunnar's appearance, Sigurd jumped on his horse and rode through the ring of fire with ease.

In the main hall was Brynhild. The Valkyrie was sitting in her high seat, sharpening her blade. As he looked at the man who had entered her hall, she quickly rose to her feet. "You're back, my dear Sigurd!" she said in excitement. Sigurd, who was wearing the disguise of Gunnar, could see the Valkyrie's glimmering eyes, but he still could not recall their pleasant time together.

"You're not Sigurd," Brynhild exclaimed in rage when she finally saw the man up close. The disguised Sigurd then introduced himself as Gunnar and explained his real intention of visiting the Valkyrie. Still holding on to the pledge that she had made with the legendary hero, Brynhild refused Gunnar's proposal cold-heartedly.

"The flames," the disguised hero said. "Did you not set it so that only the bravest of men could pass? And did you not pledge yourself to marry only the one who knows no fear?" The Valkyrie was lost for words. After all, she did swear to marry the one who had proven himself to be the bravest among all heroes, so she accepted the proposal.

Sigurd, who was still in disguise, stayed with the Valkyrie for three nights, but at night, he would lay his unsheathed sword in between them. "I swore an oath to never touch you until we are wed," said the hero. In truth, he was holding on to his honor since he was only in the keep for Gunnar's sake.

When the three nights were up, the disguised hero prepared to leave but not before he noticed the fine ring on one of the Valkyrie's fingers. Sigurd might have forgotten about Brynhild, but it was impossible for him to forget his prized treasure, Andvaranaut. Carefully, he removed the ring from her finger and swapped it with the one Gunnar had given to him earlier.

The wedding day finally approached, and when the two had exchanged their vows, Sigurd snapped out of Grimhild's spell. The legendary hero now remembered everything about the Valkyrie, but it was too late. Sigurd was clouded with disappointment and sorrow as he looked at his beloved Valkyrie in the arms of another man.

As for Brynhild, she was more than irritated to see Sigurd alive and married to another woman, so she began taunting his wife. While they were down by the river, the two women quarreled over whose husband was the bravest. Brynhild boasted about her husband, Gunnar, who had made his way through the flames just so he could seek her hand. Gudrun was enraged when the Valkyrie started to belittle Sigurd, so she revealed the truth. "It was never Gunnar who jumped through the flames. It was, in fact, my husband, Sigurd, who was in disguise!" When Brynhild accused Gudrun of lying, the latter then showed the Valkyrie the ring, Andvaranaut, hugging her finger. The Valkyrie recognized the ring instantly, and knowing that she had been deceived, Brynhild swore vengeance.

The Valkyrie later lied to her husband, saying that while Sigurd was in disguise, the hero had touched her in bed. She then demanded the hero's death, but Gunnar refused to do so since Sigurd was his sworn brother. Instead, Gunnar persuaded his younger brother, Guttorm, who was not bound to their oath, to pick up a blade and slay the legendary hero. And so, while Sigurd was sound asleep in his room, Guttorm quietly walked in with a sword held tightly in his grasp. He then plunged the blade into the hero's chest. Before he drew his last breath, Sigurd managed to reach for his own sword and threw it toward the young Guttorm, resulting in his death.

Brynhild had her hands dirty since she had killed Sigurd's son, Sigmund. However, although her vengeance was fulfilled, the Valkyrie was not at all relieved. Brynhild revealed to her husband that Sigurd was indeed an honorable man since he had never touched her while she was in her keep. She then told him about the fates of his clan, the Gjúkungs, and the other important events that were yet to happen. Having already lost her will to live, the Valkyrie decided to end her own life. When Sigurd's funeral pyre was lit, Brynhild jumped straight into the flames and lay beside him. And so, the wisest Valkyrie and the legendary hero rode to Hel together.

Chapter 11: The Fortifications of Asgard

Asgard is also known as the fortified city of the gods. It was surrounded by towering walls so strong that not even a major earthquake could shake it to the ground. These fortified walls were the ones that had kept the mighty gods of Asgard safe and sound, protected from all the unwanted threats by the giants and trolls. However, believe it or not, these strong walls were not always there.

When the gods from the tribes of Æsir and Vanir finally realized that their long war was not going to end anytime soon and that more and more destruction was faced by both sides each day, they agreed to seal a pact and coexist peacefully. But the realms did face heavy casualties before that, especially Asgard. It turns out that when the war was waged, the gods from Vanaheim managed to launch a powerful attack on the walls of Asgard and reduced them to rubble and ash. Because of this, Asgard was left undefended, free for any jötunn to attack them.

When peace was achieved between the gods, and they were done building the realm of humankind, Odin shifted his focus back to his own realm. The All-Father was worried about the safety of Asgard, and he began pondering about the best way to fortify the city. However, Asgard was so big that building a wall around it would take years. While Odin was walking from one end of the city to the other, his head overwhelmed with the matter, he saw a figure approaching the city through Bifröst. This mysterious person had journeyed all the way to the realm of the gods, and he had an interesting offer for them.

The mysterious man presented himself to the gods and claimed to be a master builder. "I could build a strong stone wall surrounding this city in just the span of three seasons, and when I'm done, neither giants nor monsters would be able to penetrate it," he declared. The gods were surprised by his claim and, at the same time, suspicious of his offer. For such a daring proposal, to finish a wall surrounding a massive city in just a short amount of time, the builder must have had something else in mind. "Well, for a price, of course," he continued. In return for building the walls, the master builder had asked for things that the gods had to think twice about before they could agree. For instance, he asked for the goddess Freyja's hand in marriage, along with the sun and the moon to bring him back from where he had come.

The gods obviously did not give an answer right away; instead, they gathered around for a quick discussion. They were in need of a fortified wall to protect themselves, but the price set by the builder was much too high. The gods had not planned to lose a powerful and valuable goddess from their pantheon and let the world turn dark and cold without the sun and the moon. Just as they were a few moments away from declining the builder's daring offer, Loki stepped in and persuaded the gods to do otherwise.

The trickster claimed that the builder was only boasting about his skills. He suggested the gods make a counteroffer; he would have to finish the walls in just one season to get Freyja along with the sun and the moon. The gods listened attentively to Loki's idea, but they were still unsure. "He won't be able to finish it," the trickster said in full confidence. "The most he could do is probably half of the work, so why not just watch him do it? He won't get his hands on Freyja, the sun, and the moon if he fails to complete it in time, but at least we get most of the walls done." Loki saw the offer as an opportunity to build the walls for free, and he successfully persuaded the gods to look at the situation the way he saw it.

The gods then met with the mysterious master builder and informed him of their decision; he was to complete the construction of the walls by the first day of summer. The builder then asked if he could bring his loyal horse to work with him, to which the gods agreed. He also made sure the gods agreed not to do him any harm as long as he was in the city constructing the massive walls. Without delaying more, the mysterious builder and the gods sealed an agreement, which was witnessed by many.

An illustration of the mysterious master builder and his horse by Robert Engels, 1919.
https://commons.wikimedia.org/w/index.php?curid=4663677

The very next day, the master builder returned to the city of Asgard with his steed, Svadilfari. The gods kept a close eye on the builder as he worked. He was, indeed, skillful in his work, but it was his horse that shone the most. The master builder was hardworking and had great strength, but his horse was twice as strong, and it could work all day and night without a second of rest. The builder would haul the stones for the walls and carefully yet steadily laid them around the city until towering walls took shape, while Svadilfari dragged all the massive boulders to the walls. The construction went extremely well and smoothly as the days went by, which made the gods worried. When winter ended, and spring approached, half of Asgard was already surrounded by tall walls. Just as promised, the walls were so strong that not even the most monstrous creatures in the world could come through.

More days passed. The builder and his horse never stopped working, and the walls almost reached the gates of Asgard. Three days were left before summer replaced spring, and the gods were beginning to panic. Even Freyja could not sit still since she was not at all ready to leave her hall and be with a suspicious man whose background was unknown. Then, the gods recalled the very reason they agreed to this high-stake agreement; if it was not for Loki's persuasion, they would not have had to deal with this problem. And so, they summoned the son of Laufey and gave him a warning. "This is on you, Loki," Odin said. "You are the one who came up with this plan, so you better think of a solution before the builder can deliver his part of the deal."

The gods began to threaten the trickster, saying that he would face the ugliest death that anyone could ever imagine should he not think of a solution right there and then. Scared of his possible fate, Loki quickly swore that he would fix everything and that nothing bad would happen to Freyja, the sun, or the moon.

Loki and Svadilfari by Dorothy Hardy, 1909.
https://commons.wikimedia.org/w/index.php?curid=9700367

Loki knew there was nothing he could do or say to the master builder to stop him from working, so he planned to trick the strong stallion, Svadilfari. The gods watched as the trickster went into the forest. After a moment, a beautiful mare came out of the very same place Loki had gone into. The mare gracefully trotted, displaying itself in front of Svadilfari, who was busy assisting its master trying to complete the construction of the walls. Once the stallion saw the beautiful mare, he immediately snapped out of his harness, abandoned the construction site, and went on to chase the mare through the forest. The gods of Asgard, who saw the entire incident, were amused since they knew the mare that managed to distract the great stallion was, in fact, Loki in disguise.

The chase between the two horses went on for hours; they galloped across the plains from day to night, and the master builder was left alone at the construction site, hauling smaller stones from one side to the other. The next day, he waited for his strong stallion to return. Hours passed by, and he was still working alone. The builder knew Svadilfari would not return to his side anytime soon, and he also realized that there was no way he could finish building the walls on time all by himself. Knowing that his plan to marry a goddess and capture the moon and the sun was about to fail, the master builder burst into a rage—one that only a mountain giant could portray. He smashed the many trees growing around him and broke the rocks and stones that he had gathered for the walls. The gods saw the builder's reaction, and they somehow were not surprised to discover that he was actually a giant—few of the gods were already suspicious of his true nature.

Even though the gods had struck a deal to not harm the builder as long as he was in Asgard, discovering that he was a jötunn completely changed the situation. They summoned Thor, who was away in the east, fighting mountain trolls, to face the builder. The giant killer arrived very quickly. He struck a deadly blow to the master builder's skull by using his hammer. The blow was so powerful that the builder's skull shattered into thousands of pieces, and his entire body was thrown into the lower depths of Helheim.

With the giant master builder gone, the gods could rest easy. Freyja could still remain in Asgard without having to worry about anyone taking her away. The sun and the moon were in place, and the world was not swallowed by total darkness. With a single smash to the skull, the builder had received his payment: instant death. However, Asgard was not entirely protected since the walls had not been finished. The gods were not expecting any more threats to their city, but the unfinished walls would cause casualties when the day of Ragnarök finally arrived.

Loki, on the other hand, was never seen in Asgard after the incident, at least not until several months later. All that time, he was presumably in the forest, heavily pregnant with a foal that came from his encounter with Svadilfari. He then gave birth to a beautiful gray horse with eight legs. This magnificent eight-legged steed was named Sleipnir (the "Sliding One"), and Loki brought it along with him to Asgard.

When the trickster arrived in the realm of the gods, he was approached by the All-Father, who marveled at the unusual horse. The

Æsir owned many steeds that they would ride over Bifröst, and they each had their own abilities. Freyr's horse, Blodughofi, could gallop through fire and get out of it unharmed. Gullfaxi, a golden horse gifted to Magni by Thor, could run as fast as the wind on land, in the air, and even on the water. But Sleipnir was the best of all, just as Yggdrasil was the finest of all ash trees and Thor the mightiest of all gods. One could ride the eight-legged horse and swiftly travel between worlds, including the realm of the dead, Helheim.

"Odin Rides to Hel" by W. G. Collingwood, 1908.
https://commons.wikimedia.org/w/index.php?curid=4740927

"Take him!" Loki said to the All-Father, offering the unusual horse to him as a gift. Odin immediately accepted the gift and welcomed the son of Laufey back to Asgard. With Sleipnir as his loyal mount, the All-Father could gallop across all nine realms at full speed. One time, Odin challenged the mightiest giant, Hrungnir, to a horse race. The god and the giant mounted their rides—Odin on Sleipnir and Hrungnir on Gullfaxi—and raced from the river streams to the steep hills and thick forests of Jötunheimr until they finally arrived at the gates of Asgard. As expected, Sleipnir won the race and held its title as the greatest horse in the universe. Later on, the All-Father, with Gungnir (his spear) held firmly in his grasp, would ride the eight-legged horse across the battlefield of Vigrid to face Fenrir the wolf and eventually fall to his demise.

Chapter 12: Odin's Sacrifice and the Mead of Poetry

"I ween that I hung on the windy tree,
　Hung there for nights full nine;
　With spear I was wounded, and offered I was
　To Odin, myself to myself,
　On the tree that none may ever know what root beneath it runs."
　(*Hávamál*, Verse 138, translated by Henry Adams Bellows)

　Humans are born with five senses, which they use to discover the world around them, but Odin was said to be blessed with the sixth sense: knowledge. The All-Father knew almost everything. He knew how to calm the crashing waves of the wild sea, he knew how to dull the blades of his enemies and render them blind, he knew how to heal and treat all kinds of wounds and illnesses that plagued the world, and he knew how to raise the dead so that they could speak and reveal secrets to him. However, this boundless knowledge was not bestowed upon him without a price. The All-Father had to go through a long, rough journey across the realms and perform the ultimate sacrifice before he could be blessed with such priceless wisdom.

　Odin's first quest for wisdom began when he realized that his thirst for knowledge was only getting stronger. And so, the All-Father set out on a journey to Jötunheimr, the untamed land of his very enemies, the giants. Odin, who was disguised as a traveler, wandered the cold misty land alone until he reached a well located right beneath one of Yggdrasil's three massive roots.

The well, also known as Mímisbrunnr, was believed to contain all of the intelligence and wisdom in the world. Its guardian, Mimir, once drank from the well using Gjallarhorn—the very same horn that Heimdall blew when Ragnarök came—and its water had granted him exceptional wisdom and endless knowledge to the point he was known among the Æsir as the wisest being. Odin knew that a sip of the water from the well was all he needed to gain all the wisdom in the world. And so, he approached the well and greeted its guardian, Mimir, who scholars also suggest might be his uncle.

"Why have you come to my well, mighty Odin?" Mimir asked.

"For wisdom, of course," the All-Father responded. "I am the All-Father and the lord of the gods. So, tell me, Mimir, how could I live up to that title if I fail to gain and absorb all the knowledge and intelligence in this universe?" Odin asked the wise being if he could drink from his well of knowledge, but Mimir claimed that although he was, in fact, the chief of all gods, Odin still had to pay a high price before he could fulfill his request. And so, the wise being demanded the All-Father to sacrifice one of his eyes.

Odin would gladly do anything just so he could possess more power and knowledge. So, the god, without even hesitating, gouged his eye out. It was said that his screams of pain echoed throughout the universe and shook the grounds of the world. Then, using his own hands, he dropped his eye into Mimir's well of knowledge.

"I have done my part," said the chief of the gods. Honoring his part of the deal, Mimir took the horn and drew the glimmering water from his well. He then passed the horn to the All-Father, who immediately quaffed the water in a single breath. With the horn emptied to the last drop, Odin gained the ultimate intellectual power that none of the gods in Asgard could ever match, except for Mimir himself. But that was not all, as he also gained a deep scar on one of his eye sockets and another name for himself: the one-eyed god.

Even though Odin was left with only one eye at the end of his quest for wisdom in Jötunheimr, the All-Father could still oversee the universe in full clarity—in fact, he could see it even better. While sitting on his throne, Hliðskjálf, another event caught his attention. It was the sight of the Norns underneath the World Tree; they were right by the Well of Urd. These three women were busy dictating the fate of all beings in the universe, and they did so by carving runes on the massive trunk of Yggdrasil. Once they were done, humans and all other creatures, including the gods themselves, would soon learn of their fate.

From his observation, Odin knew the runes were not merely a writing system made of a set of letters and symbols. He knew that the runes were also used to invoke magical powers. The runes, combined with the knowledge of magic and inscriptions, could be used to cast spells, put a curse on a person, imbue a certain weapon with great abilities, and even heal wounds and sickness. Like the Norns, a person who possessed the art of runes could also predict the future and protect themselves from terrible misfortunes.

Knowing that he still did not possess all the knowledge in the world, Odin grew envious of the Norns. He wished to acquire the mysterious knowledge of the runes, and he would do absolutely anything to make this dream come true. And so, again, Odin left his hall and set out on another quest. This time around, he journeyed to the center of the world where Yggdrasil grew and where the Well of Urd could be found. The runes, however, would only appear to those who were worthy and knew nothing of fear. Some even said that one could only see the runes in death. So, the All-Father performed yet another great sacrifice to prove himself.

An illustration of Odin sacrificing himself by Lorenz Frølich.
https://commons.wikimedia.org/wiki/File:The_Sacrifice_of_Odin_by_Fr%C3%B8lich.jpg

Odin hung himself from the branch of Yggdrasil, and he pierced his flesh with his own spear. For nine days and nights, the All-Father hung from the tree, his skin and entire body exposed to the scorching heat, the windy evenings, and the cold, stormy nights. He refused to be fed and cared for, and he forbade the gods from saving him—none of the Æsir were to come near the All-Father and provide him nourishment.

It was believed that on the ninth night, when the god died due to his sacrificial actions, all the lights in the world were extinguished. But when midnight had passed, the god came back to life, and he brought along with him a powerful knowledge of runes. Through his sacrifice, the All-Father had mastered nine spells and eighteen charms, which he later shared with his fellow gods in Asgard.

Due to his powerful knowledge of the runes and magic, it is not a surprise that the one-eyed god was associated with wisdom, war, and even death. But magic, spells, and the ability to foresee the future were not all the All-Father was after. He was also going for the mead of poetry.

After the war between the Æsir and the Vanir came to a stalemate, the gods decided to sheathe their weapons and come up with a truce through which they would coexist peacefully. To seal the treaty, the gods from both tribes spat in a vessel. From their spittle, a great being was born, and he went by the name Kvasir.

Kvasir was said to be the wisest among men, and he was also considered the best poet in the world. One could flood him with questions, and he never failed to answer each of them with ease. Because of his extreme wit and intelligence, Kvasir often traveled the world, providing men with knowledge and counsel.

However, things were about to go south when two mysterious dwarves named Fjalar ("Deceiver") and Galar ("Screamer") decided to invite the wise being to their house. Kvasir, who was completely unaware of their ill intentions, accepted their invitation right away, and when he arrived at their doorstep, he was welcomed by the two dwarves. Once they were certain that there were no extra eyes watching them, Fjalar and Galar murdered Kvasir, after which they collected his blood into three huge separate vats.

With honey, the dwarves brewed his blood until it turned into a very special drink called the mead of poetry. Whoever managed to get even a sip of the special mead would gain the ultimate skills of a poet or a scholar.

After some time, the gods of Asgard began to wonder about Kvasir's whereabouts, especially Odin. They had suspicions about the two dwarves, but both Fjalar and Galar already had their answers ready should the gods arrive at their home with questions. "He choked on his own unlimited knowledge" was what the dwarves planned to say to those who questioned them. Soon, the dwarves gained a new hobby; they started killing for sport. Their next victim was a giant named Gilling, whom they drowned to death near their house. The giant, however, was married, and his sudden disappearance caused his wife to arrive at the dwarves' doorstep.

"Have you seen my husband?" asked the poor giantess.

"He's dead," the dwarves replied with no remorse. Upon learning her husband's fate, the giantess burst into loud cries, which quickly irritated the two dwarves. And so, they killed the weeping giantess by dropping a heavy millstone on her head.

A few days later, the dwarves received another guest. He was a giant named Suttung, and he was the son of Gilling. The giant was, of course, furious when he learned of his father's murder, and he wished for the dwarves to pay for their wicked actions. So, he captured both Fjalar and Galar and carried them to the very place where his father had drowned. At low tide, he tied the two mischievous dwarves to a rock. Knowing that they would drown when the tide rose, the dwarves began to beg for their lives.

"Please, spare us!" one of them yelled. "Let us compensate for your father's death! Let us go, and every drop of the mead of poetry is yours." Suttung knew that getting his hands on the mead would make the gods incredibly jealous, so he agreed to release the dwarves in exchange for all three vats of the mead of poetry.

Odin saw the entire incident and was enraged by the fact that a giant possessed such a priceless item. The one-eyed god, who was always in pursuit of wisdom and knowledge, bent his will to steal the mead from the giant. However, the theft was not going to be easy, as Suttung had hidden the precious mead somewhere in his home, far on top of the mountain and guarded by his own daughter, Gunlod.

And so, the All-Father devised a new plan. Instead of traveling straight to Suttung's dwelling, Odin assumed a disguise—this time as a wandering farmhand named Bölverkr—and journeyed to a farmstead belonging to the giant's brother, Baugi. The moment he arrived, the god noticed nine of Baugi's servants sweating under the sun and struggling to cut the hay. Odin approached them, and from underneath his cloak, the disguised god took out a whetstone. "Try using this whetstone of mine on your scythes. You will only need to use minimal effort to cut through the hay."

All nine slaves were delighted that their scythes were sharper than before, and they managed to finish their work in just a few short moments. "This is, indeed, the finest whetstone in the world!" said one of the servants. "Would you sell it to one of us?"

"Of course," the All-Father responded. "But it comes with a high price." Before he walked away, Odin threw the whetstone in the air. The nine slaves, with their scythes in their hands, scrambled toward the direction of the whetstone, but their desperation got the best of them; they accidentally slit each other's throats.

Upon learning that his slaves were all dead, Baugi was filled with rage and disappointment. But Odin, who was still in disguise as Bölverkr, approached him and offered to help. "I can do all the work of the nine slaves," the disguised god proudly claimed.

"And the price for your help?" Baugi looked at him.

"I would like only a sip of your brother's precious mead."

Baugi went silent for a moment and told the wandering farmhand that he could not promise him the mead, but he could get him to Suttung. Odin agreed right away and began working on the farm.

Once summer ended, the disguised god returned to Baugi and demanded his reward. So, the giant led him to the mountains, and eventually, they arrived at Suttung's stone dwelling. Baugi met with his brother and pleaded his case. Suttung, however, refused to give his precious mead to the disguised god no matter how much he had helped his brother. Turning to the farmhand, Baugi claimed that he had completed his part of the deal. "I only promised to bring you here, and that's done."

Odin, whose mind was full of tricks and plans, handed the giant an auger from underneath his cloak. "The least you could do to repay me is to drill a way into the mountain where the mead is hidden." Baugi gave him a worried look and was not convinced by the plan. "Don't worry, Baugi. I'll take a sip so small that your brother won't even notice."

The giant knew the god would not leave the mountain empty-handed, so he grabbed the auger and drilled through the mountainside. After a while, Baugi stopped drilling and turned to look at the disguised god. "It's done."

Odin was suspicious of the giant's claim, so he blew into the hole. The dust, however, blew back into his face, proving that the giant had tried to deceive him. "I don't think so," Odin said, stopping the giant from leaving. "You need to continue drilling."

With no way to escape, Baugi did what the disguised god had commanded him. When the giant stopped working, Odin again blew into the hole. This time around, the dust went through. After thanking him for delivering his part of the deal, Odin transformed into a snake and slithered into the tiny hole. Baugi attempted to stab the god with the auger, but he was a tad too slow.

When the god finally got in, he assumed the appearance of an attractive young man and approached Gunlod, who was guarding the mead. He charmed the giantess with his words and false promises. The god made the giantess believe that he would soon seek her hand in marriage. So, for three nights in a row, the disguised god came to her bed and stayed with her. While whispering seductions in her ear, the god asked the giantess for a sip of the mead. On the first night, the god took his first sip of the mead and drained the entire vat. The second night, he charmed the giantess yet again, and he was again granted access to the mead. The god then swallowed every drop of the second vat. On the third night, he did the same thing once more.

Now that all three vats were emptied, Odin had to make sure the mead would not rise up in his throat, or all of his efforts would turn into nothing but a waste of time. So, he transformed himself into an eagle and escaped from Gunlod's dwelling. His flight, however, was not at all fast, as the god was bloated; his stomach was too full of mead. Suttung saw the suspicious eagle flying from his daughter's keep, so he assumed his form as a massive eagle and chased after the god.

The gods in Asgard saw the pursuit, and when Odin was nearing their walls, they quickly dragged three huge vessels out of their palace. Suttung flapped his wings as hard as he could, but he failed to catch the god and was forced to retreat. Odin, who was still in the shape of an eagle, arrived safely in Asgard. He then made his way to the three vessels and vomited all the mead that he had swallowed.

While the All-Father regurgitated the mead, a few small drops from his beak fell into the world of men. While the better mead in the vessels was shared among the Æsir, the small droplets of the mead were passed to the humans and became the source of all bad to mediocre poets and scholars.

Chapter 13: The Binding of Fenrir

Odin was sitting on his high throne, Hliðskjálf, overlooking all nine realms when he saw something alarming in the land of the giants. Deep in the wilderness of Jötunheimr was a giantess called Angrboða (Angrboda), living with her three children: Jörmungandr, Fenrir, and Hel. The All-Father could feel something dark about them, especially when he knew that the three monstrous children were Loki's offspring.

In *Völuspá*, it is mentioned that Odin once summoned the spirit of a dead Völva or seeress to appear before him and persuaded her to tell him the knowledge of the past, present, and future. Although reluctant, the Völva did tell Odin all that she knew, but the prophecy about the end of the world was what caught the All-Father's attention the most.

"There will be a day when the forces of chaos will outnumber the guardians of order," The Völva said. "Loki and his children will set themselves free and bring terror to the world. The dead ones from the dark realm of Helheim will sail to the land of the living and cause catastrophe, while the fire giants will swing their blazing swords, burning the world and reducing it to nothing but ashes." The prophecy was explained to the chief of gods in full detail, including his own fate; Odin was to perish during Ragnarök. He would be devoured by the giant wolf, Fenrir.

Ever since the gods learned of their future doom at the hands of Loki's children, they immediately declared them to be monsters and enemies of the Æsir. When Odin discovered where the three children were being raised, he ordered his fellow gods to travel to Jötunheimr and take away all of Loki's offspring and bring them to Asgard. Once they arrived, Odin was disgusted when he first laid eyes on Jörmungandr, which was, at that time, a small serpent. To deal with him, Odin threw Jörmungandr into the deep sea of Midgard, where he would dwell until Ragnarök came. Jörmungandr grew slowly, but as time went by, it turned into a massive serpent to the point where he could encircle the entire earth and bite its own tail.

Next, Odin laid his eyes on Hel, Loki's daughter, whose appearance was unusual; half of her face looked like a normal human being with fair skin, while the other half of her face was a gloomy blue, almost like a decomposing corpse, with parts of her skull exposed. Unlike Jörmungandr, which was tossed into the sea, Hel was sent to Helheim, where she would rule over those who died of sickness, old age, and accidents.

Last but not least, Odin looked at the wolf cub Fenrir, although some refer to him as Fenris. One glance at him, and the All-Father could feel a shiver in his bones since he knew Fenrir would be the one to devour him whole when the Twilight of the Gods finally happened. And so, Odin thought of an idea; he planned to keep the wolf in Asgard so that he could keep an eye on him at all times.

It was said that Fenrir actually lived peacefully among the gods in Asgard. The one who would care for him was none other than the god Týr. Each day, the god of honor and justice would feed Fenrir meat using his own hands, and sometimes, he would spend some time playing with the wolf cub after he returned home or before he set out on a journey away from the realm.

An image of Týr feeding Fenrir, illustrator unknown.
https://commons.wikimedia.org/wiki/File:Tyr_feeds_Fenrir.gif

Although Fenrir did not cause any trouble in Asgard, it was hard for the gods to look at him without terror filling their eyes. They held onto the prophecy and were sure that the wolf would bring nothing but disaster upon them. While Jörmungandr was said to take a long time to grow, it was completely the opposite for Fenrir. When the gods first brought him in, Fenrir was merely a small cub that could be held in the small hands of a child, but as the days passed by, he grew tremendously huge. Soon, no one was able to hold him, let alone beat his powerful strength.

Seeing the wolf's alarming growth, Odin began to plan for his next move. The All-Father could not just sit still while Loki's monstrous child continued to grow stronger. It would be dishonorable to shed the wolf's blood within the gates of Asgard, so he had to figure out something else as fast as he could. This was when the other gods suggested that Fenrir be bound. With haste, Odin rose from his throne and ordered the finest blacksmiths in Asgard to craft a piece of binding that was strong enough to stop the wolf from moving. A few days later, the blacksmiths proudly presented the first binding to the chief of the gods, and this binding was named Laedingr.

Odin, along with the other gods of Asgard, took the newly crafted binding and brought it to the giant wolf. Fenrir, however, had not been told of their plans since they did not want to risk the wolf going on a rampage in their realm. So, instead, the gods told him that the binding was nothing but a simple test of strength. The gods deceived him, saying that by breaking free from the binding, he would be regarded as the strongest being in the world. Wishing to be known for his mighty strength, Fenrir agreed to be bound by Laedingr.

With a huge yet slow sigh of relief, the gods of Asgard carefully approached the giant wolf and bound him. Fenrir did not move and waited until the gods had taken a few steps back. While all eyes were on him, Fenrir heaved and yanked himself out of the binding without any difficulties. It only took him one try before the binding was in pieces. Feeling as if he had passed the test of the gods, Fenrir roared with pride.

The gods, especially Odin, were disturbed and terrified by the wolf's strength. "Imagine how terrible it would be if the wolf were free to roam on the battlefield, attacking and tearing each one of us to pieces," the gods wondered. And so, the gods went to meet the blacksmiths again. "We need stronger binding!" they exclaimed. "One that is stronger than the last one."

The gods then got what they had requested. The smiths presented them with another binding, and they called it Dromi. It was twice as strong as Laedingr and much longer and wider. With the second binding in their hands, the gods invited Fenrir to test his might again. However, this time around, the wolf was more wary since the binding looked sturdier and stronger than before. But the Æsir had their ways of persuading the giant wolf, and he soon agreed to be bound.

Fenrir yanked once, but the binding was still intact, leaving the gods at the edge of their seats. The wolf heaved again, and the binding started to loosen. It took Fenrir a few heaves, but he did manage to break free. Again, the wolf had proved his might and left the gods distraught.

Almost unable to contain his fear, Odin summoned Skírnr to his hall. "Go to Svartalfheim with haste," commanded the All-Father. "There, you will find the dwarves, who are all master smiths."

Without delaying a single moment, the messenger journeyed to the realm of the dwarves, which was deep underneath the ground. He then met with the master smiths and convinced them to forge the strongest binding in the entire universe: Gleipnir.

With the air full of soot and the smell of smoke coming from the furnace, the dwarves began their work. They forged the binding using unusual resources: the sounds of a cat's footfall, a woman's beard, the roots of a mountain, the sinews of a bear, a fish's breath, and the spittle of a bird. Once it was forged, the messenger carried it back to the realm of the gods and presented it to them.

With Gleipnir in their possession, the gods went to see Fenrir once more, this time more confident than before. When the young giant wolf saw the third binding, he could not help but feel suspicious of the gods. Unlike the previous two bindings, Gleipnir looked different; the binding was almost as soft as silk, and it was as wide as a simple ribbon. Fenrir started to suspect that the gods were out to deceive him, which was why he decided to decline the challenge.

The Æsir then taunted the wolf. "You've broken free from two strong bindings before, so how difficult could a ribbon be?" This aroused the wolf's suspicion even more, but he reluctantly agreed to the challenge on one condition; he asked for one of the gods to hold one of their hands in his mouth. If he was right about the gods trying to trick him, he would bite off the Æsir's sword hand.

The gods went silent upon hearing Fenrir's request. They knew the young wolf would never break free this time, so none of them were willing to lose their sword hand. The discussion between the gods stopped when Týr, the only god who dared to feed and care for the wolf, volunteered. He approached Fenrir and calmly laid his hand in the giant wolf's mouth. Then, the other gods came to put the binding on, and once they were done, they quickly stepped away.

Tyr and Fenrir by Viktor Rydberg, 1911.
https://commons.wikimedia.org/wiki/File:Tyr_and_Fenrir-John_Bauer.jpg

Fenrir shook himself free to no avail. Again, he yanked and thrashed to break free, but the harder he tried, the tighter the binding held him. Knowing that his guess was true all along—the gods were indeed trying to trick him—he snapped his jaw close and bit Týr's right hand. None of the Æsir tried to help the wolf, and he lunged toward them, trying to attack. The gods laughed at the helpless wolf except for Týr, who just stared at him. It is unsure why Týr reacted the way he did when he saw Fenrir finally bound. Perhaps he really did care for the wolf since he was the one who had been feeding him ever since he was a cub. Perhaps he somehow knew that by deceiving and betraying Fenrir, they had sealed their own fates and were a step closer to the prophecy being fulfilled. Some sources even claim that if the gods had raised the wolf well without betraying him, perhaps Fenrir would have been on their side when Ragnarök came.

An illustration of the binding of Fenrir by Dorothy Hardy, 1909.
https://commons.wikimedia.org/wiki/File:Fenrir_binded.png

With the binding holding him tight, Fenrir could no longer move. And so, the gods took Gelgja, a chain that was said to be unbreakable, and attached it to the binding. They knew it would be dangerous to keep an angry wolf within their stronghold, so the gods dragged the poor wolf to a lonely and deserted island called Lyngvi. On the island, the unbreakable chain was tightly tied to a stone slab, and the gods later pounded it into the ground. Still refusing to give up, Fenrir struggled and tried to attack the gods nearby. Suddenly, one of the Æsir took a step closer to the wolf, and the god plunged his sword into the wolf's jaw to hold his mouth open.

Fenrir howled helplessly until his saliva flowed out of his huge mouth. From Fenrir's saliva came the cloudy river called Ván. Some believed that Fenrir's two children, Sköll and Hati, tried to break him free, but they failed terribly since the bindings were too strong. Fenrir was said to be held and bound on the isolated island with his mouth open until Ragnarök finally happened.

When Ragnarök occurred, the vicious wolf would finally break free from his long, painful binding, and he would run through the realms, devouring everything and everyone that stood in his way. His last stop would be the battlefield of Vígríðr (Vigrid), where he would wait for the god who had planned his binding. Although Fenrir was later killed by Odin's son, Vidar, the wolf did manage to fulfill his revenge by devouring the chief of the gods himself.

Chapter 14: Thor in the Land of the Giants

In return for a place to stay the night, Thor had sacrificed both of his goats and used them to prepare dinner. Although the peasant and his family were all free to share the meal with the gods, Thor had strictly warned them not to break any of the goats' bones as it would interfere with the resurrection process. Loki, however, successfully persuaded Thjalfi, the son of the peasant, to break one of the goat's bones and taste the marrow. The goats were resurrected the very next morning, but one of them appeared to be limping on one side.

After discovering this, Thor burst into anger. However, he felt pity for the peasants since he saw how miserable they were. So, the red-bearded god agreed not to do them any harm and only took the two siblings—Thjalfi and Röskva—in exchange for their wrongdoings. The brother and sister turned out to be his most loyal servants, accompanying him on a series of adventures. While little to nothing is mentioned about Röskva in the old poems, Thjalfi was said to be one of the swiftest among humans. He was fast on foot and could win many races. Thor tasked the young man to carry his wallet, which contained all the provisions and resources that the god needed during his travels.

And so, with the two young servants in tow, Thor and Loki continued their journey to the land of the giants. They left the chariot behind and headed out of the farmstead by foot. The four travelers headed east, where they had to sail across the great ocean and wade through dangerous rivers. Then, they continued their journey until they reached a thick forest. However, they were already losing light the moment they arrived at the forest since the sun was beginning to be replaced by the dim light of the moon.

"Let us rest," suggested the god of thunder after journeying from Midgard to Jötunheimr all day long.

Under the moonlight, the four travelers searched for a safe place for them to spend the night. One did not sleep in the open, especially when the land was said to be inhabited by barbaric giants. After wandering around the wild for quite some time, they came across a peculiar-looking hall. The building was massive, as was the entrance. The door was so broad that it spanned from one end to the other. Noticing that it was getting late, Thor and his companions entered the peculiar hall to get some rest.

While they were sound asleep, a loud, terrible noise woke the red-bearded god. It was midnight, and the sound got louder as the seconds passed by. Soon, the terrible noise was followed by an earthquake. The entire building shook, and it felt as if the walls were about to collapse soon. Sensing the danger, Thor leaped to his feet and shook his three companions out of their sleep until they finally realized what was going on.

"We must be on guard," said the thunder god. "Go find someplace safer!" They stumbled in the dark while the terrible noise and earthquakes continued. Then, they found themselves in front of another chamber; it was narrow and as dark as the forest outside.

Loki and the two young siblings scrambled inside and sat on the ground, their bodies trembling, terrified of what was going to happen next. Thor reassured his companions that they would remain safe as he walked to the doorway and stood guard all night long. Soon, the sun began to rise, and the sounds of birds chirping could be heard faintly. Thor rose and walked toward the broad entrance to investigate the source of the terrible noise and the earthquakes that terrorized them during the night.

As soon as Thor stepped outside, he was astonished when he saw a giant sleeping in the middle of the woods. "Finally!" he exclaimed under his breath while holding Mjölnir firmly in his hand. Ever since the start of the journey, Thor had been searching for a giant that he could kill, and he had finally found one.

The giant was still asleep when Thor suddenly heard something familiar; it was the giant's snoring that had made the terrible noise, and his snoring had also caused the earthquakes. The giant breathed out so strongly that even the largest of mountains shook. Ready to attack the sleeping giant, Thor slowly approached him with his hammer at the ready. Right before the red-bearded god could lift Mjölnir and strike the jötunn's skull, the enormous giant opened his eyes. He got on his feet as slow as a crippled old man and stared blankly at the lightning god. Unlike the other jötnar that the god had faced before, this particular one did not look threatening at all. In fact, he looked rather friendly.

And so, Thor lowered his hammer. He stood with his hands on the waist and asked for the giant's name. "Skrymir is what they call me," the giant responded. Just before Thor could proudly introduce himself, the giant cut in, "I know you! You're the mighty Thor of Asgard." Skrymir then turned to look to his side where his huge glove was. He then walked over and grabbed it but not before Loki and the two siblings scrambled out of it. This entire time, the travelers had been taking shelter inside of the giant's glove, and the chamber that they had stumbled upon during the earthquake was actually the thumb of the glove.

Illustration of Skrymir meeting the gods by Elmer Boyd Smith, 1902.
https://commons.wikimedia.org/wiki/File:I_am_the_giant_Skrymir_by_Elmer_Boyd_Smith.jpg

Having made acquaintance with all the travelers, the giant asked where they were headed to. Thor told him that they were on their way to Jötunheimr. Skrymir then offered to keep them company along the way, to which Thor agreed since he sensed no danger from the cheerful giant. Before starting their journey that day, Skrymir suddenly stopped the travelers, for he had noticed how heavy it was for the tiny beings to drag their bags.

"It'll be a long journey ahead. The least I can do is carry your provisions for you. Here, you can put them in my bag," the friendly giant offered. Since Thor did not have much food left, he agreed and handed his provisions to Skrymir. The giant then tied his bag and hoisted it across his body before walking toward the direction of Jötunheimr.

After an entire day of walking and trying to keep up with Skrymir's big steps, the travelers were exhausted and found an oak tree, which they lay under. The giant had requested some rest as well, saying that he needed a nap before they could continue the adventure. "You need some dinner," the giant said while putting his gigantic bag on the ground. "Go ahead and take your supplies," he said before walking toward a group of moss and bushes. Once the giant fell asleep, he would snore terribly.

Thor shook his head and walked over to the giant's bag to get himself and his companions some food. The god tried opening the huge bag, but the knot was so strong that Thor could only untangle it an inch. The short-fused god then tried again, using his might to unfasten the knot, but failed. His eyes were getting red, and his face tightened. He was growing immensely angry, as his attempts appeared to be futile. Thor was sure that the giant purposely did this so that his companions would see his failure. Loki was there, and everyone knew how the trickster loved to embarrass others.

Without hesitation, Thor fastened his belt of strength and grabbed his mighty hammer. He stomped his way over to the sleeping Skrymir. The god of thunder then swayed his hammer and struck the giant on the head. The blow was so hard that Mjölnir almost sank into the giant's skull. Skrymir, however, stopped snoring and slowly opened one of his eyes. He sat upright and looked around; the giant thought a leaf had fallen on his head. Thor, who was used to killing giants with only a single strike to their heads, was surprised by the giant's reaction. "Have you had your dinner, Thor?" Skrymir asked the stunned god. Ignoring the giant's question, Thor informed him that they were about to get some sleep below another tree nearby.

Illustration of Thor attacking Skrymir while he is sleeping by Ludwig von Maydell.
https://commons.wikimedia.org/wiki/File:Skr%C3%BDmir_by_Maydell.jpg

While the rest of his party slept, Thor kept his eyes open. He was puzzled by what had just happened. He was ashamed twice—once when he failed to untie the giant's bag of provisions and the second time when his strike went wrong. Finally able to brush his anger away, the lightning god tried to get some rest, but unfortunately, it only lasted until midnight. Skrymir's snoring echoed through the forest, and again, the ground shook. The god was furious, so he grabbed his hammer once again and stomped toward the giant.

Wishing to not repeat the same mistake again, Thor lifted Mjölnir higher. Doubling his strength, he laid a powerful hit right to Skrymir's skull. This time around, the giant woke up, startled. "Was that an acorn that fell on my head?" the giant asked under his breath. Again, he was startled when he saw Thor next to him. "Is everything okay, my friend? What are you doing here?" asked the giant, clueless.

Thor clenched his jaw and only said that he was going back to sleep. However, the god could not just let the giant go, especially when his powerful strike was thought to be an acorn that fell from the tree. So, he waited for Skrymir to fall back to sleep, and when he did, Thor struck another heavy blow with his mighty hammer. He laid a hit at the giant's temple until a thudding sound traveled through the dense wood. The god had been in many battles against giants before—there is even a statue of him today in Odense, Denmark, that depicts his fight—and not one of them ever survived his powerful hammer strike. So, Thor was sure that he had done it right this time and that Skrymir had met his fate.

However, to Thor's disappointment, Skrymir opened his eyes and gave his head a little scratch. "I suppose there are birds nesting on these trees, as I can feel their feathers falling on me." He then looked at Thor, who once again was standing beside him. "You don't sleep well at all, my friend," Skrymir said before he grabbed his huge bag and rose to his full height. "Come along now. We're almost there."

Once they were nearing the land of the giants, Skrymir turned to look at the god of thunder and gave him a piece of advice. He claimed that the giants within the stronghold—or Utgard as some preferred to call the land—were so much bigger and taller than himself. "So, keep your eyes open, and avoid expressing your pride," the friendly giant said before he left Thor and his companions and retraced his steps back into the dense forest. Thor, among all, felt relieved that the giant had left them, and he truly hoped that they never crossed paths again.

It was not until noon that the four travelers finally made it to the giant's stronghold. It was a massive city, and it had towering gates that kept unwanted outsiders from entering. Just as they expected, the gates were locked, and the padlocks were so huge that it was impossible for the god of thunder to break them open. However, the spaces between the bars were wide enough for the gods and the two young siblings to squeeze through. Thor thought this idea to be dishonorable, but he was left with no other choice. And so, they wriggled themselves between the bars and found themselves inside of Utgard. They made their way to the great hall, and once inside, they were surrounded by a company of enormous giants who were even taller than Skrymir and the other ones that Thor had met before.

Thor, remembering Skrymir's advice to keep his pride contained, walked over to the end of the hall where the king of the giants was calmly sitting on his throne. The red-bearded god was, of course, well known among the giants of Jötunheimr, which was why the giant king recognized him straight away. "So, you are the mighty Thor from Asgard?" He glanced at the god. "I have heard many stories of your might, but I was not expecting you to be so small." Thor only stared at him. "Come now! Let us see what you and your companions are made of. How about a few challenges?"

Loki stepped forward and boasted about his abilities; he claimed that he could devour food faster than any man alive, giants included. Some say that the trickster god was so hungry that this was his way of getting hot food served to him, while others suggest that Loki was trying to save his dignity and that of his companions. Nevertheless, the giant king, who went by the name of Utgarda-Loki, accepted the challenge and sent one of his kind to face the trickster. Loki's opponent was named Logi ("Fire"). In between the two was a huge trough of meat. The challenge was simple; the first person to devour the meat and reach the middle of the trough would win. And so, both Loki and Logi gobbled the meat as fast as they could, and they reached the middle at the same time. However, Logi earned the point since he had also devoured all the bones and the massive plate itself.

"Surely one of you could win something," Utgarda-Loki taunted the travelers once Loki lost. The next challenge was a race between Thjalfi and another being named Hugi ("Old"). They then went to the starting point outside of the hall. Although Thjalfi was said to be a swift runner, Hugi proved to be even faster than him, as once Hugi reached the finishing line, he was able to his steps about halfway to check on his opponent. The second time they raced, Thjalfi lost by a long shot, and he also lost the third one. Again, Utgarda-Loki laughed, but although Thjalfi had lost the race, Utgarda-Loki did say that he was the fastest human being he had ever seen.

Next, Thor was challenged to redeem his party's honor. He could not accept the fact that both Loki and Thjalfi had lost to the cynical giant king. Utgarda-Loki then asked Thor what he could do best so that he could prove his might. After all, every giant had been talking about him. The god of thunder told the giant king that he could drink mead better than everyone present in the hall. Looking at the size of the red-bearded god, Utgarda-Loki burst into loud laughter. "Very well," he said before ordering his servant to get a massive horn that the giants used to drink. "If you can finish the mead in a single breath, you will be hailed as a great drinker. If you can finish it in two, you're considered fair, but if you can't even finish the mead in three, then I have no words for you, mighty Thor."

Thor grabbed the horn and chugged the mead in a single breath, but when he stopped to look at how much he had drunk, only a tiny bit of the liquor had moved. The god, of course, refused to give up, so he drank it again with all his might this time. The level of liquor decreased noticeably, but there was still a lot left to be drunk. The thunder god took a huge, deep breath and chugged the mead again until he could no longer do so. He took a look at the horn, and while the mead had lowered even more than before, more than half of it was still left. Even though Thor was fueled with anger, he finally gave up.

Utgarda-Loki had another challenge in mind that was specially tailored for the mighty god. Thor was to lift the giant king's cat from the ground. The monstrous cat was immediately brought into the hall; it was gray in color and had eyes as yellow as the burning sun itself. Thor approached the hideous creature, and with all his strength, he tried to lift it off the ground. The harder the god tried to lift it, the stronger the cat arched its body, trying to stay on the ground. Thor again used his entire body to lift the mysteriously strong cat, and this time around, one of its paws lifted from the ground. However, that was all Thor could manage, as the cat's other three legs were still on the floor, as if they were glued.

The giant king was amused by the sight of Thor struggling so hard to lift a cat. "I suppose my cat is too heavy for you, god of thunder?"

Thor was moments away from reaching for Mjölnir, but he held himself from doing so. "If you giants are said to be so strong, come here and wrestle me!" the lighting god exclaimed.

"Wrestling is nothing but child's play, master Thor. None of my men would want to do that! But very well, I have someone in mind that could face you." Utgarda-Loki called upon his servant, Elli, whose name simply means "Age."

Thor felt insulted since Elli was a crippled old woman. Even her back was terribly bent, and wrinkles were everywhere on her face. When Elli first approached the god, Thor refused to wrestle her, claiming that he would never hurt a woman, let alone someone who was extremely old and incapable. However, the old woman kept on taunting the god, and the hall was filled with the giant's howl of how the mighty god was not at all worthy. And so, Thor lunged toward the old woman and tightly wrapped his thick arms around her crippled body in hopes of hearing her scream in pain. The woman, however, stood still without any emotion. Enraged, Thor tightened his grip even more so that her ribs would crack, but still, the old woman did not move.

When it was time for Elli to strike, only one attack was enough to drop the god of thunder to one of his knees. The old woman's arms were said to be as hard as a thick trunk of a tree. And so, Thor lost another challenge.

"That's enough for tonight. No more challenges," Utgarda-Loki said when the wrestling match ended. "Let us feast together. You and your companions can stay the night and make your journey back in the early morning." Even after all the insults, the giant king gave Thor and his companions the best he could offer.

The very next morning, the four travelers were ready to make their way back to Asgard. Utgarda-Loki led them out of the hall, and it was then that the giant king confessed his tricks. It was revealed that Skrymir, the giant that they had encountered in the woods, was, in fact, Utgarda-Loki himself. The giant king told the lightning god that his strength was almighty indeed, as the huge provision bag that he tried to open was magically wrought in iron. The fact that Thor had managed to open it by an inch was quite impressive. As for the hammer strikes that Thor had inflicted upon him, Utgarda-Loki explained that he successfully evaded all three of them; instead of his skull, the god had struck the mountain, and the blow had created three valleys. "Should I have failed to evade your powerful strikes, I might have already been dead," the giant king said.

The same thing went for the challenges that the travelers faced the night before. Utgarda-Loki had applied magic in all of them. Loki's performance in his challenge was remarkable since he was actually competing against fire itself, while Thjalfi was racing against thought, something that is impossible to outrun. As for Thor, the horn that he drank from was connected to the great ocean. "You lowered the tides right after you drunk from that horn," Utgarda-Loki explained. "About the cat, my mighty Thor, you were trying to lift the World Serpent itself." Even the giants were on the edge of their seats when they saw Thor lifting one of the cat's legs. Last but not least, the giants were astonished by how long the god had stood his ground during the wrestling match as, in reality, Thor was wrestling against old age.

"Now that you know the truth, I warn you to never come back to our land." The giant king looked at the thunder god in all seriousness. After learning about the tricks and illusions played by the giants, Thor's face reddened, and he was consumed by anger. He grabbed Mjölnir and was about to kill Utgarda-Loki and destroy his entire stronghold. However, the moment he turned back, the giant was nowhere to be seen, and his massive castle had disappeared. What was left were four travelers, who were angry and confused.

Chapter 15: Thor and Mjölnir

Mjölnir was a powerful weapon belonging to none other than Thor, the mighty protector of both Asgard and Midgard. With Mjölnir in his hand, the god of thunder had successfully defeated thousands of giants who wished to bring doom to his fellow gods without a single casualty. But the hammer was not only used for destruction and killing; the mighty god also needed it to resurrect his two magical goats.

Since Mjölnir was a weapon of power and acted as a divine instrument, it greatly helped the thunder god in almost all of his adventures across the realms. It was undoubtedly Thor's most prized possession, and he had Loki to thank for it. The hammer was originally forged by the dwarves, and it was Loki who had requested it. It all started when the trickster pulled a prank on Thor's wife, Sif—he had cut off the goddess's golden hair, resulting in Thor threatening to break every single bone in his body should he fail to return his wife's glorious beauty.

Upon traveling to Svartalfheim, Loki managed to get the sons of Ivaldi to forge a golden headpiece for Sif. However, that was not the only thing that he obtained from the dwarves, as he had also asked for the spear named Gungnir and the ship called *Skidbladnir*. The trickster wished to give them to the gods, and the dwarves agreed to make them and let him return to Asgard with all three magical treasures. However, before Loki left the realm of the dwarves, he again came up with yet another one of his mischievous plans. He decided to stop by the hall of Brokk and Eitri, two other master smiths and rivals to the sons of Ivaldi.

Upon arriving at the entrance of the great hall, the two dwarves quickly rose to their feet and approached the trickster. They noticed the three items that Loki had in his possession, and they quickly grew irritated since they knew the items were all forged by their rivals. Noticing the unpleasant reaction of the two siblings, Loki grinned and began taunting them. "What do you think of the craftsmanship of these items?" the sly god asked. "Have you seen any greater work?"

"Of course. Ours are better. The best even!" Brokk responded.

"So, you think you can come up with things even finer than these?" the trickster questioned. The dwarves gave him a look and continued to bluntly boast about their exquisite smithing skills.

"Then, how about a wager? Forge me three items finer than these, and my head is yours," Loki said, placing a stake that was high enough to lead the dwarves to agree right away. And so, the two siblings began hauling the resources needed for their crafts while Loki sat behind with a horn full of mead to quench his thirst. The master smiths had strictly ordered the god to do nothing except sit around and wait for them to be done with their fine crafts.

Not long after that, the air was immediately filled with smoke coming out of the furnace, for Brokk had thrown dozens of pieces of wood in it. Eitri, on the other hand, was working on a roll of gold wire before he moved to the pigskin. Brokk then began pumping the bellows, and Eitri warned him to never stop until he returned or else the item would not turn out as perfect as they had planned. The god of mischief overheard this, and he immediately transformed himself into a fly. In his new form, he flew onto Brokk's rough hand and stung him. The dwarf, however, was so focused on pumping the bellows that he did not even notice the bite. Soon, Eitri returned, and with a pair of iron tongs, he took the newly crafted treasure out of the burning forge; this was Gullinbursti, a golden boar with the ability to run across the air and the sea.

Next, the dwarves worked on an exquisite block of gold. Again, Eitri told Brokk to keep pumping until he returned. Loki overheard Eitri's warning too, so once again, he turned into a fly. This time around, he flew onto Brokk's sweaty neck, and he stung him twice as hard. The dwarf felt the sting this time, and he flinched, but his hands kept on pumping the bellows. The moments passed by, and Eitri finally returned. He pulled the gold out of the furnace, and it became Draupnir, a golden ring that could multiply itself into eight more rings of the same weight every ninth night.

Last but not least, the dwarves worked on a great pile of heavy iron. They threw it into the furnace, took it out, hammered it into shape, and carved its side. Then, just as before, Brokk was tasked to pump the bellows until Eitri returned. "We cannot risk damaging this one, for it is impossible to repair it!" he exclaimed before leaving Brokk to his task. Of course, hearing how serious Eitri was, Loki turned into a fly again and landed in between Brokk's eyes. He stung him with all his might until a stream of blood came running down the dwarf's broad forehead and into his eyes. Brokk let go of the bellows just for a quick second so that he could wipe off the blood that had hindered his sight, but the damage had already been done. Eitri came running to the furnace, and as he took the last item out, he could not help but shake his head in disappointment. This was the mighty hammer, Mjölnir, and the defect could be seen on its handle; it was rather short, but its power was still magnificent. One could throw the hammer in different directions, and it would always come back.

Seeing that only the handle was affected, the two siblings were relieved. With faces full of pride, they handed the three magical items to Loki. "Let us travel to Asgard and see whose craftsmanship is better, shall we?" boasted Brokk.

Upon arriving in Asgard, Loki and Brokk went straight into the hall where the gods had gathered. Loki presented the first three items; he gave the golden hair to Sif, gifted the powerful spear to the All-Father, and the magical ship to Freyr. Next, Brokk stepped forward and presented his and Eitri's three other crafts; the golden boar was given to Freyr, while the ring of Draupnir was gifted to the All-Father. Last but not least, Brokk presented Mjölnir to the thunder god. Thor lifted the heavy hammer and marveled at its exquisite craftsmanship. All the gods in the hall were impressed and astounded by its devastating power to the point they did not even care about its minor defect, the weirdly short handle.

With all of the gifts presented, the three gods then exchanged looks with each other and right away agreed that Mjölnir was the finest piece of work that they had ever laid eyes on. "It seems like you owe the dwarf your head, Loki," the All-Father said. Finally realizing that his stake was, indeed, too high, Loki disappeared from the hall in an attempt to escape from his own wager.

Thor was indebted to Brokk for honoring him with such a great weapon, so he immediately sprung to his feet and chased after the trickster. Only a few moments were all it took before the thunder god returned to the hall, dragging Loki behind him.

"Wait!" exclaimed the trickster. "I did bet on my head but not my neck!"

Brokk looked at him, irritated that the trickster had once again got the better of him. "Fine. Then, I would like to sew your lips, Loki. So, you can stop promising false hopes!"

Loki ended up with his lips tightly sewn by the dwarf, but it was only for a short while. When Brokk left, the mischievous god ran out of the great hall and yanked the leather threads out of his lips.

Ever since Thor was gifted with Mjölnir, he almost never set out on a journey without it. Even the gods rarely saw him walking around without his mighty weapon hanging from his waist. While the gods treasured Mjölnir since it greatly helped Thor protect their city from all sorts of threats, the same could not be said of the giants; the hammer was well known among the jötnar but only because many of their kind had been killed by it. Few of them would even dare to go near the thunder god's prized weapon, let alone steal it—except for one.

On one fine morning, Asgard was shocked by yet another temper tantrum thrown by the red-bearded god. Thor had woken up to his hammer missing. He searched his entire massive hall, barging in through one door and the next, but Mjölnir was nowhere to be found. The more time passed, the angrier the god became, and suddenly, someone came to his mind: Loki. "Who else could have pulled such a horrible prank?" Thor thought. And so, he yelled the trickster's name as loud as he could until the grumbling sounds of thunder could be heard by those who were down in Midgard.

The mighty god left his hall and went to see the trickster. "What happened, Thor?" Loki asked. For once, he looked clueless. The thunder god fiercely explained that his hammer was missing and pointed his finger at the trickster, for he was convinced that Loki was behind this mischief. "Not this time," Loki responded. "But I think I know who has your prized hammer. But first, let us visit Freyja in her hall."

The two gods then met Freyja in her massive hall, where Loki requested to borrow her magical coat of feathers. Upon learning what had happened, the goddess handed the coat to Loki without further questions. Using the magical coat, Loki transformed into a hawk, and he began his journey to the cold, misty land of the giants.

Once Loki arrived in Jötunheimr, he circled the skies in search of the culprit. A few moments later, he caught sight of a huge frost giant sitting on a burial mound, tending to his many dogs and horses. The giant was known by the name Thrym.

"Why have you come to this cold land of ours?" Thrym asked as soon as he saw Loki approaching him with such haste. When the trickster questioned him about Mjölnir, the giant laughed and admitted that he was the one who stole it. "I've hidden it eight miles underneath the ground so that it could never be found again by the likes of you," said the giant.

"Everyone has a price, Thrym. Name yours, and I shall see to it."

The frost giant gave Loki a grin. "The most beautiful goddess in Asgard," he answered slyly. "I want Freyja's hand in marriage, and in exchange, I'll return the hammer to its owner."

Shortly after, Loki returned to the fortified city of the gods bearing the bad news of Mjölnir's whereabouts. The news caused Thor to burst into rage. He was not at all pleased that a giant had managed to steal his treasured hammer. The thunder god then turned to Freyja and insisted that she get changed into a wedding dress right away. "If Freyja is who the giant wants, then so be it!" he rudely exclaimed.

The goddess responded with a snort. "How atrocious!" It turns out that Thor was not the only one in anger, as the hall began to shake as Freyja fiercely objected to the idea. Since no better solution could come out of the two enraged gods, they decided to hold a council where they would discuss the matter with the other gods of Asgard.

"I've got an idea," Heimdall, the shining god, said, stepping forward. He suggested that they play along with the giant's request, except that Freyja would not be the one to go to Jötunheimr. Instead of the beautiful goddess, he asked Thor to put on the wedding dress. The red-bearded god, of course, strongly disagreed with Heimdall's absurd suggestion. It was not at all manly for a strong god such as himself to put on a woman's dress.

"Well, do you have other ideas, Thor? Thrym is a tough enemy, even for you. I don't suppose you would like to face him without your mighty hammer?" Thor went silent, but he was still uncertain of the idea.

"Wear my necklace. This ought to convince the giant that I'm the one under the wedding veil," Freyja said.

"And I'll accompany you," Loki said, volunteering to disguise himself as Thor's handmaiden.

The god Thor dressed as Freyja by Elmer Boyd Smith, 1902.
https://commons.wikimedia.org/wiki/File:Ah,_what_a_lovely_maid_it_is!_by_Elmer_Boyd_Smith.jpg

With the plan set, the two gods then went to change. Loki happily put on a dress, while Thor unwillingly let Freyja and her maids dress him. The wedding gown was beautifully bedazzled with precious stones and gems. On his waist was a dangling set of keys, and on his finger, he wore an exquisite ring. On his neck was Freyja's brilliant necklace, the Brísingamen. While Loki could easily pass as the handmaiden, Thor's disguise was not at all convincing, especially with his bulky torso and fierce eyes—not even the finest veil could conceal his vengeful face. Nevertheless, after the makeover, the red-bearded god and his handmaiden, Loki, set on a journey to Jötunheimr, riding Thor's chariot of magical goats.

Once Thrym heard the news that his soon-to-be-wife was nearing his hall, the eager giant quickly ordered his servants to prepare for the wedding. The frost giant welcomed the two gods in disguise with a grand feast. Once his honored guests were seated, he began boasting about his wealth and strength. He claimed that he already possessed everything in the world now that he had Freyja as his wife. But when the food was served, the giant was surprised to see his bride's unusual appetite. Even dressed in a tight wedding gown, Thor devoured a whole ox, eight salmon, the entire wedding cake, and three full casks of mead.

Loki, who was scared that the giant might somehow get suspicious, came up with an excuse for Thor's barbaric behavior. "Forgive Mistress Freyja, my mighty Thrym. Your bride was so eager to see you that she had not eaten in eight days!" The giant told Loki that he had never seen such an appetite in a woman before, but he was, indeed, impressed.

Loki was relieved that the giant was not suspicious of his bride, but the trickster had to think fast again when the giant suddenly approached Thor for a kiss. Upon getting closer to his bride's face, the giant was startled when he saw two fierce eyes glaring at him angrily under the veil.

"Forgive my mistress, mighty Thrym." Loki immediately rose to his feet. "Your bride was so excited to wed you that she refused to sleep for eight nights in a row! You, out of anyone else in this hall, should know what extreme tiredness can do to your eyes." Thrym was still shocked, but he quickly brushed it off.

Thor Destroys the Giant Thrym *by Lorenz Frølich, 1906.*
https://commons.wikimedia.org/wiki/File:Thor_Destroys_the_Giant_Thrym.jpg

Later on, Thrym's elder sister entered the hall and stood before Thor. She asked for a bridal gift, which was a fee the bride and her family must pay to the man she was to marry. "Take off that golden ring of yours, and hand it to me," the giantess rudely commanded. At the same time, Thrym summoned his servants to bring in Mjölnir. He then put the heavy hammer on his bride's lap in an act to consecrate the wedding.

With his prized weapon back in his reach again, Thor's eyes lit up, and he immediately grabbed it by its short pommel. The red-bearded god broke his character as a bride, and he bashed Thrym's skull with his hammer until the giant's enormous body thudded on the floor, lifeless. His next target was the giantess who dared to ask for the golden ring. Instead of a bridal fee, Thor gifted her with a deadly blow right in her head. With his gown ripped, the god continued to destroy every giant in the great hall.

When Thrym's hall was wiped clean, the two gods returned to Asgard. Not a single giant ever dared to repeat Thrym's mistake, and Thor never let Mjölnir out of his sight again. Later on, the thunder god would unleash all of Mjölnir's power when he battled the World Serpent during Ragnarök. And when he finally died from Jörmungandr's venom, Mjölnir was said to pass down to his sons, Magni and Modi.

Since Mjölnir was considered the mightiest weapon in Norse mythology, the hammer has become a symbol of strength and power. Some even suggest that Mjölnir has religious meanings behind it, as its symbols were often found on graves of fallen warriors who had fought on the battlefield.

An illustration of a Mjölnir pendant.
https://commons.wikimedia.org/wiki/File:Mjollnir.png

During the Middle Ages, the Vikings—especially those who openly worshiped Thor—would often be seen wearing an amulet with a pendant in the shape of Mjölnir. Some even believed that those who wore the pendant would receive Thor's mighty protection and that they would remain safe from all life-endangering threats.

Chapter 16: Baldur's Death and Loki's Binding

"I saw for Baldr, | the bleeding god,
  The son of Othin, | his destiny set:
  Famous and fair | in the lofty fields,
  Full grown in strength | the mistletoe stood."
(*Völuspá*, Stanza 32, translated by Henry Adams Bellows)

The son of Odin always walked around the fortified city wearing a beautiful smile. Baldur was always known to radiate joy, and his gentle way of interacting with every being in the world made him a special god. However, one day, the Æsir noticed something different about the shining god; his face was gloomy, and the light shining out of him was dim. And so, the gods began to question his unusual behavior. Unable to hold it in any longer, Baldur informed them that he had been plagued by an ominous dream. "It feels as if my life is in danger," said the shining god.

The gods knew that they must protect Baldur at any cost. Not only because he was loved by many but also because of the prophecy; Baldur's death was an early sign of Ragnarök. Since none of the Æsir could interpret his dream, they chose Odin to discover the meaning behind it.

Without wasting any more time, the All-Father mounted his eight-legged steed and galloped to the realm of the dead. Once he arrived, Odin discovered that one of the halls in the realm was being prepared lavishly, as if the underworld was about to receive an honorable guest. Assuming one of his many disguises, the one-eyed god summoned a dead seeress to answer his questions.

"This hall, who is it for?" the All-Father asked.

An illustration of the invincible Baldur by Elmer Boyd Smith, 1902.
https://commons.wikimedia.org/wiki/File:Each_arrow_overshot_his_head_by_Elmer_Boyd_Smith.jpg

"With only the best mead served on the table and the finest throne prepared, surely it is for Baldur!" The seeress replied and then continued to tell the disguised Odin all about the events that were yet to happen: Baldur's death, his killer, and the person who would avenge his death. However, she abruptly stopped talking the moment she discovered that the person in front of her was the All-Father himself.

Now that he knew the meaning behind Baldur's premonition, the one-eyed god hurried to Asgard with a heavy heart. The other gods of Asgard were disheartened upon learning about Odin's discovery. One day, Frigg dispatched her many messengers across the realm to gather oaths from everyone and everything that they would never harm her treasured son. Once the messengers returned with the oaths, the gods gathered around and amused themselves with Baldur's new immunity.

Taking turns, the Æsir would grab anything that they could—from stones to sticks, knives, and spears—and throw them toward the shining god. Since everything and everyone had sworn an oath to never harm him, Baldur remained unscathed no matter what items and weapons were thrown at him.

Witnessing this, Loki grew irritated. "What is so special about Baldur that makes him earn such immunity?" he thought to himself. And so, he came up with another one of his schemes.

The trickster transformed into an old lady and went to see Frigg. At first, he asked the goddess why the gods were laughing in the hall. Next, he asked if the goddess really did obtain oaths from everything and everyone in all nine realms. "Why, yes," Frigg answered, having no clue who she was talking to. "Except for the mistletoe. I didn't think it could do any harm to my son, so I never asked it to swear an oath." Loki's eyes glimmered, for he had gotten the answer he was looking for.

Quickly, the trickster went to the woods and searched for mistletoe. Once he had gathered enough, Loki created a spear out of it. With a sinister grin carved on his face, the sly god returned to Asgard and approached Baldur's blind brother, Hodr.

"Do you feel left out, Hodr?" Loki asked the blind god.

"Well, there's nothing I can do, Loki. I can't even see, let alone aim at anything."

The trickster then handed Hodr the mistletoe spear that he had crafted. "Take this. I'll guide your arm so that you'll hit your mark. This way, you'll get to honor the strength of your brother."

It did not take long until the laughter was replaced by complete silence. The mistletoe spear thrown by Hodr and guided by Loki flew straight into the shining god's chest. The wound was so deep that Baldur immediately dropped dead to the ground.

Baldur's death was expected, but none would have thought that it would be this soon. They had lost their beloved god, and they had set Ragnarök in motion. Instead of dying bravely in battle, the shining god had died without a fight, which earned him a place in the bleak lands of Helheim. Hodr, on the other hand, was killed by another one of Odin's sons, Váli (not to be confused with Loki's son, who was also named Váli in some sources)—just as the seeress had foreseen. It was believed that Váli avenged Baldur when he was just a day old.

With a heavy heart, the gods prepared a funeral for their beloved god. They turned Baldur's ship, *Hringhorni*, into a pyre and laid his remains on it. The funeral began with a procession; in front was Freyr in his chariot pulled by Gullinbursti, his golden boar. Behind him were the Valkyries, who escorted the All-Father and his wife. Heimdall followed on his horse while Freyja rode on her chariot. At the back was Thor, who was on foot, ready to consecrate the pyre.

When it was time to launch *Hringhorni* to the sea, the gods had a hard time since the ship was so massive that it would not budge. The Æsir were forced to summon a giantess named Hyrrokkin to help them. The giantess, however, had pushed the ship a little too hard, causing the world to shake. This angered Thor, but Odin stopped him from reaching for his hammer and killing the giantess.

Nanna could not bear to watch her husband lying lifeless on the ship, and her heart stopped beating all of a sudden. The gods carried her body and laid her remains right by her husband's body. Odin then removed his treasured ring, Draupnir, and placed it on the pyre before whispering into his dead son's ears—what the All-Father said before sending his son to the underworld remains unknown.

Odin's Last Words to Baldr by W. G. Collingwood, 1908.
https://commons.wikimedia.org/wiki/File:Odin%27s_last_words_to_Baldr.jpg

Although Baldur was safely delivered to the realm of Helheim, Frigg was almost certain that she could resurrect her son. And so, she sent Hermod to the underworld, where he bargained with the mistress of the dead. Hel agreed to release Baldur and his wife back to the land of the living if everyone wept for his death.

So, messengers were again sent across the realms to make sure everyone in the universe shed at least a single tear for the shining god. Hel's condition was almost fulfilled, but it was ruined by the giantess named Thökk. She coldly refused to weep for Baldur's death. It was hard to believe that there was someone who hated the fair god—unless the stubborn giantess was none other than Loki in disguise.

The death of the beloved god was not something that the Æsir could forget. They grieved and fed themselves with nothing but sorrow for days. But when the sadness slowly went away, the gods decided to hold a feast in Ægir's glimmering hall beneath the rolling waves, perhaps to lighten the mood after going through a devastating incident. With the five-mile-deep cauldron that Thor and Týr had brought to him, Ægir agreed to host the feast, and he was able to brew the gods an endless supply of mead.

Loki fighting with the gods by Lorenz Frølich, 1895.
https://commons.wikimedia.org/wiki/File:Lokasenna_by_Lorenz_Fr%C3%B8lich.jpg

Almost all the gods of Asgard left their seats that day and journeyed to Ægir's hall, except for Thor, who was on his usual adventure in Jötunheimr. Odin and Frigg left their halls first, followed by Vidar, Sif, Idun, and her husband, Bragi. Then, Njord followed, along with his children, Freyr and Freyja. However, the feast was not attended only by the gods, as the elves also took their seats on the bench. Even Loki was there, with his mind full of trouble and mischief.

Soon, the feast began, and the air was filled with laughter and chatter. The guests' drinking horns were never empty, and they were served by two diligent servers: Fimafengr the Swift Handler and Eldir the Man of Fire. They moved around the hall at great speed and entertained the guests to the fullest, making sure their plates and cups were full.

The gods were so impressed by the two servers' hard work and diligence that they kept on praising them. Loki, however, was irritated that everyone loved them. His face reddened each time another compliment went through his ears. He eyed one of the servers, Fimafengr, and when he walked past Loki, the trickster lunged forward and stabbed the server to death with his knife.

The laughter was immediately replaced with a loud uproar as the server thudded on the floor with a rush of blood flowing out. The gods sprang to their feet and unsheathed their swords. Without hesitation, they chased Loki out of the hall, and the trickster ran straight into the dark forest, saving his own life in the process. When they could no longer spot the mischievous god's shadow anywhere nearby, the gods returned to Ægir's vast hall and resumed their banquet. More mead was poured, and again, the hall was filled with great laughter and conversations.

Not long afterward, the son of Laufey emerged from the dark wilderness and walked toward the hall. Loki stopped the other server, Eldir, by the door and rudely interrupted his work. "What was that noise all about?" the trickster asked. "Tell me, Eldir, what are the gods talking about in there?"

The server told him the truth. "They were comparing their strength and weapons and sharing stories of their greatest victories. That's all. You won't find any good words about you in there."

Loki's face contorted into a sinister expression. He shoved the server aside and made his way back into the hall. He stood in the doorway as if he had done nothing wrong. The gods and the elves sitting on the bench greeted the son of Laufey with complete silence.

"Can someone at least bring me an ale? I've been on the road for quite some time." None of the gods responded to him except for Bragi.

"Go, now, Loki, as the gods do not welcome you here."

Ignoring the god, Loki turned to the All-Father. "High One, are we not blood-brothers? And did we not swear oaths that we would never drink without the other? I don't suppose you're planning to sever our sacred bond."

Odin frowned and turned to his son, Vidar. "Give some space for him to sit, Vidar, before he unleashes more trouble upon us." Odin's son rose and handed the trickster a horn of mead. Loki then climbed on the table and shouted out a toast. "Hail, Æsir! Hail, Ásynjur! Except for Bragi, who knows nothing of hospitality!"

Bragi tried to persuade the trickster to stop causing more trouble. He offered him gifts of a horse, golden rings, and a sword if Loki agreed to return to his seat and refrain from spitting nonsense. The trickster, however, responded by throwing insults at Bragi's face. He accused the god of being a coward.

Loki Taunts Bragi by W. G. Collingwood, 1908.
https://commons.wikimedia.org/wiki/File:Loki_taunts_Bragi.jpg

Bragi was, of course, on the verge of losing his patience as the son of Laufey kept on insulting him. "Stay in your seat, Bragi," his wife, Idun, said, trying to calm him. "Think of our family's honor."

"Silence, Idun!" Loki pointed his finger to the goddess of youth. "You are no better than your husband either. Everyone in this very hall knows your craving for sex! You even laid in bed with your brother's murderer!" Not a word came out of the goddess's mouth. The silence in the hall was obvious, but Loki was not planning to stop his antics anytime soon. He continued insulting each one of the gods present at the feast.

His next victims were the two goddesses of fertility, Gefjun (also spelled as Gefjon) and Frigg. Loki pointed his finger and accused the two of infidelity. "You, Frigg, are a woman of no shame. I know this since you slept with both your husband's brothers while he was gone!"

Freyja sprang to her feet and warned the trickster to be careful of his tongue. "Watch your words, Loki! Frigg knows all the things that are yet to happen, although she would never reveal them!"

The trickster ignored Freyja's warning. "Silence, Freyja! For you are nothing but a prostitute. You have laid in bed with every god, as well as elves and even dwarves from underneath the mountains!"

None of the gods could escape Loki's sharp tongue, and none could stop him from his antics—except for the thunder god who had just arrived from his long journey from Jötunheimr. Thor, with Mjölnir held tight in his grasp, fiercely approached the loud trickster. "Leave, or I'll use my might to smash your skull into a hundred pieces!" the red-bearded god threatened him.

It took Loki four death threats from the thunder god until he finally left the feast. "Very well, Thor. I'll take my leave because of you, for I am aware of what you are capable of." He then took a final look at the gods in the hall. "You will never have a feast as fine as this after tonight. Soon, fire will engulf every one of you, and everything you've built will be destroyed."

The gods were speechless, and they could no longer tolerate the trickster's schemes. Some said that while he was taunting Frigg, Loki accidentally spilled the beans about his role in Baldur's death. And so, the gods decided to put an end to the trickster's antics.

Loki never returned to Asgard after the feast at Ægir's hall. He knew the Æsir would hunt him down sooner or later, so he took refuge in the untamed lands of Jötunheimr. He dwelled within a humble house on top of a mountain. This house was made out of stones, and it had four doors so that the trickster could always see if someone was breaking in.

During the day, the god of mischief would turn himself into a salmon, and he blended in with the other fish underneath a hidden waterfall. Terrified that the gods might discover his disguise, Loki spent his nights inventing tools that he thought the gods might create to catch him. One night, as he was sitting by his campfire, the trickster weaved a fishing net; the twines were finely twisted together so that not even the smallest fish could swim through. And so, the trickster began to ponder a way of an escape should the gods ever use it against him.

Suddenly, the anxious god was disturbed by a noise coming from a distance. He knew that it came from the gods; the All-Father must have finally discovered his hiding spot from the high seat, Hlidskjalf (Hliðskjálf). Panicked, Loki threw the fishing net into the flames, and he quickly transformed into a salmon before jumping into the cold stream.

Kvasir, the wise god, barged into his four-door house and came across the half-burned fishing net. Because of Loki's own carelessness, the gods knew what they must create to hunt him down. And so, the Æsir built another net, as fine as the one Loki had created, and cast it into the stream. The trickster, however, managed to evade their trap. The Æsir cast their net several more times, but they failed to catch the salmon.

At last, Thor lost his patience. He left the net behind and waded his way into the middle of the stream. Loki decided to escape to the open sea, so he made a bold leap. However, he could not escape his fate, as Thor managed to grab him by his tail while he was in the air.

The gods were not permitted to kill the troublemaker since he was a sworn blood-brother to Odin. So, instead, the gods took him to an isolated cave. Then, they dragged in three huge stone slabs and drilled a hole in each one. Before they exacted their revenge on Loki, they brought in his two sons. One of the gods turned Váli into a wolf, and as he went berserk, the wolf ripped his brother, Narfi, apart. The gods disemboweled the slain Narfi. Using his bloody entrails, the Æsir tied Loki to the three stone slabs. To make sure the trickster suffered even more, the gods turned his bindings into rigid iron.

Skadi, the daughter of the giant Thjazi, recalled that Loki had once played a role in her father's murder, so she placed a snake above the trickster's face. This snake would then drip its venom into his eyes. But Loki's wife was as faithful as ever—she stayed by her husband's side, holding up a bowl so that the venom would not touch Loki's eyes and skin. However, as time passed, the bowl would fill up to the rim, and Sigyn was left with no choice but to empty it. And every time she stepped away, the venom would drip into Loki's eyes, and he would scream in pain, causing terrible earthquakes that could be felt by the entire universe.

It was only when Ragnarök approached that Loki would break free from his punishment. Until then, he would remain in the cave, bound and in pain.

Chapter 17: Ragnarök

"The sun turns black, | earth sinks in the sea,
  The hot stars down | from heaven are whirled;
  Fierce grows the steam | and the life-feeding flame,
  Till fire leaps high | above heaven itself."
(*Völuspá*, Stanza 57, translated by Henry Adams Bellows)

The lands were fully covered in snow. The wind kept on blowing from all directions, causing the temperature to drop each second. The warmth of the sun could no longer reach the earth. No plants could survive the weather, nor could the strongest animals. Peasants, noblemen, heroes, kings, and queens stayed in their dwellings, shivering and scared of what would happen next. Another year passed by, and not even the slightest warmth could be felt. Winter had taken over the world, leaving no space for summer to bloom again. Eventually, three years had passed, and the world was still snowing.

Soon, humans began to fight each other. Wars kept on raging on the cold battlefield. Day and night, the sounds of axes, swords, and spears clashing onto iron shields echoed throughout the plains. Food supplies deteriorated, resources could no longer be gathered, and the weather only grew worse. Humans became desperate. Their morale plummeted, and justice no longer existed. Fathers killed their sons just so they could get enough food. Men slaughtered their own mothers, and brothers would slay each other just so they could survive another day.

This was neither a normal winter nor climate change. This was known as Fimbulwinter; it lasted for three years straight, with no summer. It was also one of the signs that Ragnarök was just around the corner.

The Old Norse word Ragnarök had more than one translation. Some translate the word as the "Twilight of the Gods," while others call it the "Fate of the Gods." But no matter the translation, the events that were to happen during this time remained the same. The gods of Asgard would finally battle the forces of chaos led by Loki, and the world would perish, leaving behind only blood and ashes.

The Norns had already determined the fate of all beings, including the mighty gods in Asgard, and there was no way to avoid it. The All-Father was well aware of this, so he did everything that he could to at least delay the cataclysmic destruction. He had traveled the world in search of knowledge, summoned the soul of a dead seeress to tell him about future events, formed his own brave army, and imprisoned those who were said to be a part of the forces of chaos, including his blood-brother Loki. When Baldur died, Odin knew they were all a step closer to Ragnarök, but when the strong winter came and lasted for three years without rest, the All-Father began to be shrouded by fear since he knew what would happen next.

To alert the gods in Asgard of the beginning of the war, a rooster called Gullinkambi would crow until it echoed throughout every room in Valhalla. Upon hearing this, the einherjar would quickly prepare themselves for battle. Another rooster named Fjalar would also crow in the untamed land of Jötunheimr to signal the start of the war to the giants. Unlike the gods, the giants smiled when they heard this signal. In Hel, the dishonorable dead would also get ready the moment the third unnamed rooster crowed. This time, Hel's bloody hound would bark ferociously outside of Gnipa Cavern, knowing that he would soon be free from his fetters.

The gods continued to sit restlessly on their thrones as the world turned dark. Sköll and Hati had been chasing Sol and Mani ever since the beginning of time. The wolves had never succeeded in devouring them, but it would be different this time around. Sköll would finally catch up with the chariot carrying Sol, resulting in him devouring the sun, while Hati would eagerly swallow the moon. The stars, too, would vanish from the open skies, leaving the heavens with only darkness and emptiness.

Then, it was time for the dwarves underneath the ground to leave their dwellings, for the earth started to shake terribly. The lands on every corner of the world trembled so hard that even the World Tree, Yggdrasil, could no longer stand. As the mighty ash tree tumbled to the ground, so did the other trees in the universe. Mountains would then split into two, and boulders cracked into a million pieces.

Because of the earthquake, Fenrir managed to break free from his bindings. The wolf was once raised in Asgard, but he had been betrayed by the gods when he grew too large. So, Fenrir wished for nothing except vengeance. Finally free from Gleipnir, the giant wolf ran across the realm with his jaws open wide, devouring everything that stood in his way.

At the same time, another one of Loki's monstrous offspring, Jörmungandr, let go of his own tail that encircled Midgard. The enormous serpent then rose from the bottomless sea, causing horrendous waves and a great flood, which washed over the world of men. While the World Serpent headed toward Asgard, he would spit venom along the way that could kill anything, even the gods.

While the flood brought terror to the humans, it was an opportunity for the ship called *Naglfar* to set sail. This massive ship was made out of the nails of the dead and was built by the queen of Helheim herself. Loki, who had also broken from his bindings, would be the one steering the ship through the flood. On board *Naglfar* were thousands of giants and the armies of the dead. They were all ready to taste the blood of the gods. And in the sky, an eagle would hover around and shriek to signal that the battle was nearing.

"The Giant with the Flaming Sword" by John Charles Dollman, published in 1909.
https://commons.wikimedia.org/wiki/File:The_giant_with_the_flaming_sword_by_Dollman.jpg

As the earth kept on trembling and as the trees were uprooted from the ground, the empty sky split open. Through this opening, a hoard of fire giants from Muspelheim poured into the world below. They were led by none other than Surtr, who trampled the world while swinging his blazing sword. The fire giants burned everything on the earth and turned the already destroyed lands into nothing but ashes. Surtr and his minions then marched across Bifröst, and their trails of fire caused the rainbow bridge to slowly collapse. When the blazing giants were halfway to Asgard, the frost giants led by a jötunn named Hrym, resurfaced and crossed the icy rivers, heading in the direction of the fortified city.

Heimdall, who spotted the sons of Muspelheim from afar, immediately blew Gjallarhorn to signal the gods of Asgard. Every single god in the city then gathered around for one last council except for the All-Father. Odin instead mounted his eight-legged steed and headed toward the direction of Mímisbrunnr. Once he arrived, the one-eyed god approached the wise being and sought his counsel. "There is only one ending to this destruction, and you know it," Mimir spoke. "It is high time for you to greet your fate."

And so, it began—Odin armed himself with his mighty spear and put on a shiny coat of mail and his golden-winged helmet. He then returned to Valhalla, where he prepared his brave warriors, the einherjar. The All-Father and the other warrior gods of Asgard marched to Vigrid, the empty plain where the battle would take place. Odin stood in front of the einherjar, with one of his hands wrapped tightly around Gungnir. They were, of course, outnumbered by the giants, but they firmly stood their ground. Among the giants, only one creature could turn the All-Father pale, and it was none other than his fated enemy, Fenrir.

The giant wolf stepped forward to face the one-eyed god. His menacing growl could be heard from across the battlefield. Thor, on the other hand, began to strike the World Serpent with his hammer. The god of thunder went berserk, but so did Jörmungandr, who had been waiting a long time to kill his enemy. The battlefield of Vigrid continued to tremble, as Freyr faced the lord of Muspelheim, Surtr. The Vanir god, however, was not all that determined to battle his foe since he was missing his treasured sword. If he had not given up the sword to Skírnr, his fate might have been different. Týr, the one-handed god, was also busy on the battlefield; he was fending off the bloody hound from Helheim, Garmr, who was trying to bite off his other hand. At the other end of the battlefield was Heimdall. He clashed swords with the vengeful god of mischief, Loki.

The war went on for a long time. Both the gods and the forces of chaos continued to spill each other's blood. The einherjar fought valiantly by Odin's side, but none could rescue the All-Father from his fate, for he was destined to be swallowed whole by the giant wolf. Fenrir finally got his vengeance, and he snapped his jaws shut. He howled to mark his victory, but it was cut short when Odin's son, Vidar, charged at him with eyes filled with fire. The silent god then lunged toward the giant wolf and stepped on his lower jaw with his iron-clad shoe. With his bare hands, the god ripped Fenrir's jaw open, killing him instantly.

Thor and the Midgard Serpent *by Emil Doepler, 1905.*
https://commons.wikimedia.org/wiki/File:Thor_und_die_Midgardsschlange.jpg

On one side of the battlefield, Thor could be seen lifting Mjölnir up in the sky, ready to deliver a deadly blow to the World Serpent. Jörmungandr was defeated by the hands of the thunder god, but before he dropped to the ground, the serpent managed to spit his lethal venom until the god was covered in it from head to toe. With Jörmungandr dead, Thor took exactly nine steps before his body gave up on him. For once, Mjölnir fell from his hand, and the thunder god surrendered to his fate.

The same thing happened to Týr and Garmr, as they wounded each other in battle. Both perished, and none emerged victorious. The same could also be said about Heimdall and the son of Laufey. Heimdall successfully put an end to Loki's treachery and tricks by killing him mercilessly. But before he died, Loki managed to land a couple of heavy slashes on the father of mankind. And so, the gods lost their watchman.

Both sides of the war suffered heavy casualties, and many had died. The plain of Vigrid was saturated with blood, and there were bodies everywhere—be it giants, monsters, or gods. The world began to sink into the great ocean, and there was nothing left except an empty void. The prophecy had come true; everything that the All-Father had created was destroyed.

A depiction of the new world by Emil Doepler, c. 1905.
https://commons.wikimedia.org/wiki/File:After_Ragnar%C3%B6k_by_Doepler.jpg

However, some believed that Ragnarök was not the end of everything and that the world would soon be reborn. When no more roars and cries could be heard on the battlefield, and after all of the flames lit by those from Muspelheim had been extinguished, a new world would arise from the waters. Mountains would take shape, waterfalls would be created, and new rivers would form.

The surviving gods gathered on the untouched plain of Iðavöllr. The sons of Thor, Magni and Modi, would carry their father's hammer to the plain, where they would meet with the others: Vidar, Váli, Njord, and Hœnir. Some sources even suggested that most of the goddesses, including Freyja, Frigg, and Sif, had survived the cataclysmic destruction. If that is the case, they also would have gathered at Iðavöllr.

With the realms destroyed, Baldur, his wife Nanna, and Hod were also free to leave Helheim. Together, they would walk across the barren lands to meet the remaining gods. Hœnir, the companion of the deceased All-Father, would then pass his vast knowledge to the younger gods. Together, they would build a new hall named Gimle, which was where the gods would dwell and regain their strength.

An illustration of Líf and Lífthrasir by Lorenz Frølich, 1895.
https://commons.wikimedia.org/wiki/File:L%C3%ADf_and_L%C3%ADfthrasir_by_Lorenz_Fr%C3%B8lich.jpg

Soon, the skies were healed, and another sun was born, thanks to Sol's surviving daughter, who gladly took her mother's role. In time, the grasses began to grow from the empty lands, and trees stood tall, forming new forests and woods. Flowers bloomed, adorning the fertile lands, and animals were reborn to occupy the earth. As for humans, the events of Ragnarök had destroyed them all, except for two—Líf and Lífthrasir. As they emerged out of their hiding, the two would rebuild their new lives on the new land. Time would pass, and humans would repopulate the earth.

Conclusion

Whether Ragnarök had already happened before or is yet to come remains unsure. Norse mythology is filled with mystery, which makes it both intriguing and mind-bending. Unlike the well-known stories of Greek mythology, Norse myths resurfaced much later. The stories were first shared via oral tradition by the Vikings. The Vikings are often associated with barbaric raids and extreme wars, but few of us are aware that these ancient warriors were also exceptional when it came to the arts and storytelling. The link between the Vikings and Norse mythology runs deep since they were the ones who shared the stories of the gods and the heroic legends, most of the time doing so in the form of poetry.

But since they were passed down orally, most of these stories ended up lost in history. It was only in the mid-13th century that an anonymous author collected these stories and preserved them in the Codex Regius. However, the codex was not found until 1643.

Norse mythology only began to receive attention from all over the world in the 19th century; before that, it was only widely shared within Scandinavia. The old poems were translated into various languages, and they soon became a huge inspiration for modern poets, theatrical plays, operas, films, novels, and video games.

The English writer and poet J. R. R Tolkien produced his fantasy novels based on Norse mythology, and it became a hot sensation. The Norse god of thunder, Thor, is now known by many due to his depictions in the comic books and superhero films by Marvel. Huge video game developers have also adopted many Norse tales and legends into their games; some feature their depictions of the gods, while others create a whole different character and story based on the many existing details found in the mythical legends. Even musicians, especially metal bands in Iceland, reference various Norse myths in their lyrics and songwriting. Just like that, Norse mythology survived time and is forever immortalized in literature and the modern arts.

But the world of entertainment is not the only thing influenced by the Norse myths. Scandinavia has always embraced them as part of their culture and tradition, especially Iceland. Towns, streets, and neighborhoods are named after the Norse gods. Reykjavík is not only known as the capital city of Iceland but also as the "Neighborhood of the Gods." The city has an area where the streets are named after the gods and other famous Norse figures. There's Óðinsgata ("Odin's Street"), which is named after the All-Father; Týsgata ("Týr's Street"), which is named for the one-handed god; Baldursgata; and even Lokastígur after the trickster Loki. Tórshavn, the capital city of the Faroe Islands, simply means "Thor's Harbor," and its coat of arms features the thunder god's mighty hammer, Mjölnir. Sweden also has a ship named after a goddess: *Sigyn*. The ship's name references the story of how Sigyn, the faithful wife of Loki, collected the venom dripping from the snake placed above her fettered husband. The ship was used to transport nuclear wastes from Swedish nuclear power plants.

Although their roots were never forgotten, the rediscovery of Norse myths greatly impacted the lives of the Scandinavian people. While it is possible for one to continue their higher education in Old Norse literature and mythology, it is also possible for one to explore the movement of Ásatrú. The Old Norse religion was practiced during the Viking Age before it was replaced by Christianity by the end of the 10th century. But with the rediscovery of archaeological and folkloric evidence, the old belief has been revived and is now known as Ásatrú. Re-recognized as a religion in 1973, it has become the fastest-growing religion in Iceland, with its very first temple currently in construction. And so, the stories and mythical legends of Odin and his fellow gods will continue to live on.

Here's another book by Enthralling History that you might like

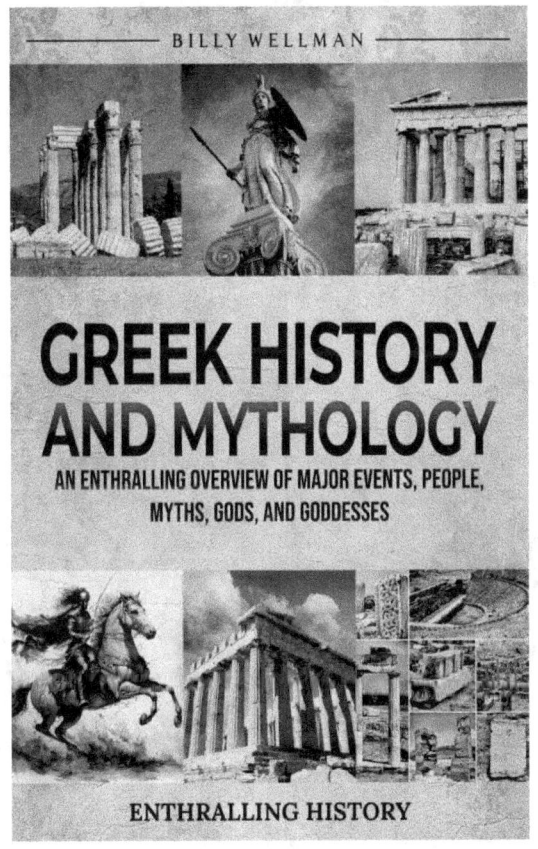

Free limited time bonus

Stop for a moment. We have a free bonus set up for you. The problem is this: we forget 90% of everything that we read after 7 days. Crazy fact, right? Here's the solution: we've created a printable, 1-page pdf summary for this book that you're reading now. All you have to do to get your free pdf summary is to go to the following website:

https://livetolearn.lpages.co/enthrallinghistory/

Once you do, it will be intuitive. Enjoy, and thank you!

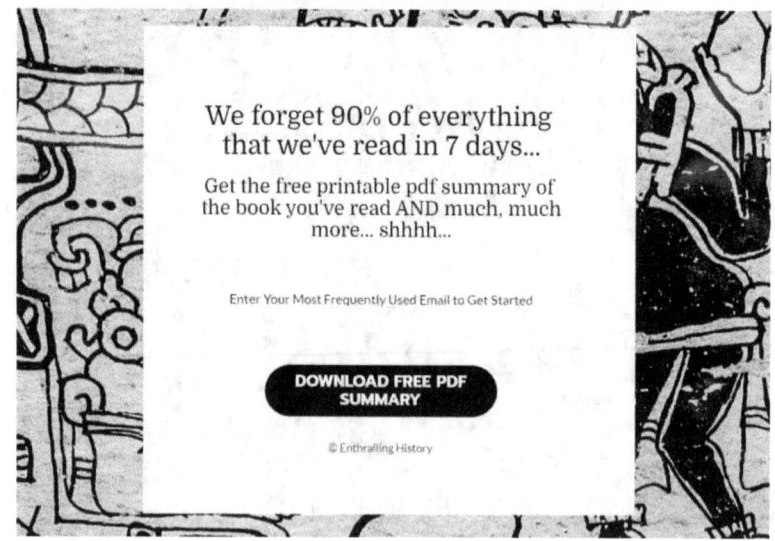

Bibliography

https://www.english-heritage.org.uk/visit/places/lindisfarne-priory/History/viking-raid/
https://www.englishmonarchs.co.uk/vikings_8.html.
https://www.followthevikings.com/discover/origins.
https://www.historic-uk.com/HistoryUK/HistoryofBritain/Invaders/
http://www.historyofyork.org.uk/themes/viking-invasion
https://www.jorvikvikingcentre.co.uk/the-vikings/
https://www.lifeinnorway.net/scandinavia-before-the-vikings/
https://www.medievalists.net/2021/11/where-did-the-vikings-go-the-decline-of-norse-piracy/
https://www.norden.org/en/information/history-nordic-region "The history of the Nordic Region"
https://nordicperspective.com/history/vikings/viking-origin-story
http://www.scandinavianarchaeology.com/the-vendel-period-the-golden-age-of-the-norse/
https://scandinaviafacts.com/scandinavia-before-the-vikings/
https://weaponsandwarfare.com/2020/07/06/the-great-raid-of-hastein-and-bjorn-ironsides/
https://www.worldhistory.org/article/1321/william-the-conqueror--the-ely-rebellion/
https://www.worldhistory.org/Vikings/
Lassieur, Allison. The Vikings. San Diego: Lucent Books 2001.
https://www.britannica.com/topic/Viking-people
https://en.natmus.dk/historical-knowledge/denmark/prehistoric-period-until-1050-ad/the-viking-age/power-and-aristocracy/
https://www.followthevikings.com/discover/culture/viking-literature-and-the-oral-tradition
https://www.historyonthenet.com/viking-society-nobles-medieval-freemen-slaves
https://www.hurstwic.org/history/articles/society/text/social_classes.htm
Lassieur, Allison. The Vikings. San Diego: Lucent Books 2001.
https://www.legendsandchronicles.com/ancient-civilizations/the-vikings/viking-food-and-diet/
https://skjalden.com/viking-social-classes/
https://smarthistory.org/viking-art/

https://sonsofvikings.com/blogs/history/viking-lore-a-quick-intro-to-norse-eddas-and-sagas
https://www.thingsites.com/what-is-a-thing
http://viking.archeurope.com/runes/the-rok-runestone/
https://www.worldhistory.org/Viking_Art/
Berger, Melvin and Gilda Berger. The Real Vikings. National Geographic 2003 Belgium
https://www.berganza.com/periods_viking.html
https://www.britainexpress.com/History/battles/index.htm
https://en.natmus.dk/historical-knowledge/denmark/prehistoric-period-until-1050-ad/the-viking-age/weapons
https://www.historyonthenet.com/viking-weapons-and-armor
https://www.medievalchronicles.com/medieval-history/medieval-history-periods/vikings/famous-viking-battles/
https://regia.org/research/ships/Ships0.htm
https://www.science20.com/the_conversation/vikings_were_craftsmen_too-153378
https://theconversation.com/vikings-were-pioneers-of-craft-and-international-trade-not-just-pillaging-37599
https://vikingsna.org/viking-crafts/
https://viking-styles.com/blogs/history/viking-battles
https://workingtheflame.com/viking-battles/
https://www.celebratepaganholidays.com/general/11-core-nordic-religion-principal-beliefs
Clare, John D. I Was There: Vikings. The Bodley Head Children's Books London 1994.
https://englishhistory.net/vikings/viking-burials/
https://www.hurstwic.org/history/articles/mythology/religion/text/practices.htm
https://lufolk.com/blogs/vikings-and-norse-mythology/skidbladnir-best-ship-in-norse-mythology
https://www.newworldencyclopedia.org/entry/Asgard
https://norse-mythology.org/
https://www.su.se/english/news/new-interpretation-of-norse-religion-1.543297
https://thevikingherald.com/article/the-most-important-viking-symbols-a-primer/318
https://vikingr.org/norse-cosmology/yggdrasil
Yasuda, Anita. Explore Norse Myths. White River Junction, VT. Nomad Press, 2015.
https://www.worldhistory.org/article/1836/ten-norse-mythology-facts-you-need-to-know/
Batista, J. V. (2020, May 3). Odin's wives. Jay Veloso Batista.
Birkett, T. (2018). The Norse Myths: Stories of The Norse Gods and Heroes Vividly Retold.
Quercus Publishing.
Britannica. (n.d.). Týr. https://www.britannica.com/topic/Týr

Britannica Kids. (n.d.). Sol and Mani. https://kids.britannica.com/students/article/Sol-and-Mani/313604

George, J. J. (2019, September 7). Norse Mythology: The Fenris Wolf. Owlcation. https://owlcation.com/humanities/Norse-Mythology-The-Fenris-Wolf

Greenberg, M. (2020, December 29). Who Was Baldur in Norse Mythology? Mythology Source. https://mythologysource.com/baldur-norse-god

Groeneveld, E. (2018, February 19). Freyja. World History Encyclopedia. https://www.worldhistory.org/Freyja

Jay, N. (n.d.). Who is Gullveig? Symbol Sage. https://symbolsage.com/gullveig-norse-mythology

Kids Britannica. (n.d.). Hermod. https://kids.britannica.com/students/article/Hermod/311662#

Manea, I. (2021, March 15). Heimdall. World History Encyclopedia. https://www.worldhistory.org/heimdall

Mark, J. J. (2021, August 27). Frigg. World History Encyclopedia. https://www.worldhistory.org/Frigg

Mark, J. J. (2021, August 30). Sleipnir. World History Encyclopedia. https://www.worldhistory.org/Sleipnir

McCoy, D. (n.d.). Ginnungagap. Norse Mythology for Smart People. https://norse-mythology.org/cosmology/ginnungagap

McCoy, D. (n.d.). The Binding of Fenrir. Norse Mythology for Smart People. https://norse-mythology.org/tales/the-binding-of-fenrirMcCoy, D. (n.d.). The Fortification of Asgard. Norse Mythology for Smart People. https://norse-mythology.org/tales/the-fortification-of-asgard

McCoy, D. (n.d.). The Mead of Poetry. Norse Mythology for Smart People. https://norse-mythology.org/tales/the-mead-of-poetry

McCoy, D. (n.d.). The Norns. Norse Mythology for Smart People. https://norse-mythology.org/gods-and-creatures/others/the-norns

New World Encyclopedia. (n.d.). Týr. https://www.newworldencyclopedia.org/entry/Týr#Major_Mythic_Tales

New World Encyclopedia. (n.d.). Yggdrasil. https://www.newworldencyclopedia.org/entry/Yggdrasill

Norman. (2009, February 14). Brunhilde. The Norse Gods. https://thenorsegods.com/brunhilde

Norman. (2012, May 18). The Building of Asgard's Wall. The Norse Gods. https://thenorsegods.com/the-building-of-asgards-wall

Norman. (2013a, January 6). The Necklace of the Brisings. The Norse Gods.

https://thenorsegods.com/the-necklace-of-the-brisings
Norman. (2013b, April 9). The Lay of Hymir. The Norse Gods. https://thenorsegods.com/the-lay-of-hymir
Norman. (2013c, November 11). Loki's Flyting. The Norse Gods. https://thenorsegods.com/lokis-flyting
Scandinavia Facts. (n.d.). Svartalfheim (Nidavellir) in Norse Mythology: Elves, Dwarfs and More. https://scandinaviafacts.com/svartalfheim-nidavellir-in-norse-mythology-elves-dwarfs-and-more
Skjalden. (2011). The Nine Realms in Norse Mythology. https://skjalden.com/nine-realms-in-norse-mythology/amp
Skjalden. (2011, June 1). Alvíss. https://skjalden.com/alviss
kjalden. (2019). Social Classes in Viking Society. https://skjalden.com/viking-social-classes/amp
Skjalden. (2020, July 22). Ginnungagap. https://skjalden.com/ginnungagap
Skjalden. (2020, July 28). Thor's battle with the Giants. https://skjalden.com/thors-battle-with-the-giants
Skjalden. (2020, September 5). Thor's Goats. https://skjalden.com/thors-goats
Skjalden. (2020, September 25). Nótt & Dagr in Norse mythology. https://skjalden.com/nott-and-dagr
The Poetic Edda, Grímnismál, trans. Henry Adams Bellows (1936). https://www.sacred-texts.com/neu/poe/poe08.htm
The Poetic Edda, Harbarthsljoth, trans. Henry Adams Bellows (1936). https://www.sacred-texts.com/neu/poe/poe08.htm
Thor's Hammer Amulets. (n.d.). Sol-Land. http://www.sol-land.org/thors-hammer-amulets.html
What is Niflheim in Norse Mythology? (n.d.). Mythologian.Net. https://mythologian.net/what-is-niflheim-norse-mythology
Wikipedia. (2021, September 23). Tiwaz (rune). https://en.wikipedia.org/wiki/Tiwaz_(rune)
Williams, J. A. (2021, September 29). Nine World of Norse Mythology Explained. Grunge. https://www.grunge.com/618744/the-nine-worlds-of-norse-mythology-explained
World History Edu. (2021, July 12). Ask and Embla: the first two humans in Norse mythology. https://www.worldhistoryedu.com/ask-and-embla-the-first-two-humans-in-norse-mythology

www.ingramcontent.com/pod-product-compliance
Lightning Source LLC
Chambersburg PA
CBHW072104050526
44107CB00099B/430